Video Enhanced Observation for Language Teaching

Advances in Digital Language Learning and Teaching
Series Editors: Michael Thomas, Liverpool John Moores University, UK;
Mark Peterson, Kyoto University, Japan; Mark Warschauer,
University of California – Irvine, USA

Today's language educators need support to understand how their learners are changing and the ways technology can be used to aid their teaching and learning strategies. The movement toward different modes of language learning – from presence-based to autonomous as well as blended and fully online modes – requires different skill sets such as e-moderation and new ways of designing and developing language learning tasks in the digital age. Theoretical studies that include practical case studies and high-quality empirical studies incorporating critical perspectives are necessary to move the field further. This series is committed to providing such an outlet for high-quality work on digital language learning and teaching. Volumes in the series focus on a number of areas including but not limited to:

- task-based learning and teaching approaches utilizing technology
- language-learner creativity
- e-moderation and teaching languages online
- blended language learning
- designing courses for online and distance language learning
- mobile-assisted language learning
- autonomous language learning, both in and outside of formal educational contexts
- the use of web 2.0/social media technologies
- immersive and virtual language-learning environments
- digital game-based language learning
- language educator professional development with digital technologies
- teaching language skills with technologies

Enquiries about the series can be made by contacting the series editors:
Michael Thomas (M.Thomas@ljmu.ac.uk), Mark Peterson (tufsmp@yahoo.com)
and Mark Warschauer (markw@uci.edu).

Also available in the series:

Autonomous Language Learning with Technology: Beyond The Classroom,
Chun Lai

Autonomy and Foreign Language Learning in a Virtual Learning Environment,
Miranda Hamilton

Digital Games and Language Learning: Theory, Development and Implementation,
edited by Mark Peterson, Kasumi Yamazaki and Michael Thomas

Language Teacher Education and Technology: Approaches and Practices,
edited by Jeong-Bae Son and Scott Windeatt

Online Teaching and Learning: Sociocultural Perspectives, edited by Carla Meskill

*Task-Based Language Learning in a Real-World Digital Environment: The European
Digital Kitchen*, edited by Paul Seedhouse

*Teacher Education in Computer-Assisted Language Learning: A Sociocultural and
Linguistic Perspective*, Euline Cutrim Schmid

*Teaching Languages with Technology: Communicative Approaches to Interactive
Whiteboard Use*, edited by Euline Cutrim Schmid and Shona Whyte

WorldCALL: Sustainability and Computer-Assisted Language Learning, edited by Ana
María Gimeno Sanz, Mike Levy, Françoise Blin and David Barr

Forthcoming in the series:

Teaching Languages with Screen Media: Pedagogical Reflections, edited by Carmen
Herrero and Marta F. Suarez

Video Enhanced Observation for Language Teaching

Reflection and Professional Development

Edited by Paul Seedhouse

BLOOMSBURY ACADEMIC
LONDON • NEW YORK • OXFORD • NEW DELHI • SYDNEY

BLOOMSBURY ACADEMIC
Bloomsbury Publishing Plc
50 Bedford Square, London, WC1B 3DP, UK
1385 Broadway, New York, NY 10018, USA
29 Earlsfort Terrace, Dublin 2, Ireland

BLOOMSBURY, BLOOMSBURY ACADEMIC and the Diana logo are trademarks of
Bloomsbury Publishing Plc

First published in Great Britain, 2022
This paperback edition published in 2023

Copyright © Paul Seedhouse and Bloomsbury, 2022

Paul Seedhouse and Bloomsbury have asserted their right under the Copyright,
Designs and Patents Act, 1988, to be identified as Author of this work.

Cover design by James Watson
Cover image © shutterstock.com

All rights reserved. No part of this publication may be reproduced or
transmitted in any form or by any means, electronic or mechanical, including
photocopying, recording, or any information storage or retrieval system,
without prior permission in writing from the publishers.

Bloomsbury Publishing Plc does not have any control over, or responsibility for, any
third-party websites referred to or in this book. All internet addresses given
in this book were correct at the time of going to press. The author and publisher
regret any inconvenience caused if addresses have changed or sites have
ceased to exist, but can accept no responsibility for any such changes.

A catalogue record for this book is available from the British Library.

Library of Congress Cataloging-in-Publication Data
Names: Seedhouse, Paul, editor.
Title: Video enhanced observation for language teaching: reflection and
professional development / edited by Paul Seedhouse.
Description: London; New York, NY: Bloomsbury Academic, 2022. |
Series: Advances in digital language learning and teaching |
Includes bibliographical references and index.
Identifiers: LCCN 2021023562 (print) | LCCN 2021023563 (ebook) |
ISBN 9781350085039 (hardback) | ISBN 9781350272316 (paperback) |
ISBN 9781350085046 (pdf) | ISBN 9781350085053 (epub)
Subjects: LCSH: Language teachers–Training of–Audio-visual aids–Case
studies. | Language teachers–In-service training–Audio-visual
aids–Case studies. | Observation (Educational method)–Audio-visual
aids–Case studies. | Peer review–Audio-visual aids–Case studies. |
Reflective teaching–Audio-visual aids–Case studies.
Classification: LCC P53.85.V53 2022 (print) |
LCC P53.85 (ebook) | DDC 371.33/5–dc23
LC record available at https://lccn.loc.gov/2021023562
LC ebook record available at https://lccn.loc.gov/2021023563

ISBN: HB: 978-1-3500-8503-9
PB: 978-1-3502-7231-6
ePDF: 978-1-3500-8504-6
eBook: 978-1-3500-8505-3

Series: Advances in Digital Language Learning and Teaching

Typeset by Integra Software Services Pvt. Ltd.

To find out more about our authors and books visit www.bloomsbury.com
and sign up for our newsletters.

This book is dedicated to my new grandchildren – Dylan Lomax
and Evelyn Lomax – with love from granddad!
Paul Seedhouse

Contents

List of Illustrations	xi
Notes on Contributors	xiv
Note on Text	xviii
Acknowledgements	xix
List of Abbreviations	xx

Part 1   Background to Video Enhanced Observation

1	Introduction *Paul Seedhouse*	3
2	Using Digital Video for Teacher Development: The Research Context *Sandra Morales*	9
3	From Teaching to Learning: The Development of the VEO App *Paul Miller and Jon Haines*	21
4	Using VEO – A Practical Guide *Paul Miller and Jon Haines*	39

Part 2   Video Enhanced Observation in Practice: Case Studies

5	Integrating VEO in Foreign Language Teacher Education in Germany *Götz Schwab and Mareike Oesterle*	65
6	VEO as Part of Reflective Practice in the Primary Teacher Education Programme in Finland *Minna Körkkö, Outi Kyrö-Ämmälä and Tuija Turunen*	83
7	VEO-integrated IMDAT in Pre-service Language Teacher Education: A Focus on Change in Teacher Questioning Practices *Merve Bozbıyık, Olcay Sert and Kadriye Dilek Bacanak*	97
8	Integrating the Video Enhanced Observation (VEO) App in Peer Observation Feedback Interaction *Jaume Batlle Rodríguez and Paul Seedhouse*	117
9	Improving Discipline and Classroom Management Using VEO in a Turkish University Pre-service Context *Saziye Tasdemir and Paul Seedhouse*	135
10	Video-enhanced Lesson Observation: Moving from Performance Management to Continuous Teacher Development *Elizabeth Hidson*	153

11 SETTVEO: Evidence-based Reflective Practice and Professional Development *Steve Walsh*	167
12 Changing Error Correction Practice over Three Lessons Using an Individualized Video Enhanced Observation Tagset on a Teacher Training Course *Paul Seedhouse and Alison Whelan*	181

Part 3   Making the Most of Video Enhanced Observation

13 A Practical Framework for Integrating Digital Video and Video Enhanced Observation into Continuing Professional Development *Paul Seedhouse, Paul Miller and Jon Haines*	199
14 Researching Using the VEO App *Paul Seedhouse, Paul Miller and Jon Haines*	217

Notes	228
References	229
Index	251

Illustrations

Figures

3.1	Teacher training in Ghana	25
3.2	The Kirkpatrick model for evaluating training	25
3.3	Lesson debriefing using VEO-tagged video as a stimulus for discussion and professional development	28
3.4	Tagging and annotation of this particular moment highlighting a behavioural incident, and the trainee teacher's own response to the issue	30
3.5	Annotations can be viewed as a string of notes which can be commented upon further as shown above	30
3.6	Tagging and annotation which draw the trainee's attention to the need to develop a stronger approach to questioning	31
3.7	Training with teachers from Kazakhstan	32
3.8	Using VEO with teachers from Kazakhstan	33
3.9	Using VEO for clinical practice	34
4.1	'Tag' buttons to the left and right of the video	40
4.2	Tags with 'Subtags'	41
4.3	Adding a note against a tag	42
4.4	'Possession' tags beneath the screen	42
4.5	Percentage slider, showing 'Engagement' in this example	43
4.6	Interactive tagged moments to navigate the video	44
4.7	Highlighted key moments	44
4.8	Notes popping out onto video	45
4.9	An example of Note Conversation	45
4.10	Bar chart showing positives and negatives in a teaching session	46
4.11	'Possession' pie chart example	47
4.12	Changes in 'Engagement' over time	48
4.13	Selecting users and groups with whom to share a video	52
4.14	Tagging live with the VEO app	56
4.15	Achieving different types of learning through VEO	59
5.1	Screenshots of tag set	70
5.2	Stats from lesson 1 and 3, P1	71

5.3	VEO tag set, taken from Treetzen (2016, p. 63)	74
5.4	Model A	80
5.5	Model B	80
6.1	Integration of theory studies, methodological studies and teaching practicum in teacher education (Kyrö-Ämmälä 2019)	86
6.2	The procedure of guided reflection with VEO	88
7.1	IMDAT: A classroom interaction-driven, technology-enhanced and reflective teacher education framework (Sert 2019, p. 223)	102
7.2	The first version of the 'Language Learning and Teaching Tagset' used in this study	102
7.3	A sample tagged lesson on a tablet computer	103
	Appendix I: The tag set that focuses on the teacher: 'L2 Teacher – Hacettepe University'	116
	Appendix II: The tag set that focuses on the learners: 'L2 Learner – Hacettepe University'	116
8.1	Alb looking at Fra	123
8.2	Alb looking at the tablet	123
8.3	Alb touching and scrolling down the tablet	123
8.4	Alb touching and scrolling down the tablet	123
8.5	Alb looking at Fra	124
8.6	Jul and Rog looking at the screen	125
8.7	Jul and Rog looking at the screen, and Jul pointing the screen	125
8.8	Rog looking at Jul	125
8.9	Rog looking at the screen	126
8.10	Jul looking at the screen	126
8.11	Rog looking at Jul; Jul looking at the screen and putting her hand on the mouse	126
8.12	Jul looking at Rog; Rog looking at the screen	126
8.13	Alb and Fra looking at the tablet	129
8.14	Alb looking at Fra	129
8.15	Alb touching the tablet and scrolling down	129
8.16	Alb looking at Fra	129
8.17	Fra and Alb looking at the tablet	129
8.18	Jul signing the screen	130
8.19	Jul signing the screen	130
8.20	Jul and Rog looking at the screen	131
8.21	Jul putting her hand on the mouse	131
9.1	Practicum structure	139
9.2	Detailed practicum structure using VEO	139

Illustrations xiii

9.3	Language Learning and Teaching Tag Set	140
9.4	L2 Teacher Tag Set	141
9.5	Data collection and analysis	142
9.6	Lesson 1 VEO tag data	145
10.1	Example of a lesson observation form for recording outcomes and feedback	158
10.2	Lesson observation using VEO during the performance management cycle in the case study school	159
11.1	Screenshot of the SETTVEO tagset	171
12.1	The DELTA tagset	187
12.2	Visual representation of how VEO was used for self-directed CPD	194
13.1	Scaffolding processes of reflection among pre-service teachers	200
13.2	The procedure of guided reflection with VEO	201
13.3	IMDAT: A classroom interaction-driven, technology-enhanced and reflective teacher education framework (Sert 2019, p. 223)	202
13.4	Detailed practicum structure using VEO	202
13.5	Lesson observation using VEO during the performance management cycle in the case study school.	203
13.6	Visual representation of how VEO was used for self-directed CPD.	203
13.7	A practical framework for integrating digital video and Video Enhanced Observation into CPD	204
13.8	Reviewing and reflecting, with notes produced	205
13.9	A meeting with multiple sources and types of data	206
13.10	Actions agreed for the following lesson	207
13.11	Making scoring decisions on VEO using the IELTS tagset	211
13.12	Adding notes on VEO using the IELTS tagset	211
13.13	Comparison of decisions for four criteria by four examiners for the same candidate	213
13.14	Ethical approval processes within an organization	215
14.1	Example of screenshot of VEO quantitative tag data	221

Tables

3.1	Comparison of text-based and video-based observation	29
5.1	Tally of taggings, taken from Treetzen (2016, p. 68)	75
9.1	Lesson 1 VEO tag data break down	145
9.2	Lesson 1 Classroom and reflective essay excerpt	147
9.3	Lesson 2 Classroom and reflective essay excerpt	149

Contributors

Editor

Paul Seedhouse is Professor of Educational and Applied Linguistics in the School of Education, Communication and Language Sciences, Newcastle University, UK. His monograph *The Interactional Architecture of the Language Classroom* (2004) won the Modern Languages Association of America Mildenberger Prize. He has worked with colleagues in Computer Science at Newcastle to develop ilab:learn, a centre for digital educational technology. He is the editor of *Task-Based Language Learning in a Real-World Digital Environment: The European Digital Kitchen* (Bloomsbury, 2017).

Volume Contributors

Kadriye Dilek Bacanak is Associate Professor at the Department of English Language Teaching at Gazi University, Ankara, Turkey. Her research interests include lexical competence, teaching reading skills, socio linguistics and discourse. She has presented at national and international conferences and published in several journals.

Jaume Batlle is Assistant Teacher at the University of Barcelona, Spain. He is also a teachers' trainer in Spanish as a Foreign Language Masters degrees, working specifically in classroom discourse and basic concepts for foreign language teachers. His earlier work has mainly focused on the study of the foreign language classroom interaction from a conversation analysis perspective and the development of reflexive practice in teachers' professional development.

Merve Bozbıyık is Research Assistant at Middle East Technical University (METU), Turkey. She currently works in close collaboration with HUMAN Research Centre as an Associate Researcher and as a member of the DISCORE Research Team. Her research interests include classroom interaction, teacher education, medical interaction and call-centre interaction.

Jon Haines is PGCE Subject Lead for Science in the School of Education, Communication and Language Sciences, Newcastle University, UK, and is also Co-Founder and Director of Video Enhanced Observation Ltd. He was a secondary science teacher for thirteen years and head of a successful science department in a large comprehensive secondary school in the north east of England for eleven of these. As co-founder of VEO, Haines is keen to support teaching and learning through reflection and effective coaching practices, both within and beyond traditional educational settings.

Elizabeth Hidson is Senior Lecturer in Education in the Faculty of Education and Society at the University of Sunderland, UK, where she specializes in international teacher education and distance learning. Hidson's research interests include technology-enhanced learning and digital pedagogies, computing education, video-enhanced lesson observation and the use of digital and visual research methods. She is a committee member of the Technology, Pedagogy and Education Association and Senior Fellow of the Higher Education Academy.

Minna Körkkö achieved a PhD at the Faculty of Education at the University of Lapland, Finland. In her doctoral thesis, she studied reflection guidance during teacher education, with special focus on how the video-application VEO can be used for promoting reflection as part of guided professional experience for teacher students. Her research interests include research-based teacher education, teacher students' reflection and professional development. Körkkö has worked as a researcher in relevant international and national projects at the University of Lapland, Finland. She is currently working in the private sector as an educator and trainer.

Outi Kyrö-Ämmälä is Lecturer in Teacher Education at the University of Lapland, Finland. She is also the Vice Dean responsible for teaching at the Faculty of Education. She has played an integral part in developing the model of research-based teacher education at the University of Lapland. Kyrö-Ämmälä's research interests also include inclusive education. Over the last decade, she has participated in several international projects relating to inclusive education and teacher education. Recently, she has been involved in Finnish nationally focused projects developing and researching teacher education. She is a member of the Teacher Education Forum organized by the Ministry of Education and Culture of Finland.

Paul Miller is Co-Founder and CEO of Video Enhanced Observation Ltd. Miller has overseen development of the VEO concept from the idea's inception through to university spinout and business growth. With a career spanning business, education and research, recent consultancy for Newcastle University, UK, involved designing and delivering both large-scale teacher CPD programmes and educational research across slum areas in west Africa. His interests lie in creating innovative and scalable learning platforms to meet twenty-first-century needs.

Sandra Morales received her PhD in Educational and Applied Linguistics at Newcastle University, UK, where she is now Visiting Lecturer. She is an experienced English language teacher and teacher educator and has worked with undergraduate and postgraduate TESOL students in her home country, Chile, and the UK. Her area of research is computer-assisted language learning (CALL), mainly, teacher education and the use of online and blended learning models for teaching and learning. Morales has worked in several educational technology research projects and has published her work in international journals and books. She has also presented in conferences such as EuroCALL, WorldCALL and BAAL.

Mareike Oesterle is a PhD student and Research Assistant at the University of Education Ludwigsburg, Germany. She has a degree in primary and secondary teaching and has been involved in a number of different projects (e.g. proPIC, VEO Europa and Beyond School), mainly aimed at developing innovative formats to support (future) teachers' in their own continuing professional development (CPD). In her PhD, she currently investigates a transient professional community of teacher educators and explores possible ways to foster professional learning in a transnational context. Further interests include language learning and teaching, and the use of mobile technologies in teacher education.

Götz Schwab is Professor of Applied Linguistics at the Institute of English, Ludwigsburg University of Education, Germany. He worked as a secondary school teacher before starting a career at the university where he received his PhD in 2008. He is currently head of the Institute and is involved in a number of transnational projects. Schwab has a wide range of research interests, including conversation analysis for second language acquisition (CA-SLA), telecollaboration and the use of mobile technology, syntax, low achievers and students-at-risk, especially at secondary schools, ELT/FLT methodology in primary and secondary schools as well as content and language-integrated learning (CLIL).

Olcay Sert is Associate Professor of TESOL and Applied Linguistics at Mälardalen University, Sweden. He is the editor of *Classroom Discourse* and is the author of *Social Interaction and L2 Classroom Discourse (EUP)*, which was shortlisted for the BAAL Book Prize and AAAL first book award. He is leading Mälardalen INteraction & Didactics (MIND) Research Group and is currently the PI of *Digi-REFLECT*, a research and development project that aims to enhance teachers' roles and leadership in classrooms.

Saziye Tasdemir is a PhD student at Newcastle University, UK, and is currently writing her thesis on English language teachers' reflective practices using the VEO app. She has three years of experience as an EFL teacher and a master's degree in Applied Linguistics and TESOL from Newcastle University. Her research interests include foreign language teaching and learning, CALL, reflection and teachers' professional development.

Tuija Turunen is Professor of Teacher Education at the Faculty of Education of the University of Lapland, Finland. She leads the University of the Arctic (Uarctic) network on *Teacher Education for Social Justice and Diversity*, and the UNITWIN/ UNESCO network by the same name, which currently host over twenty-member institutions across the circumpolar north and global south. She has led several national and international research projects, with funding by the Academy of Finland, the Nordic Council of Ministers, the Danish Agency for Science and Higher

Education, etc. Turunen's current research interests focus on teacher education, professional development in higher education, educational transitions (especially starting school), multi-professional work in schools and preventative school welfare work.

Steve Walsh is Professor of Applied Linguistics and Communication in the School of Education, Communication and Language Sciences, Newcastle University, UK, where he was, until recently, Head of Department. He has been involved in English language teaching and English language teacher education for more than thirty years in a range of overseas contexts, including in China, England, Hong Kong, Hungary, Ireland, Poland and Spain. Walsh's research interests include classroom discourse, teacher development, second language teacher education and professional communication. He has published ten books and more than 100 research papers, including, with Steve Mann, *Reflective Practice for English Language Teaching: Research-Based Principles and Practices* (2017) and *The Routledge Handbook of English Language Teacher Education* (2019).

Alison Whelan is Research Associate in the Research Centre for Learning and Teaching (CfLaT) in the School of Education, Communication and Language Sciences at Newcastle University, UK. Formerly a secondary MFL teacher, her research interests include language learning and teaching, project-based learning, teacher training and development, and the creation and implementation of research-based, innovative, creative curriculums in primary and secondary schools.

Note on Text

Companion Websites

This book has two companion websites with complementary resources:

The VEO Europa website, www.veoeuropa.com, has a wide range of resources produced by the project team including:

- App training handbook and training resources, including how-to video tutorials
- Research publications
- Teacher education resources
- Teacher briefings
- iBook

The VEO website, https://veo.co.uk/, provides:

- Access to the VEO app
- Demo request facility
- Information about the app
- Contact with the VEO company
- Case studies

Acknowledgements

The VEO Europa project was funded by an EU Erasmus+ grant from September 2015 to September 2017: KA201 – Strategic Partnerships for School Education 2015-1-UK01-KA201-013414. Partners were Newcastle University (UK); EdEUcation Ltd (UK); Paedagogische Hochschule Karlsruhe (Germany); Lapland University (Finland); Hacettepe University (Turkey) and Regionalen inspectorat po obrazovanieto-Haskovo (Bulgaria).

Many thanks to the innumerable people who were involved in the VEO Europa project and who made valuable contributions in many different capacities.

Many thanks to Alison Whelan for her excellent editing, proofreading and indexing of the manuscript.

Many thanks to Maria Giovanna Brauzzi, Evangeline Stanford and Zeba Talkhani from Bloomsbury Publishing and to Suriya Rajasekar from Integra Software Services for their excellent work in taking the manuscript through many stages to publication.

Paul Seedhouse

Abbreviations

Community of Practice (CoP): 'groups of people who share a concern or a passion for something they do and learn how to do it better as they interact regularly'. This learning that takes place is not necessarily intentional. Three components are required in order to be a CoP: (1) the domain, (2) the community and (3) the practice (Lave and Wenger 1988).

Computer-Assisted Language Learning (CALL): an approach to teaching and learning in which the computer and computer-based resources such as the internet are used to present, reinforce and assess material to be learned. It usually includes a substantial interactive element.

DELTA (Diploma in Teaching English to Speakers of Other Languages): DELTA is an advanced blend of theory and practice that provides professional development for teachers with at least one year's experience.

IMDAT: enables student teachers to reflect on their classroom interaction practices and pedagogical decisions by focusing on recorded and tagged lessons and engaging in feedback (both with supervisors and peers) and reflection practices (Sert 2015, 2019).

Interactional Competence (IC): the ability to jointly communicate in setting-specific ways; it is about using communicative resources to co-construct understanding and co-accomplish context-specific goals.

Peer Observation: a form of peer review characterized by a symmetrical relationship between the observer and the observee and focused commonly on observing each other's practices with the aim to develop reflective practice conducting to a teachers professional development.

Post-observation Feedback: Feedback given after a lesson observation and carried out with the aim to assess the teacher's performance or to develop a specific reflective practice for teachers' professional development.

SETTVEO: enables teachers to reflect on their practice through the use of SETT (Self Evaluation of Teacher Talk) and VEO (Video Enhanced Observation). The use of an effective teacher development framework such as SETT with the innovative video technology of VEO (i.e. tags and online community) will help teachers to gather and interpret their own teaching evidence and that of others. This will foster teachers' necessary skills to identify and make meaning of what is relevant and what can be improved in their teaching through individual and collaborative reflective practice.

Tagsets: sets of Teacher Talk tags and subtags used within the VEO app which allow for professional dialogue based on specific examples from a teacher's practice.

TESOL: Teaching English to Speakers of Other Languages.

Part One

Background to Video Enhanced Observation

1

Introduction

Paul Seedhouse
Newcastle University, UK

How can you use the latest digital technology to record the spoken interaction in your professional setting; tag, analyse and evaluate the talk; and use it as the basis for reflection and professional development? This book explains how to do this, covering how and why the Video Enhanced Observation (VEO) app was designed and built, what it can do, how you can use it and how you can adapt it to improve your own professional practice. Video tutorials on the accompanying website https://veoeuropa.com/ give you a hands-on introduction to using the app and making the most of all of its features. Book chapters provide detailed case studies tracing how teachers in many different settings have used VEO with digital video for recording, evaluating and reflecting on lessons. The chapters provide clear research evidence of the professional development of many education professionals from around the world.

Written by experts in education, educational technology and applied linguistics, the book explains the principles and procedures involved, enabling professionals in other contexts to integrate digital video and the VEO app into their own environment and practice in the same way. If you are a teacher and want to use the latest digital technology to record the spoken interaction in your teaching and learning setting; tag, analyse and evaluate the talk; and use it as the basis for reflection and professional development, this is the book for you! In-depth research studies show how the system was actually implemented in seven different countries (Chile, Finland, Germany, Spain, Thailand, Turkey and the UK), using five different languages and with a wide range of types of learners and subject areas. There are numerous photographs of the app in use. There is also evidence of the ways in which many users around the world integrated VEO into their professional practice and models and flowcharts, illustrating how anyone can apply VEO to their own context. So you can learn from the experiences of others and apply VEO to your own situation.

The central argument of the book is this: although individual projects may be ephemeral because of the pace of technological change, the analyses in this collection draw out general principles and a framework in relation to using digital video and the VEO app in particular for professional development and reflective practice. These principles may then continue to be applied to other professional settings in the future.

The book therefore provides a model, principles and procedures which professionals in any area may use to adapt digital video to their own professional environment for capturing talk, professional development, change and reflection. The whole book is pedagogically conceived as a model, which will enable others to design and implement practical frameworks for implementation, with research and illustrative case studies providing examples in the individual chapters. These culminate in Chapter 13, which makes explicit the practical framework, which is of general applicability for professional practice. This will allow readers to create their own customized VEO-based professional development programme. Chapter 14 also provides a framework for researching using the VEO app.

The Structure of the Book

The structure of the book is designed to deliver on the aims stated above. **Part I** provides all of the relevant background and history to the VEO app. **Part II** provides case studies of how the VEO app has been used in practice in a wide range of countries and educational settings. **Part III** explains to readers how to make the most of using the VEO app in their own contexts, introducing a framework for the use of digital video, and the VEO app in particular, for professional development and reflective practice. In addition, a framework for researching using the VEO app is provided.

Within Part I, Morales's **Chapter 2** introduces the existing research literature and background, looking at the approaches which have previously been employed in this academic area and their research findings. The focus then narrows to the specific area of the use of digital video for teacher development and reflection, the area for which VEO was developed. **Chapter 3**, written by VEO Group co-founders Haines and Miller, illustrates the development and application of the VEO system since its inception. A number of small case studies and personal stories show how in all cases there has been a visible shift from teaching to learning, on the part of the leader, the teacher trainer, the teacher trainee, the teacher and pupils. In **Chapter 4**, the same authors provide a practical introduction to how the app works and can be used for reflection and professional development. The introduction is written for beginners with no previous experience of using the app, or digital video for teacher development. The text is illustrated by photos and screenshots.

Part II starts with **Chapter 5**, in which Schwab and Oesterle discussing two possible ways to use the VEO app in the context of foreign language teacher education at the University of Education Karlsruhe, Germany. First, they discuss the integration of such a mobile application in practical internships to observe pre-service English teachers and to initiate their professional development. Second, they discuss and demonstrate how the VEO app was used as a research instrument to observe and analyse teaching and learning at a primary school, focusing on classroom interaction. In **Chapter 6**, Körkkö, Kyrö-Ämmälä and Turunen present the results of VEO trials in the primary teacher education programme at the University of Lapland, Finland. Twenty student teachers participated in the trials, which followed the phases of the reflection procedure. Two students who used the VEO app during the Advanced Practicum were followed as case studies to determine how they experienced the reflection procedure and the extent to which their professional development was supported by VEO. The chapter is based on data from Körkkö's (2020) doctoral thesis, a major success associated with this project!

Chapter 7 sees Bozbıyık, Sert and Bacanak report the findings of a VEO focus on teacher questioning practices during a pre-service teacher education programme in a Turkish university. The use of VEO is integrated with the IMDAT reflective teacher education framework. In **Chapter 8**, Batlle and Seedhouse show how VEO is used by a group of teachers in a Spanish language school for peer observation feedback. The app moves to occupy a central position in the teachers' management of the activity and changes the way in which feedback interaction is managed. In **Chapter 9**, Tasdemir and Seedhouse show how a pre-service teacher makes use of VEO to reflect on her teaching as she develops her classroom management skills in a school in Turkey. By reflecting via VEO, the teacher is able to reflect with a level of detail which would not have been possible without the use of tags. In **Chapter 10**, Hidson focuses on the innovative use of VEO in the annual cycle of teacher performance management in a UK school. Hidson shows how VEO can help move the focus from a stressful focus on individual performance to a focus on continuous teacher development which incorporates a broad range of perspectives. **Chapter 11** (Walsh) describes how English language teachers reflected on and improved their practice and Classroom Interactional Competence through the use of VEO with the SETT tag set in Spain, Turkey, Chile and Thailand. The chapter provides a clear example of how an existing theoretical framework for reflective CPD via interaction can be developed and employed as a VEO tag set. In **Chapter 12**, Seedhouse and Whelan show how an individualized VEO tag set was created, which helped a teacher improve her correction practice over three lessons on an in-service teacher training course in the UK. The tag set customization facility of the VEO app proved useful in enabling the development of the targeted skills. Overall, the studies feature a wide range of methodologies and data collection instruments, which were used to analyse and evaluate professional development in the range of settings investigated.

In Part III, we present models and frameworks to enable the reader to use VEO for professional development and/or research in their own settings. Seedhouse, Miller and Haines present in **Chapter 13** a framework for the use of digital video, and the VEO app in particular, for professional development and reflective practice. The framework is broadly conceived, so as to be applicable to any profession in any country. Seedhouse's concluding **Chapter 14** draws together all of the points which have emerged from the discussions and presents a framework for **researching** using the VEO app. One clear finding from this project was that the VEO app is an extremely flexible and useful tool for carrying our research into professional practice, in addition to its core function of promoting professional development.

The Funded Projects Underlying This Volume

The empirical case studies in Part II were developed as part of the *VEO Europa* project, the outcomes of which can be found in this volume's companion website https://veoeuropa.com/about/. This was an EU Erasmus+ funded project which ran from September 2015 to September 2017: KA201 – Strategic Partnerships for school education 2015-1-UK01-KA201-013414. As VEO Europa sought to promote teacher education with technology in educational contexts, the project strategic partnership involved six partners in five countries: Newcastle University (UK); EdEUcation Ltd (UK); Paedagogische Hochschule Karlsruhe (Germany); Lapland University (Finland); Hacettepe University (Turkey) and Regionalen inspectorat po obrazovanieto-Haskovo (Bulgaria).

It aimed to improve the quality of teaching and learning by using the VEO app to support initial teacher training and professional development. The main outputs of VEO Europa have been:

- an enhanced version of the VEO app with interfaces in four additional European languages (free demo version from iTunes)
- a set of training modules downloadable from this website together with a training handbook
- a portfolio of best practice resources (videos on the project's YouTube channel)
- a series of case studies
- research outputs (reports, conferences and publications)
- our interactive iBook (available free on iTunes)

The materials produced were tested with twenty trainees or existing teachers in each of four schools or training organizations in each country, a total of 400 teachers throughout Europe. In addition, through the dissemination strand, the project reached a further 250 key stakeholders, including School Leadership teams, Teacher Training Organizations including HEIs, NGOs, Teaching Unions and National Ministries.

The rationale for the VEO Europa project was that the quality of education will only improve if the practice of teachers improves by:

- improving teacher performance through upskilling by sharing best practice
- identifying the specific needs of individual teachers and using peer learning and observation to improve their performance and competences
- using the technology to monitor engagement and motivation
- providing a low-cost and time-efficient model of CPD which does not involve teachers leaving school to go on expensive courses, to leave their classes or require expensive supply cover staff
- providing in-house CPD which is focused on the individual teacher, is ongoing and not subject to one-off courses or single in-service days
- using the technology for self-evaluation, monitoring of teacher performance and setting performance management targets
- using the technology to implement and monitor new approaches to pupil learning
- demonstrating how this digital tool can be effective in improving the performance of both teachers and their students
- Furthermore, the project could only be effective at an EU level if carried out transnationally as the approach to professional development and teacher monitoring varies from one country to another. Partners were selected to test both

Introduction 7

the technology and methodology in a range of different curriculum, pedagogic and cultural contexts and the outcomes were then adapted to ensure that they meet both country-specific and wider generic European needs. The project had five different strands, which tested in these countries with different target groups.

- Trainee teachers – the app was used as part of the classroom observation of trainee teachers
- CPD – the app was used for peer observation and analysis, based on classroom observation. The focus for each individual teacher was identified through self-evaluation and peer discussion.
- Monitoring of performance – the app was used by school leaders and inspectors for making judgements on the quality of teaching and learning through classroom observation
- Innovative pedagogies – the app was used to observe pupil activity to share innovative approaches to learning
- Research and Development – research into the methodology and its impact was conducted and further developments to the app introduced, to ensure maximum access at a European level and inform policy development.

The overall picture is that the project resulted in a comprehensive set of tried-and-tested training and support materials, which are freely available via the VEO Europa website to support teaching and learning throughout the world. The emphasis throughout this book is on the principles and procedures of designing, implementing and researching VEO-based professional development and reflective practice programmes. The VEO Europa project provided many detailed illustrations of successful, functioning environments, so there is a continuous interplay between theory and practice.

The book also incorporates VEO-based research from two other funded projects, with permission: the SETTVEO project (Walsh, Chapter 11) funded by British Council; the IELTS Joint-Funded Research Programme project entitled 'Which specific features of candidate talk do examiners orient to when taking scoring decisions?' (Seedhouse, Chapter 14).

Note on Photographs

In the photographs in this volume, some authors have used a range of methods to anonymize the participants. These include blurring of participants' faces and blurring of the whole photographs.

2

Using Digital Video for Teacher Development: The Research Context

Sandra Morales
Newcastle University, UK

Introduction

The current digital era presents innumerable resources educators can apply in their lessons in order to improve students' learning experience. Also, in these unprecedented times of emergency remote teaching due to Covid-19, technology has become indispensable. Teachers all around the globe have been faced with the challenge of selecting and implementing digital tools to support learners with social, digital, educational and emotional requirements. Bao (2020) explains that in the current health crisis, it is essential that teachers understand their students' needs and apply technological resources accordingly. Furthermore, from their experience in Spain, Diez-Gutierrez and Gajardo-Espinoza (2020) suggest that teachers should redefine technology-based feedback and evaluation processes in emergency remote teaching. With this in mind, today, more than ever, it is crucial that teachers are provided with the most appropriate technological tools and training to face online teaching demands during and post-Covid-19. Innovative resources such as VEO (Video Enhanced Observation), therefore, will allow teachers to implement meaningful distant learning and reflective experiences with colleagues and students now and after the crisis.

For decades, technology has had a significant impact on learners' second language acquisition processes as it facilitates communication, interaction and genuine cultural exchange. In this sense, language teachers are not only able to produce online materials for teaching, feedback and assessment, but also to have access to authentic communicative situations via tools such as YouTube and virtual communities in social networks like Facebook or Twitter. In addition, the multimodality (i.e. the combination of communication modes such as video and audio) of digital resources can complement language learning with contextual factors to increase the possibilities of meaningful interaction and collaboration.

Mobile resources are another example of how technology has contributed to language learning in terms of accessibility and location. For example, portable devices, such as mobile phones and iPads, allow learners to conduct tasks inside and outside the classroom in their own time and convenience (Kukulska-Hulme and Shield 2008). Therefore, traditional patterns of instruction changed when this modality was incorporated into the language classroom. Technology has also been considered as an important element when using the different language learning approaches in language teaching, as digital tools support the implementation of real-world activities, learner participation, motivation and interaction. For instance, research by Seedhouse (2015) used task-based language teaching (TBLT) and cutting-edge technology (e.g. artificial intelligence) to create a smart kitchen to foster language education and culture through collaborative cooking.

However, the effective implementation of technology in the language classroom can still be challenging for teachers and students. On the one hand, teachers have to deal with digital resources that become obsolete fast due to the ongoing evolution of technology, while learners may struggle with applying digital resources for educational purposes.

In terms of teacher preparation in technology, Kessler (2018) suggests that language educators should familiarize themselves with research in language learning and technology. He explains that this could help them to determine which resources may be useful and/or challenging considering their teaching context and what their learners require. Simultaneously, he also indicates that teacher education in technology can be problematic due to the array of resources teachers have at their disposal.

This perception is not new as Hubbard (2006) pointed out that teacher education in technology was challenging. At that time, he suggested questions regarding the preparation of teachers in computer-assisted language learning (CALL) that are still difficult to answer today. For instance, Hubbard speculated about what teachers should learn to develop their skills and knowledge of CALL. This is certainly complex to establish nowadays due to the rapid evolution of technological resources and the characteristics of the digital learners. It is important, therefore, that teachers have the opportunity to try different virtual tools in their teaching and professional development experiences. With this in mind, current technology allows educators to have formal and informal options for professional development. For example, technological knowledge has been progressively democratized as language learning associations often organize online conferences, talks and webinars that are accessible to the teaching community. In addition, virtual online communities of practice on social media have become fairly popular channels of continuous learning today. Rosell-Aguilar (2018), for example, studied a group of teachers that used Twitter to engage in professional development. After analysing the results of a survey about the teachers' perceptions and data from a follow-up interview, he concluded that the teacher participants benefited from being part of an online community on Twitter as they shared ideas and collaborated together. The teachers also felt supported, which reduced the sense of isolation they sometimes experience, particularly, if they do not engage in constant professional development. Rosell-Aguilar's (2018) findings regarding the advantages of social networks support Hubbard's (2006) concern about 'when' and 'where' teachers should learn, as by being part of a flexible online community, they have the possibility to construct meaningful knowledge at anytime, anywhere.

Using Digital Video for Teacher Development   11

Another aspect that Hubbard (2006) discusses in his questions regarding teacher preparation in CALL has to do with the knowledge that teachers acquire and what or how it is determined. As there are so many resources to which teachers can have access, their competence in technology may be difficult to measure and classify. For example, considering Compton's (2009) taxonomy for teachers' technological proficiency (e.g. expert-proficient-novice), some educators may be experts in one particular resource, but proficient or novice users in others. So, how competent are they? In which category do we place them? In order to identify teachers' CALL skills, standards and skills development models have been proposed (Hampel and Stickler 2005; Healey, Hanson-Smith, Hubbard, Ioannu-Georgiou, Kessler and Ware 2011); however, there is not a clear consensus yet on how to assess teachers' technological and pedagogical CALL competence. With this in mind, more than developing specific skills to master technology, teachers should learn about strategies that would work best for them not only to construct their knowledge continuously, but also to maintain it. As reflective practice is essential for any kind of teacher professional development, it should be included in educational experiences with technology. From Dewey's (1933) perspective, reflection is based on individuals' experiences that after being examined become meaningful instruments to face future situations. For teachers, this can be interpreted as an analytical and continuous cycle that allows them to identify potential problematic situations and find solutions.

Today, portable devices allow teachers (pre- and in-service) to capture and keep records of their teaching practices on audio and video at any moment. Marsh and Mitchell (2014) discuss the impact of video technology in initial and continuous teacher preparation and conclude that the use of this digital resource not only fosters reflection and pedagogical knowledge, but also helps teachers to focus on their students' learning experience. Educators can examine how technology is applied with their students and identify effective materials and strategies for instruction. As digital video has improved over time, classroom observation and analysis become more effective. For instance, it is possible for teachers to record lessons from different angles in the classroom, tag teaching events and share clips with colleagues and trainers on virtual communities.

In sum, the incorporation of technological resources for language teaching and learning has allowed teachers to implement innovative activities in order to motivate and support students. However, due to digital tools constantly changing, it is important that teachers are well prepared to use them in a sustainable fashion. Technology has also opened doors for teachers' formal and informal professional development opportunities, as training workshops and online communities proliferate. Nevertheless, the task of educating pre-service and in-service teachers in CALL has remained a challenge since Hubbard shared his concerns in 2006 regarding what educators should know, who should teach them and how their competence is developed and evaluated. With this in mind, it is crucial that teachers should experience technology for both teaching and professional development through reflective and collaborative opportunities.

The aim of this chapter, therefore, is to introduce the different concepts and views that served as theoretical foundations for the Video Enhanced Observation (VEO) Europa project. The main objective of this project was to use the VEO tool to support pre- and in-service teachers in their professional development in order to improve their pedagogical practices. The implementation of such an innovative tool as VEO in a variety of teacher education environments makes a valuable contribution to some of the issues that the fields of CALL and teacher development have faced over time. For this reason, firstly, we will further elaborate on CALL and teacher education in technology. Secondly, reflective practice and the use of digital video and learning communities for the professional development of pre- and in-service teachers will be discussed. Finally, concluding thoughts are presented in order to connect the reader with the inception of the VEO project that will be discussed in Chapter 3 of this volume.

Computer-assisted Language Learning: Concepts and Affordances

Computer-assisted language learning (CALL) is the term used to describe the field that deals with the meaningful incorporation of technological resources in second and foreign language instruction (Levy 1997). Although originally CALL referred exclusively to the use of computers or software for language education, as technology has dramatically changed over the years, the term now encompasses resources from the internet, mobile apps and social networks. Hubbard and Levy (2005) make the case that CALL is considered a global label as it incorporates other tools and suggests a focus on the learning of a language specifically. However, this view has caused some tension in the field as Jarvis and Krashen (2014) suggest, the CALL nomenclature may be out-of-date as it suggests the computer as the main tool for instruction and that it is used mainly for intentional learning. Their argument revolves around the fact that students can also learn a language unconsciously when they, for example, interact with non-academic online content in English (e.g. music and entertainment, chat, games). Jarvis and Krashen's point is valid if we take into account that many 'real-world' activities that incorporate technology (e.g. using a recipe app for cooking) can support language learning, particularly, outside the classroom. For the purposes of this chapter, we will use CALL as an umbrella term for the incorporation of technology in language learning and teaching.

As technology changes, the affordances of CALL allow teachers to foster language skills in an integrated manner as resources become more multimodal (Blake 2016). Reading comprehension and vocabulary can be fostered using virtual texts and mobile apps (Cobb 2007; Smith and Wang 2013; Yang, Park and Hsieh 2014) and, at the same time, collaborative online texts, blogs and forums can support writing (Sun and Chang 2012; Aidyn and Yildiz 2014). Video technology (e.g. YouTube, Skype, WhatsApp) has also been largely used to foster students' proficiency in speaking and listening (Blake 2016). The cultural aspect that accompanies language instruction has been supported by videoconference and chat as they allow learners to interact with peers around the globe (Helm 2015). In addition, CALL has empowered teachers to implement different models of learning to support language instruction. For example, a strategy that combines face-to-face lessons with instruction using technological resources is blended learning (Hinkelman and Gruba 2012). This model can be used to optimize the amount of exposure of the learners to the target language and the development of their skills. For instance, online tasks to promote language skills can be assigned outside the lesson while face-to-face time can be used to foster communication and learner interaction. Blended learning also promotes autonomy, which in turn will help learners to better understand how they learn and what strategies to choose for learning.

As well as for blended learning, language instructors need to develop pedagogical and technological skills to include e-learning into their teaching. This kind of instruction takes place entirely online and, according to Salmon (2012), it is planned, guided and purposeful, as opposed to the informal use of internet language learning resources. For this reason, multimodality plays a key role in online learning as teachers are to select the means and materials of the course in order to make the best use of, for instance, virtual learning environments (VLEs). This can be challenging for teachers because they should be able to (1) provide accessible and clear materials, (2) establish and maintain interaction in an online community of students and (3) provide feedback so that students' learning is meaningful (Hampel and Stickler 2015). Therefore, if well-organized, online language learning experiences can be highly beneficial for students, particularly, for those who cannot access traditional forms of instruction. In addition, online learning allows students to opt for different alternatives of instruction as formal and informal virtual communities, massive open-online courses (MOOCs) and apps become more popular amongst language learners (Hockly 2015). This is why it is crucial that teachers try technological resources and read about research in the field, so that it is possible for them to implement and guide online courses effectively. In this sense, Hampel and Stickler (2005) suggest that language educators have to develop their basic CALL skills and knowledge and learn about specific resources in order to facilitate learning and deal with the obstacles it can bring. They also state that as maintaining online interaction is no easy task either, it is imperative that teachers experience online communities in order to understand how to manage them in order to foster communication and learning.

In terms of resources used in fully online and blended models of instruction, mobile learning has played a key role in the incorporation of digital tools for language education. Today, as most people have portable devices such as mobile phones, teachers have been able to include them in their courses. Also, as technology is now pervasive, mobile tools are fairly easy to use inside and outside the language lesson, connecting teachers and learners at any moment and place. Nevertheless, Stockwell and Hubbard (2013) suggest that even though mobile tools are accessible, the difficulty for teachers lies in designing tasks that consider the appropriate capabilities of mobile resources in order to make the most of the language learning experience. They also reaffirm the idea that digital learners need support from their teachers in order to use technology for learning purposes effectively. At the same time, the authors point out the 'social nature' of the use of mobile devices to interact in virtual communities such as Facebook or Twitter.

Because of the prominent use of mobile learning in second and foreign language acquisition, mobile-assisted language learning (MALL) studies have been conducted so as to better understand its effectiveness for developing language skills. For instance, Burston (2013) carried out a literature review of MALL research that shows how research on podcasts, text messages, social networking and mobile apps has helped language learners from different educational contexts. For example, Fouz-González (2017) used Twitter in an English for Specific Purposes (ESP) course to improve 121 students' pronunciation. The study also sought to explore students' perception about using Twitter for such purposes. In order to achieve the study's aim, Fouz-González sent the learners daily pronunciation features over Twitter and applied pre- and post-tests to evaluate knowledge and surveys to examine the learners' views. His findings show that there was improvement in the learning process and a positive response from the learners towards this virtual network as a teaching resource.

The use of MALL can be advantageous for fostering language competence yet challenging for students. This is mainly because they have to work autonomously outside the classroom where there is usually little direct monitoring from the teacher. One such example is seen in Botero and Questier (2016), who examined how university students used the language app Duolingo for self-study. The data collected through a survey and interviews revealed that students perceived the app as useful, but they stated that they needed motivation to work with it in their own time. This is why it is crucial that teachers provide learners with training and guidance so that MALL effectively supports personalized instruction and interaction in the digital classrooms.

As evidenced in this discussion, technological resources have enriched language acquisition in terms of materials, teaching techniques, cultural inclusion and communication. In addition to language learning, digital tools and learning models can, and have been, implemented for professional development purposes, so that teachers become acquainted with technology and use it for their own benefit. As Kessler and Hubbard (2017) suggest, due to the abundance of CALL resources nowadays, the preparation of teachers in technology becomes fundamental. This enables teachers to improve their teaching practices with language learners by deciding which instructional approaches are the best and whether, how and when to incorporate technology into their lessons.

Using Video Technology to Support Reflection and Professional Development in Teacher Education

Currently, we live in times where technology plays a key role in people's connectivity all around the globe. This became especially evident during the 2020 coronavirus pandemic. Since the advent of the different technological resources, the interactions that occur online have progressively taken a social turn. That is to say, digital technologies are not perceived merely as tools, but as resources that promote communication and dialogic construction of knowledge amongst individuals. This social paradigm is not new to language teaching and teacher education as Vygostky's (1978) sociocultural theory has supported instruction and training for decades. It is just that today, more than ever, the educational use of technological resources is aligned with the social view of learning based on collaboration and experience. Thus, it is crucial that teachers, researchers and students come together to share and discuss technology-mediated teaching and learning experiences, so as to find strategies and resources that are beneficial for the teaching community.

As Freeman, Webre and Epperson (2019) state, there is an inseparable bond between English language teacher education and language teaching, as the former usually establishes what knowledge and principles teachers should acquire. This relationship can be controversial as there is constant discussion on how, and how much, each 'community', as the authors call it, contributes to the field of language teaching. This view is connected with the idea of closing the research-pedagogy gap that Kessler (2018) presents to educate teachers, as they should become familiar with theories and studies in technology. Ur (2019) also suggests that it is usually assumed that practice should often be informed by research-based theory; however, teachers sometimes think that such theories may not be applicable in their contexts and that researchers cannot relate to what really takes place in language classrooms. Nonetheless, her view suggests that there should be a balance between the use of theoretical approaches and teaching practices rather than a contraposition. She recommends that improvement in language teaching should come from the sharing and discussion of effective ideas amongst teachers and teacher educators. Therefore, in order to bring these communities together, they have to work in collaboration. For example, teachers can work with researchers on projects and learn to conduct classroom-based research so as to understand and improve their own teaching. In the same way, researchers and practitioners can learn from school teachers' daily experiences with students in order to suggest approaches and techniques to refine language instruction in a sustainable fashion. By doing this, teachers and researchers would engage in an ongoing reflective dialogue which, in turn, could lead to transformational professional practices. With this in mind, the VEO Europa project is aligned with the idea of empowering teachers and researchers so they continuously construct knowledge in community via reflection (see Chapters 5 and 6 of this volume).

Reflective Practice in Teacher Education

The general consensus in language teaching concerning reflective practice (RP) is that reflection helps teachers to become aware of their actions in the classroom in order to improve their instruction (Dewey 1933; Schön 1984). According to Schön (1984), teachers can reflect on their past lessons (on-action), current lessons (in-action) and future lessons (for-action), so as to identify teaching events that allow them, for example, to change their classroom behaviour or detect their students' needs. In this regard, Farrell (2018: 1) states that teachers engage themselves in reflection when they 'subject their own beliefs about teaching and learning to critical analysis, take full responsibility for their actions in the classroom, and continue to improve their teaching practice'. This follows Dewey's (1933) perception of reflective practice as an act of contextual self-analysis and collaborative discussion in order to find solutions to teaching concerns. In this process, therefore, teachers construct knowledge based on their own experiences and those of others (Finlay 2008). As a result, cycles of individual and/or shared examination could promote a dynamic transformation amongst teachers who, in turn, will be able to implement sustainable pedagogical actions for their students' benefit (Mezirow 2000).

Reflective practice, therefore, has been considered a vehicle for transformative and efficient teaching, although its application is not exempt from concerns. For instance, questions around the kind of reflection (i.e. individual or collaborative) that is more effective for teachers, the tools that are the most valuable for reflective practice, whether reflection should be guided and/or based on certain criteria and even if there is pedagogical change without reflection have sparked an ongoing discussion. As reflective practice has been ingrained in teacher education in many countries for years, it is important that we address these matters of contention and decide on strategies that support pre-service and in-service teachers to apply reflection effectively. In relation to this, Mann and Walsh (2017) explain that the issue with reflection has to do mainly with (1) the purpose and (2) the procedures. The authors state that there is a grey area regarding why reflection is conducted as, for instance, it can be used to assess teachers or promote development. Although there are many traditional and technology-mediated mechanisms that teachers use to reflect, such as blogs, journals, observations and forums, it is still necessary for educators to acquire the skills to use them effectively.

Mann and Walsh (2017) also suggest that the predominance of written reflection may deflect the focus of the reflection towards the effectiveness of the writing rather than the actual pedagogical analysis. For these reasons, they suggest that reflection is done in collaboration, using specific data from a lesson, with appropriate tools and a clear focus of analysis. With this in mind, technology can provide the tools to foster peer reflection. For instance, in a case study with pre-service teachers in Turkey, Mumford and Dikilitaş (2020) explored how the participants developed their reflective skills through multimodal online interaction in a blended course. Data were gathered using the pre-service teachers' contributions to online sessions with the tutor, the written reflections they produced and interviews upon course completion. Data coding and analysis suggested that factors such as the participants' attitudes towards technological resources and its use to reflect, as well as language learning online, had an impact on the development of reflection. For this reason, it is important to explore teachers' perceptions and beliefs about technology and reflection, as these may determine the motivation of teachers to engage in reflective practice through digital tools.

Reflection helps teachers to identify and examine teaching moments for professional development. Therefore, the observation of classroom contexts will allow them to better understand the language learning process in order to implement effective pedagogical strategies. In this sense, reflective practice via classroom observation using technological tools such as videos, for instance, becomes essential to improve teachers' pedagogical interaction with the students, how content is delivered, classroom management and the creation of learning opportunities. Teachers can also use lesson observation with different objectives, depending on 'who' is observing; for instance, a headmaster would probably focus on the structure of a lesson, whereas a head of the language department on methodological aspects of teaching. Educators can also conduct peer observation and self-observation to examine different elements of their pedagogical actions in the classroom. As a result, teachers will build up their own meanings of teaching and, as they continuously reflect, will be able to adapt to different contexts, making their practices more sustainable. For these reasons, it is relevant that teachers make use of technological resources such as VEO so as to incorporate digital video into their reflective processes and development with technology (see Chapters 8, 10 and 11 of this volume).

Digital Video as a Reflective and Developmental Tool for Pre- and In-service Teachers

Breen, Hird, Milton, Oliver and Thwaite (2001) suggest that it is crucial for teachers to think about their views on teaching, so they develop skills that support deep reflection rather than mere description of what happens in the classroom. The authors state that the analysis of teaching experiences helps teachers not only to understand their pedagogical actions, but also to justify them in relation to educational approaches and models. This is what Jackson and Cho (2018: 1) propose as teacher 'noticing', that is to say, the 'awareness of features of second classroom interaction that may influence student learning'. Van Es and Sherin (2002) explain that noticing has to do with the identification, explanation and reflection on classroom moments, but also with how educators are able to link them with teaching principles to anticipate issues that can affect the students' learning process. In this context, Hockly (2018) suggests that the easy access that teachers have today to digital and mobile technology can support their development as, for instance, they are able to take videos of classroom practices using their own phones. She also states that video-based observation is crucial for pre-service and in-service teachers as by having teaching evidence, it is possible to identify classroom episodes (i.e. noticing), use these for reflection and also to inform decisions regarding teacher education and language teaching. She further states that video repositories (i.e. at a course or institutional level) are useful for shaping policies at a course or institutional level. In addition, sharing videos in virtual environments can enhance continuous development and group reflection. In this sense, video observation helps to bridge the gap between teacher educators and language teachers suggested by Freeman, Webre and Epperson (2019).

With regard to the use of video for both initial teacher education and continuous professional development, Marsh and Mitchell (2014) suggest that one of the benefits of recording lessons has to do with authenticity. Teachers are able to reflect using concrete evidence, thus reducing any personal biases and interpretations that may occur, for instance, in written reflection. They state that video-recorded lessons can be valuable not only as reflective tools, but also as training resources, as recordings can be used, and played, multiple times. This is particularly relevant for connecting what takes place in schools with the training that pre-service and in-service teachers receive. Video observation, therefore, provides data from experiences in the classroom that sometimes can be difficult to obtain, and opens opportunities for pre-service and in-service teachers to engage in meaningful reflection that goes beyond perceptions. Although Marsh and Mitchell (2014) acknowledge the value of video-based classroom observation, they also point out that, as video recordings are usually done from one specific location in the classroom, some aspects of what takes place in the lesson might be lost. For this reason, it is important to use technological resources that allow teachers to record the lessons from different angles. In this sense, VEO meets this need as its mobile nature allows educators not only to move around the room to cover many aspects of the lesson, but also to tag specific moments that can be of interest for teachers' further exploration (see Chapters 7 and 9 of this volume).

Hockly (2018) explains that for pre-service teachers, video observation can be beneficial as it creates spaces for self-reflection, discussion with practicum supervisors and peers. For example, Baecher, Kung, Jewkes and Rosalia (2013) explored thirty pre-service teachers' self-analyses on videos of their teaching sessions during their TESOL training. The researchers conducted a mixed methods study where participants had to write a reflection based on clips from students from previous years and their own. The participants' videos were also given a score by their supervisors. After coding and using correlations to analyse the data, findings showed that the participants' evaluation of their performance was done in an objective and realistic manner, as the videos showed them concrete evidence of their practices. This suggests that video not only supports noticing at early stages of training, but also less biased analysis. Also, in order to examine teacher noticing and the conditions in which it takes place, Jackson and Cho (2018) conducted a mixed methods study with pre-service teachers. The authors used video-recorded lesson observation and stimulated recall to observe how the participants developed noticing when teaching. Data from the recall sessions were transcribed and coded. The findings suggest that the sooner participants analyse their lessons, the better they engage in noticing, so it is important to have multimodal tools that allow teachers to record and reflect on their lessons without much delay. Also, the participants seemed to notice more when they were interacting with the students themselves, as opposed to self, group or peer interaction. When identifying students' reactions to the lesson, it was easier for the teachers to think about how to proceed in the classroom. In terms of the quality of the reflection, the participants were able to make connections between what took place in the classrooms and what they had planned in the first place. Thus, links to pedagogical principles were considered by the participants when analysing their performance. As noticing has to do with teachers identifying relevant incidents in the classroom, it is important that they are able to reflect on concrete evidence that allows them not only to observe their teaching practices, but also to be aware of the impact these have on the students' learning processes. For this reason, digital video technology can help capture real teaching experiences for post-hoc analysis, interpretation and understanding.

Taking into consideration that the observation of different aspects of a lesson is relevant for teacher training and development, Balzaretti Ciani, Cutting, O'Keeffe and White (2019) studied the use of 360-degree video in initial teacher education. They explored how pre-service teachers developed noticing based on videos from their microteaching sessions shown from different perspectives. Their argument was supported on the fact that usually video recordings are static and only take a snapshot of what happens in the classroom. For that reason, they used cameras that recorded from a 360-degree perspective. The participants also used annotations to analyse their teaching in more detail, as they considered, for instance, their gestures and teaching presence. The findings suggest that this multimodal analysis supported pre-service teachers' own examination and also fostered their noticing skills.

As for in-service teachers, video observation can promote collaborative reflection that makes teachers engage in a developmental examination of practices instead of just evaluating actions. As a matter of fact, even though videos are actually used for assessment purposes, the end goal should always be the analysis and discussion of actions for teacher transformation. In this context, Major and Watson (2018) agree with Marsh and Mitchell (2014) that video recordings are valuable as they grasp authentic moments of a lesson in order to facilitate analysis and reflection. They also explain that videos support the development of teachers' beliefs, classroom performance and pedagogical knowledge. While video technology in pre-service teachers is often used to coach and show future teachers features of teaching practices, videos can be considered a valuable resource for in-service teachers to promote collaborative reflection through learning communities. In this context, the focus on in-service teachers' use of video recordings is transformational and oriented towards meeting learners' needs. For instance, Mosley Wetzel, Maloch and Hoffman (2017) highlight that videos serve to foster dialogue amongst experienced teachers and provide a framework that includes observation for general development, learner improvement, teaching strategies and potential classroom problems. In order to understand what takes place in a lesson, they suggest having a focus of observation; for instance, teachers can annotate specific parts of the video lesson they want to analyse. They also explain that it is useful to prepare some questions as well to build up discussion, particularly when working with pre-service teachers. The authors also indicate that mobile devices are a better alternative to record videos, and that it is important to consider video size and storage. In this light, data privacy is also crucial when teachers exchange videos, so the technological resources they use as repositories should ensure information security.

In terms of collaborative examination of practices, Van Es (2012: 182) states that 'teacher learning communities promote individual and collective capacity and can lead to improved student learning'. She also suggests that developmental collaboration amongst teachers should be sustainable over time due to the limited training opportunities to which they can access or afford. In this context, Steeg (2016) explored reflection in teachers who were part of a video-based learning community from a sociocultural perspective. She explains that collaborative professional development can have an impact on teachers' ongoing training, as reflection is contextualized and engages teachers in meaningful data-driven analysis. Therefore, teachers are able to interact in a support network that can support them from an emotional and pedagogical perspective. The author examined the participation of three in-service teachers and one pre-service teacher in a learning community. The participants had to record their lessons and share them over six meetings during one semester. They watched the videos together and identified critical classroom episodes to discuss in each session. Data from these encounters showed that the teachers used video clips to scaffold their learning in order to improve their actions. Also, the dialogues in the learning community allowed the participants to notice their students' needs, so they were clear about what and how to plan their future lessons.

From this perspective, technology opens doors to teacher collaborative behaviour, as virtual communities can be implemented on a variety of online platforms (e.g. VEO) so as to share and discuss videos. It is crucial, therefore, to enable teachers to watch their recordings as many times as they need, in order to identify and discuss teaching actions from different perspectives (Gaudin and Chaliès 2015). This will contribute to the development of teachers' reflective skills and will also encourage them to become involved in activities where they can construct their pedagogical knowledge and identity continuously. This view is shared by Seidel, Stürmer, Blomberg, Kobarg and Schwindt (2011), who observed teachers learning from their own videos and those shared by others. The objective of the study was to support teachers in their noticing skills for professional development. One important finding was that teachers are able to reflect on their own practices, but that it is somewhat problematic for them to find their own classroom problems compared to those of their peers, when they analyse others' videos. That is why building up a community when using video technology for the education of teachers is relevant, as the collaborative reflection that occurs will impact teachers' individual cognition and continuous pedagogical transformation.

Conclusions

Technological resources and CALL have supported language teaching and learning for many years. As technology evolves, teachers have had to learn how to use different digital tools for teaching practices and also to create professional development opportunities. Currently, it is essential that teachers foster their pedagogical and technological competence as well as apply technology for their own learning in a sustainable fashion. This will allow them to apply technology in a variety of teaching scenarios. In terms of teaching and learning, CALL supports learners in the development of speaking, listening, reading and writing skills as well as in the acquisition of grammar and vocabulary. These features of language can be fostered by E-Learning, Blended Learning and Mobile Learning models. In terms of professional development, technology provides teachers with elements such as digital video, which serve as an efficient way to gather information about classroom events and to trigger teacher reflection. In addition, individual and collaborative reflective practices can take place in virtual learning communities, as teachers from all places can gather together to carry out meaningful data-based discussions to become competent and reflective digital educators.

In this sense, technological resources such as VEO promote the unification of teacher networks for professional development by facilitating the recording of teaching events with refined mobile technology. In addition, VEO supports lesson observation in an innovative fashion as teachers can use the tag set creator, which is embedded in the VEO tool, to produce their own reflective criteria based on their needs and interests (see Chapter 13 of this volume). All in all, VEO is a unique and safe platform in which teachers can connect and interact to improve teaching practices that will, in turn, support their students' learning processes.

3

From Teaching to Learning: The Development of the VEO App

Paul Miller,
VEO Group
Jon Haines
Newcastle University, UK

Introduction

The VEO app and methodology was conceived and designed by Jon Haines and Paul Miller while colleagues at Newcastle University. With years of classroom teaching experience, and a shared passion for teaching and mentoring teachers and trainee teachers, the app emerged from a chance meeting at a university funding event aimed at helping academic staff develop commercially viable, impactful projects. Both were seeking funds to support similar outcomes: the development of a system which was easy to use, flexible and readily available, to enable the sharing of good practice within, and from, the classroom.

This chapter will outline the journey of the app's development from both Jon and Paul's perspectives and how their own personal practices, experiences and professional development coalesced into a new system for learning at all levels. This subsequently leads on to four illustrative case studies of adoption in diverse settings, each with lessons for improving practice at scale, explored in further discursive depth as the chapter progresses. The following sections represent Jon Haines' and Paul Miller's personal journeys as founders of VEO and therefore take the first person style.

Jon Haines' Perspective

As a science teacher and head of department at Longbenton Community College in the north east of England, and as a former trainee teacher at Newcastle University, I had long been aware of the value in self, peer and mentor; lesson observation; and reflection through the use of video. During my own training, Rachel Lofthouse (now Professor of Education at Leeds Beckett University) was a course tutor, and her interest in the impact of reflection, coaching and mentoring on the professional development of pre-service teachers was developing. She later formalized findings in the article 'The

Camera in the Classroom' (Lofthouse and Birmingham 2010) stating 'the outcomes of the video intervention are seen as positive and substantial by the majority of participants'. Indeed, it was a specific requirement of the course I was undertaking at the time and, for reasons both of discomfort (who doesn't feel at least slightly uncomfortable being filmed?) and professional development, it was a memorable and significant experience in my own growth as an effective classroom practitioner.

Back then, in 1999, accessing video for recording and playback purposes was complicated by primitive, often unwieldy and unreliable technology. Sharing, even locally never mind over distance, was similarly challenging. Nonetheless, recording one's own practice was possible, and my first experience was with a Betamax tape and camera system, used to record one of my first ever science lessons. While the tape is long gone, my early efforts to communicate the topic of electrical current to a class of thirty 11–12-year-old pupils are still very memorable, and literally visible in my mind's eye. This was partly because the video enabled me to see myself from an observer's perspective, and partly because my school mentor was able to help unpick things that were happening in a very objective and clear manner. It was also striking how disconnected the pupils were from my teaching ... Nothing I was saying was wrong, nor particularly difficult, but I quickly saw that what I was doing was talking at, or to, my class, and not talking with them ... I had made the assumption that a degree of engagement, enthusiasm and understanding would develop, simply through my presentation of the scientific ideas. It was a simple lesson, but one which helped me take a big step forward in subsequent lessons. I began to talk more effectively with my pupils, learning about their existing knowledge and misconceptions, and responding to these in a way which engaged, challenged and supported them. I realized that they were as much a part of the lesson, and their own learning, as I was.

When, as a qualified teacher and Head of Department, my role in the department and across the school developed, I continued to strive for better classroom practice, both in my own teaching and that of my colleagues. However, sharing classroom experiences and approaches, the 'moments', rather than just the 'resources', continued to be difficult. Describing classroom experiences and interactions is subject to inconsistent interpretation and recall, and the only way to share this effectively is either by being there, or by watching the events captured on video. Although, in my experience, even being there is still fraught with challenges – the differences in perception, rationale and purpose of the observer and the teacher, and the accuracy of recall, can all be hugely variable. We are often heavily influenced by preconceptions, emotions and our own conditioning. Furthermore, on a very practical level (as many teachers will testify) finding time to observe each other is a luxury most often only afforded to inspection teams and, at a stretch, senior leaders, and least of all to those less experienced teachers who might benefit from the opportunity the most. The capacity to film lessons, until recently, was also undermined by the fallibility and limitations of the technology available. Sharing any video literally meant handing over a video tape and the recipient having to watch through it. Over time, companies started to sell camera systems to schools for this purpose. These usually included a video camera, motorized tripod and motion detector, a local server, and came with a significant demand for technical support. These systems were also very expensive and inefficient, especially as more time was wasted on setting up the equipment, and subsequently having to watch the whole video to locate the key moments, than it was spent on developing one's own phronesis or practical wisdom.

Some sense of the limitations of reflection without video can be illustrated by considering a lesson-debrief held between myself and a newly qualified teacher, following a formal lesson observation undertaken as part of her Newly Qualified Teacher (NQT) assessment. As I watched Jill teaching, it was clear to me that she had a powerful questioning style, an approach that allowed, encouraged and enabled her pupils to engage in whatever question she posed. In the simplest example, this class of Year 7 pupils were being introduced to the topic of Photosynthesis. Here, she enabled the class to work out the meaning of the word themselves, providing nothing but questions to fuel their own exposition of this biological process through the dissection of the word into its component parts ('Photo' – from light, and 'synthesis' – the making of). Capturing this process in action was impossible and transcribing the discussion which took place was a challenge, but it became obvious during the subsequent debrief that even the questions themselves were largely unimportant. What **was** important was the way these questions had been presented and sequenced, the enthusiasm and encouragement evident within the tone of Jill's voice, the way she allowed pupils time to think, share and reflect, build upon and develop each other's answers, and the way she responded to the pupils' initial thoughts and suggestions. It was this process of learning, facilitated by skilled questioning, rather than the specific content, that enabled most, if not all, pupils to reconstruct and recall the scientific meaning of photosynthesis fully at the end of the lesson. At the time, this image was difficult to encapsulate and express adequately in my feedback and in our debriefing conversation. My reflections on the experience highlighted the limitations of relying on the observer's and my own recollections of the lesson, which created a very incomplete and unhelpful mental image. As a result, I think much of what was truly important was missed in our discussion, because the description and the accompanying scene weren't readily visible during the debrief. Furthermore, as is symptomatic of many 'formal observations', Jill was largely just grateful that the lesson had gone to plan, and that she had convinced me that she was a capable teacher. The final questions from her, as is often the case, were about the overall judgement/grade of the lesson and when the next observation would be, rather than about the key moments of the lesson and how we could work together to develop her practice further and share her positive teacher-characteristics with others.

Within a relatively short space of time, powerful and portable smart devices and faster cloud-computing services had become commonplace. On becoming a full-time teacher educator at Newcastle University, alongside my long-standing and ongoing interest in the use of technology to support teaching and learning, I saw an opportunity to explore the possibility of developing an app which would help me support my trainee teachers in their professional development. Readily available, inexpensive and flexible technology that everyone was already familiar with was the stepping-stone towards being able to realize my goal.

Four months after starting work at the university, I attended a business development meeting and submitted my idea, literally on the back of a postcard, asking for funds to support the development of an iPad video app for use on the PGCE programme, which could also become a commercially viable product. Paul happened to be at the same meeting, pitching almost the same idea and, coincidentally, while we hadn't spoken to each other, our offices were in the same building. So, once a colleague on the development team had spotted the similarities in our proposals and made introductions, we were able to collaborate with ease and get the project moving. Paul takes up the story of his journey from here.

Paul Miller's Perspective

As Jon's ideas and experiences developed in the UK, I was exploring ways to improve practice in multiple international contexts, most notably in impoverished settings within West Africa. I had taken a similar journey to Jon, through a PGCE, but continuing on to studying for a masters in Education at Newcastle University. Exposed to and inspired by the different ways at looking at education and learning – such as self-organized approaches being explored by Sugata Mitra – my background in teaching English as a foreign language (on and off for five years) had given me further diverse perspectives on how learning could be achieved.

Subsequently consulting for Newcastle University, I designed and delivered large-scale teacher and leadership training programmes in 2012 across multiple schools in Ghana and Sierra Leone. Moving on from an original brief to transmit knowledge to teachers, I aimed to develop cascaded and self-perpetuating training programmes, based around the kind of collaborative activity being introduced to pupils concurrently.

In some of the poorer locations, bright and enthusiastic teachers' English reading and writing ability was limited and it became clear that asking them to assimilate their own understandings and communicate them to pupils in this medium could not lead to successful learning. Learning in the schools in question, as in vast swathes of the developing world, was dominated by rote methods, the teacher as the dominant purveyor of knowledge. Observing several lessons across months, it could be seen that a majority of pupils were understanding little despite spending six hours a day, five days a week in stifling classrooms!

Therefore, the goal of the training programmes was to introduce more pupil-centred forms of learning and teaching. This would involve for many, a huge change in mindset. In Ghana, we started the mammoth task of organizing large-scale training sessions in the largest building in the area – a huge half-finished, church building – inviting teachers from across the Central Region and beyond. Lead teachers, selected for their ability to grasp and share new teaching methodologies, were trained to deliver group sessions to other teachers, using the participative methods that we aimed for the teachers to adopt themselves. This catalysed lively discussion of practice leading to trial implementation in microteaching sessions and followed by robust yet constructive peer feedback.

The resulting large-scale enthusiastic training days received very positive feedback from the vast majority of participants. However, there was a sneaking thought that this warm reception was simply the gratitude of largely untrained teachers having had rare time dedicated to professional development! This suspicion grew when we travelled around schools after the training, observing lessons and hoping to see the more

Figure 3.1 Teacher training in Ghana.

participative methods – involving some group work and peer learning – in action. Unfortunately, we found that the training had actually resulted in very little change in practice.

We realized that the size of the intended changes in approach, and multiple factors involved in putting them in practice, required shifts in mindset and would put teachers outside of their comfort zone, particularly when faced with the reality of upwards of forty pupils and the expectations of the local community. Therefore, if the training resulted in little or no change in teaching or resultant improvements in pupils learning, then it had largely been a waste of time, despite positive externalities deriving from bringing teachers together. Improving pupil learning was our aim and purpose.

Years later, we analysed this with respect to the Kirkpatrick model for evaluating training (Kirkpatrick 1996).

Figure 3.2 The Kirkpatrick model for evaluating training.

In receiving positive feedback, we had achieved Level 1 (above). It appeared, from the participants' engagement in the concepts during the training, that Level 2 had also, to an extent, been reached. However, practical behavioural change (Level 3) would require something different, perceptions of the value of enacting methods and frameworks being heavily influenced by teachers' immediate circumstances and the ingrained social and cultural environment. A new model was needed.

An advantage of working in West Africa was that I was given great access to observe the teaching and learning environment across several schools, both independently and through the eyes of the school leaders. Looking through glassless windows set in the breezeblock classrooms, I could see different, but inspiring learning environments created by novice teachers' own ideas, commitment and strong relationships with the children. Some teachers had developed their own specific techniques – such as a peer buddy system for catching up with absentees – and developed highly energetic and engaged learning environments that swept along all children with the learning.

As well as providing an entirely different frame to expand own my ideas on creating learning environments, I started thinking about how there was already a rich seam of teaching and learning to be built on across the schools. Immersive observation was key to realizing this, and I felt this experience needed to be extended across the wider community of teachers so that all could benefit and adapt from the experiences in classrooms like theirs.

I started experimenting, sharing practice via authentic in-classroom video clips captured on the fly, illustrating successful techniques to share with a wider community of teachers. Beyond the immediate benefits, this engendered great excitement about sharing, with teachers seeing each other teach and developing together. Breaking down the walls of the classroom through video was a bottom-up approach that recognized the strengths of existing practices and built confidence among teachers. Firstly, they were gratified that some things they were doing were worth sharing, and secondly, they could now imagine embedding the successful techniques they'd seen their colleagues enact, having viewed them in full detail, in similar classrooms to their own.

We organized sessions to give feedback on practice and encouraged lead teachers to actively make suggestions to teachers, based on a growing bank of videoed practice. Some schools were even able to follow up by capturing the attempts of teachers to implement new techniques, in a rudimentary action research model that guaranteed that changes in practice would be attempted and then embedded in new classrooms.

By developing such a methodology from the ground up, the scale was theoretically limitless and the 'facilitated user network' model so disruptive to the status-quo – as outlined by Christensen et al. in 'Disrupting Class' (2008) – that I was keen to refine and develop the system to generate lasting change in how teacher, leader and practical learning could happen.

Like Jon, I put together my business ideas on returning to Newcastle University and was happy that we could weave our overlapping perspectives into concrete product and

The Development of the VEO App 27

business plans. Bringing our ideas together allowed us to conceive a system combining the immediacy of key 'lightbulb' video learning moments, with the scale, reach and impact of easily shareable practice.

Shared Aims and the Resulting System

From our experiences, observations, hopes and frustrations, the initial idea for VEO was born. Our goal was to create an opportunity to capture, annotate, analyse, store and share videoed episodes of professional practice. Most importantly, this should use existing, readily available technology which was accessible, flexible, relatively inexpensive and easy to use.

Once the initial idea had been brought to fruition in the shape of an iPad app (as described in Chapter 4), the next step was to seek a second round of funding to support the development of the online storage and sharing functionality that would take VEO from being a useful tool to a learning platform. This came quickly from a local firm of venture capitalists who saw the potential of the product, and after a period of six months development, the fully integrated app and secure online sharing portal were ready to be used, safely and at scale.

Because it derived from both UK and international (local and global) perspectives, we have been able to develop a system which is universally applicable, irrespective of the domain and context in which it is used. The system has been designed to enable full translation of the interface, the use of international keyboards and characters, and all users are free to adapt the terminology used to suit their purposes, languages and cultures.

From trainee teachers, to experienced teachers, from school-leaders to school governors, the use of VEO to support reflective practice has now grown to include professionals in the clinical, commercial, legal and industrial sectors. Through early experiences showcasing VEO at Newcastle University and at other networking opportunities, medical professionals and clinical educators quickly identified that VEO would provide an apposite solution to accelerating practical learning. There follow four mini-case studies showcasing examples of how VEO has been deployed in the real world, with the benefits to each approach outlined.

Case Study 1: Improved Student Teacher Lesson Observation Debrief Using Video

Overview

Most observations made when watching a teacher in the classroom are recorded by hand, pen on paper, or typed. Trying to transcribe elements of dialogue is challenging enough; endeavouring to capture other unspoken interactions is even harder and subject to misinterpretation. Interpreting the notes made during a lesson debrief is similarly difficult. As an initial teacher educator, I was keen to enable my student teachers to develop a more open and constructive approach to reflecting on and evaluating their own lessons. I was also keen to move the conversation from mentoring-style instruction to a coaching-style conversation (Lofthouse, Leat and Towler 2010), reducing the dependency on others to inform future practice.

Approach

After gaining permission and consent from those involved, lessons are filmed by the observer using VEO. The observer is free to circulate and gather video footage of various aspects of teacher and pupil activity and interaction. Key moments are tagged to highlight features, questions and characteristics of teaching and learning. Depending on the stage of training, these moments can be ad-hoc, or focused on particular areas of interest and need.

Outcome

Rather than the conversation being based upon two different recollections of the same lesson, mostly guided by what was written down, tagged aspects of the lesson were viewed. Normally, the trainee would view these independently while I discussed the lesson and trainee's general progress with the school mentor. The moments were then watched again together, and a collective understanding and interpretation were developed through a series of rich and open questions. In my experience, the conversation was noticeably different and far more productive and less one-sided.

Figure 3.3 Lesson debriefing using VEO-tagged video as a stimulus for discussion and professional development.

Table 3.1 Comparison of text-based and video-based observation

Text-based lesson observation	Video-based observation
One-sided – led by the narrative of the observer	Balanced/Flipped – the trainee teacher can be encouraged to look at the moments through the lens of the observer or the pupils
Defensive – the trainee teacher can at times become very defensive of any observations	Candid – discovering and identifying our own strengths and weaknesses seem less likely to be such a debateable issue
Accepting – the trainee teacher can often appear to simply accept suggestions for improvement, developing a sense of dependency – relying on others to solve the problems and highlight the positives	The trainee is encouraged and enabled to develop their own solutions and way forward. There seems to be a greater sense of understanding of why things work or do not, and a greater capacity to improve

Case Study 2: Self-observation and Lesson Evaluation during Teaching Placements/Practicum

Overview

Student teachers are regularly observed by school mentors, other teachers and University tutors. Normally, there is at least one formal observation per week as part of the UK's Initial Teacher Training programme. The depth of reflection on, and development resulting from these lessons is variable, and unless they include the methodology suggested in the previous case study, are likely to maintain and build a culture of mentor-dependency. While these observations are an important assessment and measure of a trainee's progress towards meeting the Teachers' Standards, they are not always as helpful in developing and changing, understanding and practice. More frequent opportunities to observe lessons would simply add to an already demanding workload for trainee, mentor and tutor, so getting more from observations requires a more efficient approach. Video and the VEO app have proven very helpful in doing this.

Approach

The trainee teacher videos a lesson and uses VEO to retrospectively tag and add comments to moments that they believe to be significant. These moments may provide evidence of good practice, evidence of progress towards meeting previously established targets, or highlight aspects of the lesson which are either interesting, or that raise questions and issues for discussion and development. The tagged video is then shared with both the school-based mentor and the university tutor using VEO's secure online portal. Additional tags and comments can then be added by the mentor and tutor alongside, and in response to, those added by the trainee teacher. This enables a synchronous assessment, evaluation, review, reflection and discussion. This shared experience can then be used to inform and support subsequent face-to-face (or telephone) conversations.

Outcomes

The most notable outcome has been the ability to focus on aspects of the lesson which are most likely to lead to improved future practice. If the mentor and tutor can see which characteristics and aspects of the lesson the student is most positive or negative about, the coaching conversation can then focus on those which are more problematic. In my very first experience of this process, it was clear that while the management of pupil behaviours was not a strong point of the lesson, the trainee teacher was already aware of this, and had already identified appropriate strategies to pursue. On the other hand, the type of questioning was an issue that they were less aware of but needed to progress.

Figure 3.6 shows tagging and annotation undertaken by myself, drawing the trainee's attention to the need to develop a stronger approach to questioning. This is

Figure 3.4 Tagging and annotation of this particular moment highlighting a behavioural incident, and the trainee teacher's own response to the issue.

Figure 3.5 Annotations can be viewed as a string of notes which can be commented upon further as shown above.

Figure 3.6 Tagging and annotation which draw the trainee's attention to the need to develop a stronger approach to questioning.

something we then discussed further in a face-to-face conversation while watching the moment together. Interestingly, I had to do very little. The trainee teacher had already started to script rich questions within their lesson plans and presentations, stimulated by my comment on the video.

This approach also saves considerable time normally spent travelling to and from the placement schools, time which can then be invested in communication with our trainees, both through the VEO system and telephone conversations.

Case Study 3: Cross-national Training and Implementation of New Pedagogy

Overview

VEO now works with several training providers across diverse fields within education (and beyond). Once such London-based group partnered with VEO to train several hundred teachers from across Kazakhstan in new pedagogy and approaches to learning. Areas included assessment strategies, utilizing cognition in the classroom and implementing CLIL (content and language-integrated learning). Given that Kazakhstan is larger in area than the whole of Western Europe, the need to train teachers from all corners of the country had provided the training company with huge challenges! They turned to VEO, and by working in partnership we were able to create and apply an effective and engaging remote training programme that was able to evidence considered application of new teaching techniques in classrooms across Kazakhstan.

Approach

The several hundred teachers were brought together for initial face-to-face training over four days, each day dedicated to four new areas of pedagogy. Initial activities involved being grouped into peer groups of six to eight teachers. Together, using VEO, they tagged the trainers' videos which had been created to demonstrate the new techniques in action and to exemplify differing degrees of successful implementation.

Returning to their schools across Kazakhstan, teachers were then tasked with capturing a small number of lessons and tagging just three moments of their choice within each which related to their training. They then added a short paragraph of annotation on the moment, describing how and why they had implemented the technique. They tagged using simple tag sets, directly related to their training.

Through VEO, the video was then shared with a trainer-coach and their peer group, now dispersed across Kazakhstan. Peers added their feedback, with the coach prompting further exploration and discussion of concepts and practice through carefully selected questioning. As a result, each teacher would gain feedback on twelve moments of new practice spread across four video lessons, while benefiting from active discussion and insight from a further five to seven teachers, each sharing twelve moments of their own.

Outcome

What we achieved through this collaboration was a highly efficient way to introduce new practice across great distances. By tagging and analysing practice, teachers could continue to develop, way beyond the time spent in face-to-face training. This evidenced that the new techniques and strategies were not only embedded in teachers'

Figure 3.7 Training with teachers from Kazakhstan.

Figure 3.8 Using VEO with teachers from Kazakhstan.

practice, but that continuous learning was also embedded within the teacher role with minimum disruption.

In this engaging and effective programme, learning happened in recurring classroom activity, and from sharing reflective feedback from and to peers. This simple teacher (as learner) led process drew in participants and allowing them to interact on their own terms and practice, since they were able to select the moments they wanted to share. The clarity of task (select three moments to tag and annotate) meant that busy teachers could fit their professional learning easily into their busy days. This was aided by the task's asynchronous nature.

VEO continues to work with training partners with backgrounds from corporate and communication-based learning, to medical and educationalist specialisms. By embedding a simple learner-centred approach, VEO becomes a highly engaging platform to share and feedback on practice, interaction and process across any distance.

Case Study 4: Improving and Assessing Skills and Human Factors in Clinical Practice

Overview

VEO was quickly identified by clinical practitioners and lecturers as having significant application in the field. Trainee doctors, nurses and paramedics all need to acquire progressively more complex technical and procedural skills through experience, whether simulated or real. Alongside technical skill, human factors (such as communication skills, teamwork, leadership and self-management in stressful situations) are increasingly understood to be critical to optimizing patient outcomes.

Figure 3.9 Using VEO for clinical practice.

These aspects, which combine interaction and process, lend themselves to improvement through the rich feedback offered by video, with VEO's time-specific tags augmenting access to key learning moments and evidence for assessment.

In this field, the margin for error is low. Student paramedics, for example, face a rush to acquire the required skills and techniques, in preparation for their placement experience on ambulances, where they face real situations with the potential for life or death consequences for the patient.

VEO has worked with universities such as Sunderland and Gloucestershire to provide an efficient and effective means for students to reflect and improve on their practice, and to continuously evidence their competency, through to certification in degree-level courses and beyond.

Approach

Clinical learning is heavily simulation focused; while learning through experience requires repeated practice, the seriousness (and unpredictability) of real-life scenarios justifies students' initial participation in high-fidelity simulated experience. Working with course leaders and lecturers, tag sets were developed to match the frameworks and competencies used in the different areas, which ranged from 'basics', such as checking a pulse and providing CPR, through to multi-service scenarios acted out across several locations.

In these settings, VEO enables easy capture, using readily accessible devices, with self and peer reflection then available either in the moment, or later. Accessing tagged video later allows students to take stock of their practice away from the more pressured simulation environment. Tagging key moments of strength, as well as areas for improvement, gives the student a considered basis for discussing progress with, and seeking help from course tutors.

Furthermore, VEO's use extends to assessment. Replacing paper-based observation in the standard OSCE (objective-structured clinical examination) assessments, VEO enhanced the efficiency and objectivity of the marking process, while generating evidence to underpin grade decisions.

Outcome

VEO has proven popular with students and has allowed universities such as Sunderland and Gloucestershire to continue providing practical clinical courses throughout the Covid-19 pandemic. The way course lecturers have adopted the system has increased learner independence as they are newly able to identify their strengths and areas for improvement. As with the Kazakhstan example (above), sharing with peer groups meant that students could learn from one another, adopting the best practices into their own, while increasing their awareness of diverse actions and scenarios. Furthermore, the ability for video to capture interaction as well as skill has meant that learning can happen in both areas simultaneously.

As opposed to a 'film studio' approach used previously, with expensive fixed cameras providing limited reach, universities have been able to extend, accelerate and democratize learning through VEO, by taking a secure 'YouTube' approach to learning. This has since been shown to result in improvement in skills assessment performance (Clegg et al. 2018).

Discussion – The VEO Value

The four mini-case studies outlined above indicate how VEO can be used to support learning at multiple levels across diverse fields. Common themes can be seen in the focus of learning being through experience, in action and interaction. Video gave important advantages in being able to see and understand a situation, with learner focus heightened by tags, customized to the scenario, accentuating key moments. This simple innovation has been shown to open up new models of learning, created in partnership with educators to solve existing limitations and to improve learning experiences. These are extended at scale and across distance-secure global connections, enabled via the web and having been normalized by the pioneering social media giants. This allows coherent learning and objective assessment to derive from a range of complex situations, as exemplified in the case studies above, and through the experiences of Jon and Paul that led them to develop the system.

With practical origins, VEO has always focused on ease of use and simplicity. Understanding practice in complex and busy environments is challenging, and VEO's quasi-qualitative-quantitative tagging and annotation system provides great opportunities for stimulating valuable practical development and change – bringing practitioners together and moving practice forward. From a design perspective, the users of VEO are quickly rewarded with lightbulb moments, and simple but telling statistical feedback. This draws them in to participate and share in reciprocal processes based on easily accessible learning points. Simplifying the experience reduces barriers to adoption and learning, since using the system requires little additional mental effort, so the time spent reflecting on practice is productive and powerful.

Other solutions using video for professional development tend to focus heavily on the hardware for capturing and storing video, quickly becoming obsolete and unnecessary in an era where any smartphone, tablet or laptop has powerful video recording capabilities. VEO has always strived to be an affordable and cost-effective solution. Through focusing on the user experience, the system and software functionality, rather than the hardware, we have created a system which is both accessible and effective.

The VEO system allows the upload, tagging and annotation of any video, captured on any device. The bulk of this is user-generated but can also include licensed video footage from third-party sources. The ability to share this footage among peers and those with appropriate authorization within and beyond the organization extends VEO's ability to positively impact on classroom practice and systematic change. Users can choose to use VEO in isolation, developing their understanding and practice thorough self-evaluation and reflection; seek the opinion and views of others for peer observation and reflection; or curate and share examples of classroom practice which can inform, educate and stimulate others to inform their classroom practice too.

One of VEO's unique selling points comes in the form of the flexible tagging system. This means that VEO can be used to tag and address commonly accepted characteristics and behaviours of teaching and learning in the classroom using the default tag sets. Alternatively, the tags can be modified and refined to focus on, or use the language of, an organization's specific teaching and learning habits, or those of interest to its departments, subject areas or teachers. Equally, this greatly extends VEO's use across diverse learning environments, from developing leadership traits or abilities in communication, to clinical or vocational skills.

With VEO, all those engaging in the process of videoing, tagging and annotating are learning, and are developing a clearer understanding of and rationale for the moments they observe and comment on. Those watching the videos are supported in their understanding through the annotations and tags left by others. The tagged moments within the shared catalogue of videos are searchable and can provide quick and easy access to examples of moments captured across the organization, enabling further learning by, and in support of, others.

Experienced and inspiring teachers and leaders finally have the means through which they can disseminate good practice and provide the tools through which better practice can emerge and be shared. Consistency in understanding of what good practice looks like can be more readily developed and perceptions and prejudices discussed, creating a system that supports teachers to maximize learning and progress for their students. At every level, the participants can be seen as continuously learning, with video bringing visibility to intentions, actions and consequences, while the tag-data brings a focus on themes, strengths and areas for development.

Conclusions

The story of VEO since its inception in early 2013 shows the importance of design being based on needs, first identified by our own professional experiences. This has ensured relevance across multiple levels of learning. In meeting complex requirements within the classroom, VEO fulfils a key learning need across sectors and environments, principally to aid learning through experience.

This has been expanded upon in the examples above, each showing how a simple technology can change and improve learning methods, approaches and collaborations, bringing both efficiency and deeper learning at scale. The mini-case studies show how VEO brings immediacy to practical learning and build effective communication and collaboration around learning, enhancing conversations either in person or asynchronously at distance.

VEO has become a system of learning, built on key moments of lived experience, which generates evolving shared or negotiated perspectives, as well as mindfully changed activity in continuous cycles of feedback and improvement. Twenty-first-century technology allows an almost infinite scalability to this, bounded only by the availability of the system in practical terms. Following its origins, VEO's technology will continue to adapt to meet needs by enhancing ease of use and adoption, both through the experiences of its initial user pioneers and newly identified opportunities to learn at scale. The ongoing purpose will be to direct efforts towards providing easily acquired phronesis and associated deeper learning.

4

Using VEO – A Practical Guide

Paul Miller,
VEO Group
Jon Haines
Newcastle University, UK

Introduction

VEO is at its heart a video tagging web app, with associated iPad, Android and iOS apps. The basic elements that generate VEO's key and unique features will be described in this chapter, alongside the support within the system which is designed to augment learning. Processes for using and deploying are described so that this chapter may serve as a guide to implementing the system. These cover many of the considerations for deploying any means of video learning. Finally, there is discussion of the different types of practical learning that can be achieved, building up from recognition and understanding, through to mastery of practice.

As the chapter progresses, it builds up a description of VEO's learning system as a whole. The chapter is broken down into smaller discrete sections to aid understanding. The sections are laid out as follows:

1. VEO Video Tagging – The Basic Elements Defined
2. Video Review – The Results of Tagging
3. Processes for Tagging and Annotating a Video
4. Additional VEO Features for Generating Learning
5. Processes to Support Learning from Tagged Videos
6. Capturing the Video
7. Processes for Uploading Video
8. Types of Learning Generated
9. Processes for Implementing Different Types of Learning

Taken together, these sections act as a guide through the basic elements within VEO, building understanding of their functions, their place in relation to collaborative features, and revealing how these elements can work together to enhance learning activities.

1) VEO Video Tagging – The Basic Elements Defined

At its most basic level, VEO allows users to place time-related data onto video. This makes your videos much easier to work with, as we will see below. This data takes different forms, allowing discrete and continuous data to be captured as needed for the user's purpose.

Timestamp Tags

VEO provides the opportunity to timestamp 'tag' moments in video. What this means in layman's terms is that a user would click on a tag button while watching a video through VEO. This leaves a timestamp that can be returned to at a later point when watching back, effectively bookmarking the video with the tag. This makes it much easier to locate the events you want to return to in the video. As will be shown later in Section 2, the discrete data created by these tagged moments can be aggregated into statistical evidence to help with analysis of the video. All of these tags are customizable in the system, so that they can be made appropriate for different contexts and professional fields.

Example tag buttons are shown to the left and right of the video in Figure 4.1.

Simple Tags and Subtags

These timestamp tag buttons can be created in one of two forms within VEO:

1) The tag buttons themselves can directly timestamp the video on pressing. This form of tags has come to be known as a 'simple' tag.
2) The second form of tag is more complex as it opens up a menu of 'subtag' options to define the moment further. A menu of subtags is shown in Figure 4.2. In this example the user has clicked the 'Questioning' tag on the left of the screen and is able to select whether the moment relates to an open question, closed question or an episode of eliciting.

Figure 4.1 'Tag' buttons to the left and right of the video.

Using VEO – A Practical Guide

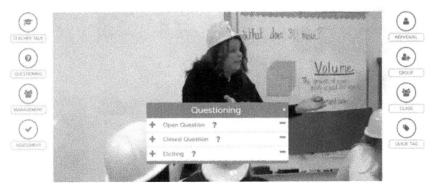

Figure 4.2 Tags with 'subtags'.

Subtag Ratings

As can be seen in Figure 4.2, subtags can be rated either '+', indicating a positive moment; '?', indicating a question arising at this moment; or '–', indicating room for improvement or an opportunity missed. Implications of rating moments in this way are discussed in Section 2.

Tag Timing

For both simple tags and tags with subtags, the timestamp is left on the video five seconds before the first click by the user. When tagging while watching the video, the bookmark would be left on the video five seconds prior to the click on the buttons to the left or right of the screen. If the tag has subtags, the timestamp tag would already be created five seconds before the first click, so the user then has time to click a second time define the tag further.

The rationale for this five second difference is to allow the viewer to see the run up to the tagged moment on review. Furthermore, the delay means that when tagging a video as it is playing, the user does not feel rushed to find and select the tag since the moment should still be captured in time.

Tagged Notes

At any time while tagging the video, notes can be added to the tags. These allow further description, analysis or questioning of the moment to be developed through text notes associated with the timestamp tag in the video. These build potential for collaborative online interrogation and discussion of videoed activity, situated within the key video moment. This will be outlined further in the video review Section 2. Figure 4.3 shows how a note can be added to the tag. Tags appear to the right of the video screen as they are created by the user. By clicking 'Notes' the user can then enter text against the tag.

Figure 4.3 Adding a note against a tag.

'Possession' Tags

The user can also use continuous tag measures to unpick the action in the video. These tags appear beneath the video on the screen and can be selected and changed over time. When conceiving the idea in the design phase, the analogy of possession in football (or other sports) was used. Here, statistics track how much time one team or another has the ball, and similarly these continuous tags allow the user to track the amount of time spent in different interactional modes. The first use for this in VEO was to track the amount of time spent in the classroom with the teacher talking, compared with in group work, individual work or whole class activities. An example of how this is displayed on the video is shown in Figure 4.4. Again, these tags are completely customizable to fit different contexts and goals.

These buttons can be seen beneath the timeline of the video and in this example the 'Teacher' tag has been clicked and appears yellow. This would be changed by the user if,

Figure 4.4 'Possession' tags beneath the screen.

for example, the class moved on to a group activity. Therefore, the total amount of time spent in these different modes is captured, the system counting the amount of time in a mode, until the user changes the mode. The system then aggregates the total amount of time for each once tagging is completed. The data that results from this is therefore continuous and comparative, rather than discrete. This is discussed in further depth in Section 2.

Slider

Another means to capture continuous data in the video is provided by a percentage slider located at the bottom of the screen. This is used as a measure of how well an aspect of the videoed activity is going at any one time, as judged by the viewer. This has been used in several different ways by users, but one example from the classroom would be to measure an estimate of overall pupil engagement. In language learning this has also been used as a measure of spoken language fluency. What the slider measures is completely customizable by the user. The slider is moved left and right during the video to provide an overall view on how the quality of whatever is being measured has changed over time. The position of the slider is shown in Figure 4.5.

Summary

Through the VEO interface, the user can tag and evaluate action within a video by adding three simple data types. Discrete and continuous data leads to an enhanced 'video reviewing' experience, as described in the next section (2). These are derived through user interaction with the three tag types and are augmented by the notes facility to build conversation into the key identified moments.

Figure 4.5 Percentage slider, showing 'Engagement' in this example.

2) Video Review – The Results of Tagging

Tagging and annotating video is not done without purpose in mind. There will be intent from the user to get something further from the video. The tags mark up the videos in ways that make it more accessible, informative and insightful, with benefits across use cases and contexts. The following section will describe the enhanced features of video review that VEO's tagging can provide.

Bookmarking and Annotating Key Moments

Tagging key moments in the video using the buttons to the left and right of the screen allows users to jump straight to these on reviewing the video. This means that key episodes can be crystallized as learning moments. The tags are displayed on the right-hand side of the video and are clickable. The value of this for time-poor learning professionals has proven to be significant. This layout is shown in Figure 4.6.

Figure 4.6 Interactive tagged moments to navigate the video.

Figure 4.7 Highlighted key moments.

Furthermore, as the video plays, the tagged moments are highlighted on the main video screen. This makes the moment more concrete for the viewer and indicates a step change in focus, as defined by the tagger. This is illustrated in Figure 4.7.

Notes are also displayed on screen against any of these key moments. These pop out into the screen, maintaining the viewer's attention on the activity in the screen (as shown in Figure 4.8).

Figure 4.8 Notes popping out onto video.

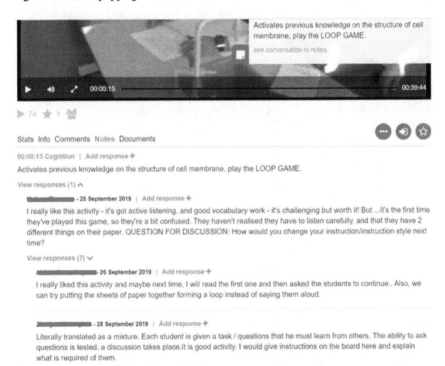

Figure 4.9 An example of note conversation.

Where notes already exist on the tags, these can be responded to. The note is also shown beneath the video and the user simply clicks 'Add response', as illustrated in Figure 4.9. This builds up conversation trees in the notes as shown. This is beneficial for asking questions in video, generating feedback and building deeper discussion of issues, whether in a teacher-student relationship, among peers, or both. This is explored further in Section 8.

Statistical Insight and Deeper Discussion

Beyond bookmarking the video to make key moments more accessible, tagging the video generates statistics that can be interacted with on review. The three main types of statistical presentation provided are described below.

Strengths and Areas for Improvement

When users timestamp-tag the video for discrete key moments, the system is able to aggregate these by category. Where this involves simple tags, their frequencies can be displayed in a bar chart. However, where the tags have subtags, these can be formulated into a grouped bar chart showing frequency of positive or negative moments (however these have been termed [see below]). An example of this is shown in Figure 4.10.

This can then give the user an indication of relative strengths and areas for improvement. The intention behind VEO is not to provide a fixed judgement, but to provide the basis for repeated conscious attempts that can lead to improvement in practice over time. The bar chart aids reflection during this process by drawing out a clearly and instantly memorable picture from lengthy video episodes.

The strength of the summariness of message provided by quantitative data is combined with the easily accessible qualitative video data. As such, it is important to remember that each tag is itself a judgement, opinion, approximation or analysis of

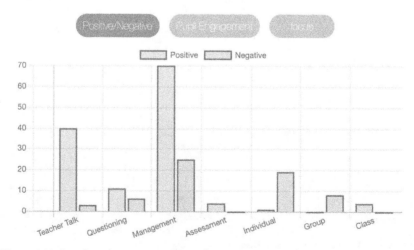

Figure 4.10 Bar chart showing positives and negatives in a teaching session.

what happened in the video. Therefore, in most cases the tags and their aggregation are open to interpretation.

Nevertheless, graphs can give quick and clear insight, for example, pointing a student teacher to areas for improvement or highlighting to a language learner that while their vocabulary is improving, there are still areas to work on in their spoken use of grammar.

As alluded to above, the '+' and '–' tags can be customized to refer to other terminology than simply 'positive' and 'negative'. More developmental examples include 'Strengths' and 'Developments'. When designing the system, there had been some discussion with academic colleagues over whether a 'negative' tag should be included at all, when considering VEO's original use case of supportive teacher development. However, feedback from teachers and lecturers has shown that users do appreciate the opportunity to see where they could improve or do something different. Regular analysis of the ratio of positive to negative tags across the whole VEO system consistently shows a 9:1 ratio. This indicates that VEO is being used in the supportive manner that was originally intended.

'Possession' Pie Charts

The 'Possession' tags shown in Figure 4.4 collect and aggregate continuous time data for each of the modes. These data feed naturally into a pie chart, showing respective percentage of the total time spent in each mode. Examples of this being used to good effect include capturing the amount of teacher talk time for novice teachers, evaluating the ownership of a conversation between a corporate professional and their coach, or the talk time between patient and clinician.

As with the bar charts above, these provide a clear profile across the video and lead therefore to actionable insights. This is most usefully deployed to motivate change in further VEO sessions in cycles of continuous improvement. The clarity of display is shown in Figure 4.11. Within the system, the precise percentage will appear when the cursor is hovered over the relevant segment.

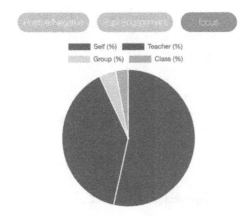

Figure 4.11 'Possession' pie chart example.

Percentage Slider: 'How Good' Over Time

The third means of capturing data on the video is via a percentage slider, through which reviewers would capture their view on the quality of what they are observing. This is customizable, and usually the definition of what this slider refers to will reflect the key observable indicator for success in a videoed session. For example, in teaching sessions this might refer to an overall view on class engagement (as seen in Figure 4.12). For sales training this might refer to likelihood of sale, and for customer service training this may reflect customer satisfaction over time.

The output for this data is an interactive line graph. The line can be clicked, taking the user to the different moments in the video where the percentage slider was changed. This allows the user to quickly access periods in the video where it was working out well or not, allowing them further insight and enhanced reflection on causes, effects and clues to actions to take forward. In addition, by analysing multiple videos in VEO, patterns in performance may be observed. For example, a presenter may start off sluggishly, but gradually win over their audience – or vice versa.

Attaching Files

As hinted by Figure 4.9 screenshot, documents and other files can be uploaded and associated with the video. From the several contexts in which VEO works, we have examples of this being used to upload, for example, lesson plans and materials, clinical assessment rubrics, language speaking activity outlines, presentations, or even verbal feedback via audio file. The intention with this feature is to centre the

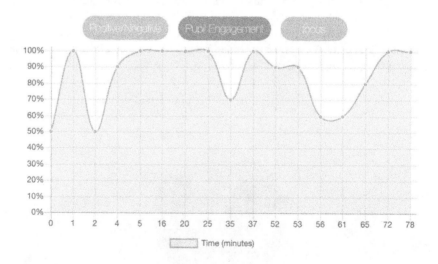

Figure 4.12 Changes in 'Engagement' over time.

learning on the video so that all necessary artefacts can be easily accessed from there, alongside the tags.

Summary

VEO aims to provide clear and actionable insights into practice. Tagged video makes key moments accessible to learn from, while statistics and graphs can give a clear summary picture. This aids reflective processes and can motivate changes in action towards the user's goals, whatever their context and purpose. Practical processes behind the features are now outlined in Section 3.

3) Processes for Tagging and Annotating a Video

VEO was designed to generate learning from action, using video as the most insightful yet accessible technology medium. To achieve this aim at scale and for a diverse cross-section of users, it is essential that it is as easy as possible to use. An indication of the simplicity of the system is given by the user processes outlined below. These also illuminate how the system would be used in practice and can serve as a primer to those wishing to understand more, as well as a guide to VEO account holders.

Logging In

- Go to https://veo.co.uk on your web-connected device (phone, tablet, laptop, PC, etc.)
- Click 'login' at the top right of the screen
- Enter your email address and password

Beginning Tagging

- From the VEO homepage https://app.veo.co.uk/#/, click into the video you wish to tag.
- If the video hasn't been tagged before, click the 'Tag Video' button.
- If the video has previously been tagged, click on the 'New Tag Session' link.
- Select a tag set (see Section 4) from the dropdown.
- Click Continue

Tags

- Play the video and click on the tags buttons to the left and right to tag key moments in the video. This will timestamp the video five seconds before the first click.
- Some tags are 'simple' tags and some tags are 'subtags'
- Clicking Simple tags immediately tags the video

- Clicking tags with subtags allows you to select a further subtag and whether the moment is '+', '?' or '–'
- Tags can be annotated – see below

Possession Tags

- Select tags at the bottom of the screen to capture data that will feed into a pie chart. These tags will continuously measure until another tag is pressed. These can be used for measuring, for example, the percentage of total time a teacher is speaking, or the amount of time spent in group work mode.

Slider

- The slider at the bottom of the screen can be shifted left and right to capture a continuous per cent measure. Often this is to evaluate overall engagement of a class, quality of learning, behaviour management or any focus which indicates 'how well' the episode is going.

Notes

- Tags can be annotated. Click the red 'Notes' link beneath the tag. Then type your notes in the 'Notes' section beneath the video. This can be used to insert short or long commentary, feedback, questions or comments.
- Click the Play icon in the video to continue tagging.

Saving Tags

- Click 'Submit tags' when finished tagging
- Click 'Submit tag session' to save the tags

Processes for Viewing a Tagged Video

These processes further illuminate how a user might achieve quick understanding or insights by accessing and interacting with the tagged video.

Accessing the Tags

- From your VEO homepage https://app.veo.co.uk/#/, click into the video you wish to view.
- If the video has been tagged, you will be able to see the most recent tag session.
- To select different 'tagging sessions', click 'Select Tag Session'. You will see a dropdown of the different times the video has been tagged, the tag set used and the name of the tagger.
- Select the tag session you wish to see.

Using VEO – A Practical Guide 51

Interacting with Tags

- Click on the tags on the right of the screen to jump to these key moments.
- You can organize these in the default timeline or by category (top-level tag).

Viewing and Responding to Notes

- View any tags with notes by clicking on the 'View Note' link beneath those tags.
- The note will pop out onto the video screen.
- You can view notes and interact with them by selecting the 'Notes' tab beneath the video screen.
- From here you can jump through the tags with notes.
- You can respond to notes by clicking 'Add Response'.
- Responses can be given at multiple levels so that conversation threads can form.
- Multiple responses to the same note by different people can be seen by clicking 'View Responses' beneath the note.

Statistics

- Statistics from the tags can be viewed by clicking the 'Stats' tab beneath the video.
- Toggle between a 'key moment tags' bar chart, 'possession' pie chart and an 'engagement' line graph.
- The line graph is clickable, allowing you to jump to moments on the line.

Documents

Clicking on the 'Documents' tab under the video gives the opportunity to upload documents, PDFs, video and audio files to be associated with the video. These can be used to provide audio feedback, or to supplement the video with associated plans or materials.

4) Additional VEO Features for Generating Learning

Beyond VEO's unique selling proposition (USP) of video tagging, the system deploys social features common on social media platforms to enhance and multiply learning possibilities. Furthermore, the tags themselves are organized into customizable 'Tag Sets', meaning that rubrics and frameworks can be used repeatedly over time, adding further meaning to the data generated.

Sharing in VEO

This chapter has so far described VEO's functionality in terms of its combination of video and tag data for reflection and continuous improvement. This can clearly be augmented through appropriate collaboration and sharing, depending on the situation.

Tagged video can be shared to support a teacher-student, expert-novice, coach-coachee or peer-peer relationship. This allows the video owner to gain valuable feedback from their colleagues, while the user who is feeding back develops understanding of the practice by seeing it performed. This provides scalable learning experiences based on real-life events. These user-generated resources can be more authentic than anything overly staged.

In addition, sharing video opens up a range of learning activities, since anyone who has had a video shared with them can tag it. For example, a course leader could share an interesting video, tagged up with questions, for their students to respond to. The potential for this is explored further in Section 8 below.

Sharing is accessed via a widely recognized 'share' icon from the video page. As shown in Figure 4.13, the video can be shared with individuals or groups according to the video owner's preference.

It is important to note that the video owner has full control over who sees the video, and can revoke sharing permissions at any time. Users who have had videos shared with them cannot go on to share the video themselves.

Groups

Sharing is supported by the ability to create groups within VEO. As can be seen in Figure 4.13, tagged video can be shared with groups. Furthermore, videos can be organized by group, meaning that learning communities can be formed at distance.

Fortunately for VEO, the concept of creating groups to communicate is widespread in today's common social media platforms. VEO aims to go beyond the purely social, to empower these connections with a focus on learning. Tagged videos are seen when a user clicks into a group page, and notifications indicate when your video (or a video

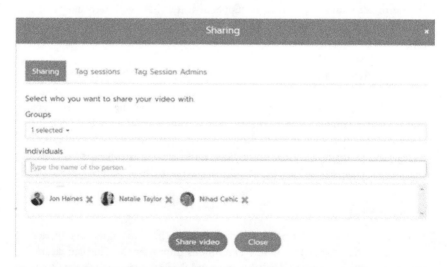

Figure 4.13 Selecting users and groups with whom to share a video.

shared with you) is available or has been tagged. This social-media style functionality is again designed with simplicity in mind. On creating a group, users are simply added by typing their names.

Tag Sets

'Tag sets' are collections of tags created together and crystallized into a set such that they can be re-used any number of times. They can consist of any combination of the data types introduced in Section 1. Re-using tag sets provides consistency for data added to video, so that changes can be seen over time.

Tag sets are often used to reflect frameworks or rubrics that are already in use by organizations. These can include teaching standards, IELTS grading systems, clinical examination criteria, vocational qualifications or desired corporate behaviours. Nevertheless, tag sets are fully customizable and can be personalized to match individual performance or progress. For example, a teacher tagging her practice with respect to a generic teaching tag set might decide to delve deeper into her questioning techniques. She could then create a tag set that focused on different question types or make use of an existing one if available.

The tag set creation process itself is very visual and consists of creating tags and inserting them into a mock-up of a video screen. Further details are available in Section 6.

Summary

While the tag set is a concept unique to VEO, the other features (groups and sharing) are commonplace. However, VEO combines these with a strong focus on learning. Simplicity of process is paramount for making this learning easily accessible. The practical system processes surrounding these features are described below.

5) Processes to Support Learning from Tagged Videos (367)

Sharing a Video

- From your VEO homepage https://app.veo.co.uk/#/, click into the video you wish to share.
- Click on the 'Share' icon beneath the video.
- Type the names of individuals you wish to share the video with into the box beneath 'Individuals'. Type their first and second names, rather than email addresses.
- You can share the video with anyone in your organization, but not across the whole of the VEO community.
- You can share the video with pre-created groups. Click the 'Groups' dropdown and select the groups you wish to share the video with.
- Click 'Share Video' and close the pop-up.

Unsharing a Video

- This can be done by following the above procedure in reverse.
- Click on the 'Share' icon beneath the video.
- Click the red 'x' next to each of the individuals you wish to unshare the video with.
- Click the dropdown to untick any groups you wish to stop sharing the video with.
- Click 'Share Video' and close the pop-up.

Creating a Group

- From your VEO homepage https://app.veo.co.uk/#/, click the 'Groups' tab at the top of the screen.
- Click 'Create a New Group'.
- Give the Group a name and optionally a description.
- Click the 'Users' dropdown.
- To create a Group consisting of all members of a Course, click the dropdown beneath 'Add entire Courses'.
- To create a Group of selected individuals, type their name beneath 'Add Users'. Type their first and second names, rather than email addresses.
- Click 'Save' when finished.

Viewing Videos in a Group

- To view all videos that have been shared to a group you are part of, first navigate to your VEO homepage https://app.veo.co.uk/#/
- Click into the Search Bar in the top left of the screen.
- Click the 'Select' dropdown beneath the 'Filter Options' section.
- Select the Group(s) to view videos shared therein.

Creating a Tag Set

This process is best illustrated by accessing the following video: http://bit.ly/VEONewTagSets. This is a little involved, but simplified as far as possible. It is a one-time effort to create a tag set that is available across users and over time, as any framework would be.

6) Capturing the video

Approach

In keeping with a desire for simplicity of user experience, VEO aims to allow flexible video capture and upload, with the intention that this could occur anytime, anywhere. This follows the many-many approach of social media organizations and platforms such as YouTube, rather than a top-down 'film-studio approach' required in video solutions.

For example, if a teacher is filming within the class we don't want the teacher to need to learn to become a cameraman while dealing with the live complexities of their true role! Equally, if a student paramedic is practicing techniques through simulation and role-play, we don't want their thoughts to be diverted onto the technical aspects of film. In keeping with this philosophy, shorter more informally captured video clips can often illuminate key moments of authentic practice and learning better than anything staged.

For example, teachers could choose to record only a specific activity; a starter, feedback session or plenary, or to focus on a corner of the room where their attention wouldn't always be throughout the lesson. We want users to be able to start recording if they feel an interesting episode is developing in their own specific context.

Video can be captured using any device and uploaded into the VEO system. This can be via bespoke VEO apps, with certain advantages outlined below, or directly into the VEO web app by accessing this online via the recording device, be that a phone, tablet, laptop or PC.

VEO Capture Apps

Basic VEO Capture Apps can be downloaded from the Apple App Store and the Google Play Store. These will work respectively with iOS and Android phones and tablets.

iOS app: https://apps.apple.com/gb/app/veo-capture/id1496585017

Android app: https://play.google.com/store/apps/details?id=com.veo.capture&hl=en_GB

The two main benefits of the VEO Capture app are that it automatically compresses the video file size to ensure faster upload, and also allows a user to immediately upload the video to their webapp without exiting and logging in separately. Aside from this, the functionality is designed to be similar to phone or tablet camera apps, such that new users will already be familiar with the functionality.

VEO iPad App

The VEO iPad app is based on the original VEO prototype app, conceived in 2013. It has since been re-developed, but the key advantage remains. This app allows the user to tag video while recording. The same tags and tag sets as are available in the web app are overlaid onto the app's recording screen, as illustrated in Figure 4.14.

After recording, the video can be played back in the iPad app, with the same review functionality as exists in the web app. The user can also add notes to the tags retrospectively. In order to share the tagged video, the user can simply upload it directly into the web app at the touch of a button from the review page. Tagging live can provide a powerful, immediate experience if there is a tagger on hand to do this.

Video Upload into VEO

Any existing video file can also be uploaded directly into the VEO Web App, by accessing this online on the device that is storing the file. Upload time depends solely on the size of the video file and the speed of the internet connection. Therefore, if you

Figure 4.14 Tagging live with the VEO app.

are recording the video on a phone or tablet, it is recommended to reduce the video quality to the minimum setting. This is usually more than good enough to understand what is going on in a workplace situation or classroom. If the internet connection is interrupted during the upload, then the process will fail (this is also true for YouTube, etc.). By reducing the video file size this risk is reduced. The VEO Capture and iPad apps do this automatically as part of their processing.

The Practicalities of Filming

Some guidance follows on filming in professional situations, using the example of a teacher to provide context. The approach taken by VEO is to make filming in the workplace, training room or classroom as easy, flexible and convenient as possible. Teachers, students and learning professionals are busy people, managing complex environments made up of several students each with their own individual and changing needs.

Device

We therefore recommend filming with whatever device is most convenient and available in the classroom. You can use phones, tablets, laptops and digital cameras to do this. VEO Capture apps, available for iOS and Android phones and tablets, make this a smoother process by automatically compressing the video file for easy upload.

Position

There is a little trial and error in finding the best position to film from. It will also depend on what you are focussed on in the recording. For example, teachers have used VEO in several different ways:

- Filming from the back, side or front of the class to get an overall view of what is happening in the classroom.
- Focussing the camera on one particular area within the classroom, capturing, for example, a group of students or an activity station.
- Focussing on the teacher for a particular activity.
  Generally a phone or tablet's audio will pick up what the human ear can hear from that position. It is therefore worth considering whether towards the front or back of the classroom is best, or whether an inexpensive Bluetooth microphone could enhance the sound.

Stands

There are several very affordable 'Gorilla Grip' stands for phones or tablets which can be clipped to tables or chairs and keep the device steady while filming.

A 'Cameraman'

If there is the opportunity to have a colleague film the episode, or elements of it, then this can work very well. For example, for trainee teachers, this can work particularly well as part of team teaching, or if there is a lab technician or learning assistant available. The person filming doesn't have to hold the camera for the full duration but can capture important episodes. Some teachers have even had pupils operate the camera and involved them in the process.

Data Protection

The relevant data protection laws should always be fully considered before filming. Further guidance on requirements for recording and capturing under the EU GDPR is outlined in this accompanying link: https://app.veo.co.uk/#/gdpr/en-GB.

Summary

Video capture is intended to be a seamless experience for VEO users. Minimizing friction and thought around video capture increases attention on, and potential for, the learning purpose to be realized. Processes are outlined in the following section (7).

7) Processes for Uploading Video

Uploading a video

- Go to https://veo.co.uk using a web browser on the device your video is stored on (phone, tablet, PC, etc.).
- Click 'login' at the top right of the screen.
- Enter your email address and password.
- Click 'Upload video'.
- Select the video from your device.
- Give the video a title and optional description. The title can be used to search for the video so that it can help to give a title that will help with this.
- Click upload. The video will upload. You can navigate to other browser tabs in the meantime, but shouldn't close the upload tab before upload is complete.

Uploading a video with VEO Capture Apps

- Log in to the Capture App on your phone or tablet using your usual VEO email and password.
- Tap the '+' button.
- Record a new video or select an existing video.
- On saving the video, the app will compress the video file.
- Tap the Upload icon to upload directly into your VEO account.
  You will need to be connected to the internet to upload from the app to the online VEO Portal.

8) Types of Learning Generated

From VEO's origins, the founders' goals aligned in seeking to help people get better at what they do. The learning was situated in recorded action and experience and involved reflective cyclical processes to improve performance across a range of sectors and fields. As has been noted, this originated in teacher training, but has found widespread use in student feedback, medical and corporate training, as well as language learning and vocational assessment.

Exposure to such diverse fields has led to different ways of learning to be considered, beyond practising action, interaction and performance. This section includes a brief summary of other ways that VEO can be used to promote learning and leads into a further section on how this learning might be planned and enacted.

Discussions with customers led the VEO team to consider the power of the video tagging functionality in new ways. It was helpful to consider different hypothetical types of learning around video. Firstly, the video did not have to be 'user' generated. It could include exemplars or educator-created video. The

To Achieve Competence (Reach a Level)	Action Learning (Continuously Improve)
Observe / Consume Content	**Observe / Consume Content**
To see for the first time	To Explore
To become acquainted with something new	To view with fresh eyes from a new perspective
To see key elements of new activity	To gain an overall impression
Identify	**Identify**
To recognise specific actions and techniques	To pick out key moments
To notice specific elements	To notice specific elements
To analyse and breakdown action	To analyse and breakdown action
Understand	**Understand**
To evaluate and critique action	To evaluate and critique action
To reason about action	To reason about action
To gain deeper learning	To gain deeper learning
Perform	**Perform**
To Achieve Competence	To try something new
To Demonstrate Competence	To put ideas into action
To Identify Gaps in Competence	To critique and evaluate new action

Figure 4.15 Achieving different types of learning through VEO.

tagging functionality would serve to focus attention onto learning moments, but for a variety of purposes.

Figure 4.15 lays out the different possible levels of learning, loosely linked to the learner's position on a continuum from novice to expert. Firstly, the learner sees a skill or activity for the first time. Then they become more familiar with the skill or activity and are able to recognize it and break down its constituent parts. Next, they begin to understand the activity or skill and its significance. Finally, they become able to perform and then master the activity or skill themselves.

All of these processes should be seen as continuous and overlapping. For example, repeated performance may be necessary to achieve mastery. The figure below is divided into two broad learning goals; VEO is used for both. These indicate slightly different learner activities.

VEO's tags can bookmark and make learning visible, both in the video action itself and in the learner's reaction to it. Therefore, a multitude of valuable learning experiences can be generated through VEO, and several use cases have emerged and been embedded throughout VEO's existence.

Some generic outlines for use in creating learning steps are shown for illustration below. Experiences with these have shown that using VEO with simple but effective processes can generate transformative learning and change at multiple levels.

9) Processes for Implementing Different Types of Learning

Trainees Explore Video (Written from the Educator's perspective)

- Upload a relevant video.
- Assign the video to the relevant course (or at a smaller scale, share the video with a group or a number of individuals).
- Change the tag session visibility settings to (2), so the 'video owner' can see all tag sessions against a video. Those who have had the video shared with them can see their own tag sessions and the video owner's tag sessions.
- Ask trainees to tag the video e.g. to identify certain techniques, or to highlight more generally what they notice or are curious about in the video. It can be a good idea to limit the number of tags – e.g. 'Tag three things you noticed about the teacher's positioning (or differentiation, etc.) in this classroom and say why you thought it interesting'.
- Respond to any notes in the trainee's tag sessions.
- Change the tag session visibility settings to (1), so anyone who can see the video can see all tag sessions.
- Ask trainees to view how others have tagged the video and to respond to their notes to build up discussion.

Trainees Respond to Questions in Video (Written from the Educator's perspective)

- Upload a relevant video.
- Tag the video at key moments with questions.
- Share the video with a group, or a number of individuals (or at larger scale, assign the video to a course group).
- Ask trainees to answer the questions in the video – without viewing other responses if preferred.
- Ask students to feedback on others' answers to create discussion.
- Discuss all responses with the trainees.

Students Tag Their Own Video

- Students record themselves performing an activity and upload to VEO.
- Students tag and annotate key moments to reflect on their practice or skill. It might be worth limiting the number of tags they use – e.g. 'tag six things that you were happy with, and tag 3 things you'd like to work on'.
- The student shares the video with their lecturer.
- The lecturer feeds back on the tagged moments in the notes and encourages further discussion in the notes.
- This can be modified to work with peer feedback. The trainee would share to a group of peers who are encouraged to feedback. It is useful for these to be moderated by a lecturer within the group, and to limit the number of tags further.

An example of such an activity is described in video format at: https://veo.co.uk/case-study/british-study-centres/

Conclusion

This chapter has consisted of a walkthrough of the basic features and processes within VEO and its associated apps. Screenshots, examples and process outlines have been used to illuminate this further, such that an understanding of how the system works might develop.

This chapter has shown that the VEO system allows its users to generate learning from the basic but key concept of timestamp-tagged video. Through simple and flexible design, multiple means of learning have been generated from the system. The pathways to creating this learning have been laid out. By focussing on ease of use and borrowing from the best of social media platforms, an efficient and effective learning platform has been created. When combined with appropriate learning processes, this leads to a scalable system that provides value across contexts and continents.

Part Two

Video Enhanced Observation in Practice: Case Studies

5

Integrating VEO in Foreign Language Teacher Education in Germany

Götz Schwab and Mareike Oesterle
University of Education Ludwigsburg, Germany

Introduction

Since the 1960s the use of video in teacher education has been recognized as a unique possibility to support pre- and in-service teachers in their own professional development (Hosenfeld and Helmke 2008). Despite a number of obstacles, for example, strict data policies or lack of technical support, video-based observation and reflection has been increasingly integrated in teacher training programmes across Germany (Hilzensauer 2017; Schwab 2020a). This surge has been facilitated by numerous technological developments, making the use of video easier and much more convenient. In line with these developments, Hockly (2018) points out additional values of new technologies: 'Access to relatively inexpensive hardware, such as compact digital cameras and mobile devices, as well as the emergence of software supporting the use of digital video in professional development, has led to increased interest in the use of digital video in language teacher education' (Ibid., 329). In Germany, this has led to a broader (though not nationwide or even university-wide) integration and use of innovative video across teacher training programmes. The developments are thus highly diverse and often dependent on individual professionals or institutes.

In addition to videography's wide accessibility, an important added value of videotaping is that it can be used in several ways and for various purposes in teacher education. In this chapter, we will demonstrate how a specific video software application, the VEO app, can scaffold processes of reflection among student teachers, as well as serve as an innovative research instrument. This chapter will focus on the integration of the VEO app by detailing two scenarios from the Erasmus+ project in Germany in which we utilized videography. We commence by addressing some of the major developments and formats of using videography to promote Continuing Professional Development (CPD) in German teacher education. Next, we discuss two scenarios that make use of the VEO app in the context of Foreign Language Teacher

Education at the Karlsruhe University of Education (KUE), referring to data from two case studies based on the VEO Europa project in Germany. Here, we first review the integration of the mobile application in practical internships to observe pre-service English teachers with the goal of initiating their professional development by raising awareness and fostering the capability to become an active agent of development. In presenting the second scenario, we will demonstrate how the VEO app can be used as a research instrument for student teachers to observe and analyse teaching and learning at a bilingual primary school, focusing on feedback in classroom interaction. In so doing, we will identify a number of aspects that either impact or result from the use of such a mobile application at our institution. The chapter then discusses these aspects based on the premise that VEO can be used effectively in a German teacher education programme to, for example, scaffold the process of gaining reflective competencies for the future teacher. The case studies from Germany that are examined in this chapter model two ways in which the VEO app can be used to bridge the gap between theory, research and practice, thereby promoting development of (future) teachers.

Integrating Video in Teacher Education in Germany

Researchers and practitioners alike regularly criticize the divide between theory and practice in teacher education. Many pre-service teachers feel that they are under-prepared and lack sufficient competence upon completing university training and entering the teaching profession (Allen and Wright 2014).

In the German education system, this debate is driven by two main positions. On the one hand, there are those who believe that the first phase of teacher education should be primarily theory-based and research-oriented in order for the students to distance themselves from their own experiences as pupils in school (Baumert and Kunter 2006; Terhart 2006). This position has long endured. However, emanating from the Bologna process, a change of focus to bachelor/master programmes resulted in an increasing practice-orientation in teacher education (Gröschner et al. 2015). Welcoming this, many argue on the other hand that theoretical knowledge needs to be applied before being internalized and becoming sustainable. This position essentially draws on competence-oriented models, including inclusive and collaborative approaches (Bresges et al. 2019). Addressing the general lack of practice in teacher education and lack of investigations of field experiences in teacher training in Germany, Gröschner et al. (2015) argue that it is not enough to combine theory and practice. Instead, practice needs to be implemented in the various modules and courses and related to scientific knowledge (Ibid., 643). Based on work undertaken by Breidbach (2007), Caspari (2016) describes what the former called *theory of practice*, meaning establishing a reciprocal connection between theory and practice (Caspari 2016: 365). Many consider this connection to be vital in achieving reflection of practical experience, which is theory-based and evidence-driven, and in the long run, in developing as a (future) teacher professionally (Sherin and van Es 2009; Mann and Walsh 2017).

Videography or video-based observation is thereby seen as an effective instrument to document and analyse (future) teachers' practices, as well as to scaffold the process of reflection and thus to initiate processes of professional development (Schramm and Aguado 2010; Seidel et al. 2010; Häusler et al. 2018; Schwab 2020a). Summarizing the current state of research with regard to using videos in teacher education, Blomberg et al. (2013) claim that the use of video can strengthen the teachers' content knowledge and help develop reflective knowledge of teaching and learning (Ibid., 92ff.). The authors believe that videos can be a 'window' into teaching (Ibid., 93) and like others argue that the use of video in teacher education can support bridging the gap between theory and practice (Abendroth-Timmer 2011; Mühlhausen 2012; Blomberg et al. 2013).

This authenticity is further noted by Seidel et al. (2011) who studied the specific effects of video analysis on teacher learning, including recordings of teachers' own and other teachers' teaching in Germany and Switzerland. In their paper, they argue that video 'allows learners to make multiple connections to their own teaching and to activate prior knowledge and experience' (Ibid., 260). Hockly (2018) stresses this argument by stating that video recordings can serve as an authentic and effective 'vehicle' to promote pre- and in-service teacher professional development: 'On a micro level, recording digital videos of classroom practice gives teachers easy access to authentic teaching events in their own or others' classrooms, which can then be used for analysis and reflection. On a macro level, recordings of real classroom events can help to shape and inform educational policy or to support institutional reforms' (Ibid., 329). Supporting previous research, the findings of Seidel et al. (2011) further substantiate and consolidate the hypothesis that many 'watched their own teaching to experience stronger activation in terms of immersion, resonance, authenticity and motivation' (Ibid., 266).

Research Context: Using VEO in Foreign Language Teacher Education at the University of Education Karlsruhe

The teacher training programmes at Karlsruhe University of Education[1] (KUE) comprise five years of bachelor and master studies. During three different internships, class teachers observe student teachers, often together with a university lecturer. After each session, student teachers receive oral feedback based on institutional guidelines and individual experiences. However, there is no underlying grading system and the decision regarding whether someone has passed or failed his or her practicum is very much up to the supervisors. Furthermore, the given feedback does not in any way count towards the students' academic achievements. If a trainee fails the classroom practice, he or she gets one more chance to pass. In general, there are no binding standards or criteria for observing and evaluating these internships. At KUE, a number of lecturers have started integrating video observation in their internships or seminars. Their motivation originates from their own experiences of using video or from projects or research activities they are involved in. However, due to increasingly strict data policies, use of video at university and in schools has become a rather complicated and sometimes frustrating endeavour in Germany. In the context of the VEO project, we contacted about thirty-five schools and fifty individual teachers. In order to be able to

68 *Video Enhanced Observation for Language Teaching*

film in schools, we had to follow certain steps prescribed by the Ministry of Education of Baden-Württemberg (Germany) before even being allowed to contact the schools.

The data presented here stem from two case studies conducted in the course of the VEO project. Each has a different focus and together they provide two distinct applications of VEO in teacher training programmes. The first case study focuses on the individual teaching experience of trainee teachers during a compulsory semester-long internship. The second aims to show how students can use VEO when conducting a research project on their own. In this investigation, the research was related to the student's final thesis about observing lessons in a bilingual primary school in order to discover how feedback and repair mechanisms are used in such settings.

The multimodal data that we have used in this chapter is based on thirty-three VEO recordings, written and spoken feedback expressed by our participants, and pre- and post-questionnaires. The participants in our case studies took part in the project from 2016 to 2017. In total, eleven student teachers participated in the project at our university. However, the data for this chapter feature a selection of only six student teachers presented as two case studies. All relevant audio and video data have been transcribed and then collaboratively been analysed. In the following, we will illustrate some major aspects of our findings along with three assorted 'critical moments' (Mann and Walsh 2017) in order to discuss them in the wider context of our research data and results.

Findings

Scenario 1 – Using VEO in Teaching Practice Groups

In line with what might be called the 'practicum turn in teacher education' (Mattson et al. 2011), students at a University of Education in Germany must complete three different internships over the course of their degree programme. At the very heart of it, a so-called integrated semester practicum (ISP) has been implemented where students work at a local school for a whole semester while attending university classes which accompany and support their teaching endeavours theoretically as well as practically. During this time, students are put in groups of three to five participants according to their chosen subjects.[2] These groups are overseen by a mentor at school together with a lecturer from the university who provide mostly oral feedback and advice based on regular lesson observations. Two of these ISP groups were selected to take part in the VEO project. In addition to the regular lesson observation by the mentor and/or lecturer, students had to record three lessons of their own and watch them at home and/or discuss them afterwards with their fellow students. Additionally, they were asked to comment on their teaching and their experience with VEO in an audio diary. In practice, this was rarely done (in fact only three times) as students reported afterwards that there was little time left to do so.

The following data set is based on one such group of five students (P1–P5) who completed their practicum requirement at a rural primary school where they taught English to pupils in class two (age: 7–8; this was also their second year of English instruction). All practicum students took part in two preparatory workshops where they learned about VEO and its distinct features, in particular how to develop one's own tag set. Furthermore, they completed two questionnaires (pre/post) and submitted a written evaluation of the app at the end of the project. One student (P1) also recorded a video diary wherein she provided her evaluation of the project and the software being used. Furthermore, students were interviewed after the internship, either individually or in focus groups.

The student group chosen here was composed of four female and one male undergraduate student, all in their second year. They were asked to take part in the VEO project as we regularly observed them during their ISP. The project work was in addition to the general workload and had no impact on their regular coursework. At the beginning of the intervention, all students received the following tasks: (1) develop a tag set for their own lessons; (2) video tape at least three of their own lessons with an iPad mini; (3) discuss the tagged recording with a peer or watch the video at home, paying attention to the chosen categories; and (4) record an audio or video reflection about the lesson. As mentioned before, the participants in this case study did not complete Task 4 due to reported time pressure. (This is in contrast to the group in the second case study whose practicum was completed at a different school who did reflect on at least one of their recorded lessons.) Additionally, most of the participants in this group opted to watch their videos at home rather than discuss their recordings with a peer (Task 3) because, again, they felt they were pressed for time and had to quickly move on to the next lesson or meeting.

Although students were encouraged to develop individual tag sets for their specific purposes (Task 1), this group decided to develop a single communal set which was used for all recordings. The students explained later that they chose this option in order to make tagging easier for the observing students as there was a clear focus and understanding of what was to be looked at. Furthermore, they all agreed on the importance of providing clear and easy-to-understand instructions, as this seems to be a common problem among teachers in the initial stage of their careers (Fantilli and Dougall 2009). Consequently, this aspect had top priority when developing the tag set.

The importance of clearly defining categories seems to be an essential characteristic of tagging in general; in fact, other project participants also pointed out how important it is that tags are well defined in advance. As VEO was developed for easy access and use (Batlle and Miller 2017), observers are usually not as thoroughly trained in coding as they would need to be in other research projects (Dörnyei 2007). Thus, some kind of training is inevitable before and during the recording phase. The screenshots in Figure 5.1 show the customized tag set developed by this group. Only a few of the tags have a subcategory as students tried to keep the whole design as simple as possible ('to find key moments', according to P2). This is also the reason why they did not add possession tags or include the engagement bar.

The following categories appear on the left (from top to bottom), with subtags in brackets (translated into English here): (1) body language (±/? clear body language), (2) time management, (3) instruction (±/? clear; ±/? brief). The categories on the right are: (1) motivation (±/? high; ±/? low), (2) understanding, (3) L2 students (±/? when is L2 used?).

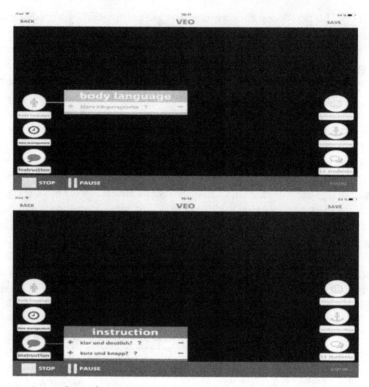

Figure 5.1 Screenshots of tag set.

The tag set was not changed over the course of the practicum and was thus used for fourteen recordings in total – sometimes a complete lesson, sometimes just certain sequences. The two graphs in Figure 5.2 provide an overview of the tags used in the first and last lesson of P1, both recorded by the same observer (P3). However, in the last session, the observer used the blurring function of the app. Unfortunately, this means that the scenery becomes less visible as observers usually watch the lesson on the screen of the iPad and not directly. This might be a reason why there are fewer instances of tagging.

Excerpts 1 and 2 are of tagged sequences. Both feature P1 and are taken from recordings 1 and 2. Excerpt 1 deals with 'instruction' as the tag which students in their written feedback identified as of utmost importance, often in connection with the 'body language' tag. The second excerpt presents the category 'L2 students' which was linked to the participation structure of the interaction in general and the student talk time (STT) in teacher fronted interaction. Students explained that they were interested in 'when and in what way students use the L2' and 'how their language competence develops'.

Integrating VEO in Germany

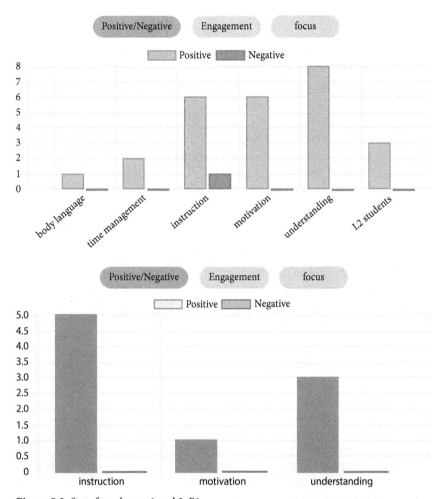

Figure 5.2 Stats from lesson 1 and 3, P1.

Excerpt 1 from the data[3]: lesson 2, tagging No. 6+7, tag: 'instruction/clear?'

Pupils in year 2 have just heard the story 'Froggy gets dressed' while sitting in a semi-circle at the front of the classroom. Now the teacher is moving on to the next phase:

```
01   T:   [tag 6] <<loud, but slowly> nOW- (2.0)
02        plEAse- (.) go BACK to your seats, (-)>
                  _____|
                        |
          showing with her hands to children's seats
```

72   *Video Enhanced Observation for Language Teaching*

03   VERY quiet- (2,5)
    |_____|

       |

   putting index finger to her lips

04   [tag 7] then> (-) i'm gonna tell (.) what comes next. (.)
    |_____|

                       |

  still holding her index in front of face

05   go <<whispering> back to your seats- very quiet>
   |_____| |_____|

         | |

  forming a circle with her arms | indicates where seats are

06   ((students are going back to their seats, though many of them are talking))

With the beginning of a new phase, the teacher is giving instructions on what comes next. The observing student thus used the tag 'instruction' twice (tagging No. 6 and No. 7), both times pressing the subtag 'clear' with a question mark as she seemed to be in doubt whether it is positive or negative. When going through the transcript, we are actually able to identify two different instruction sequences which were tagged separately. The first one from lines 01 to 03 (tagging No. 6) is dealing with content, the second, in line 04 (tagging No. 7), with manner. In line 05 there is a repetition of what was said in line 02 though this time the observer did not tag the event. Taking a closer look at the first two incidents, we see the teacher makes intensive use of body language in order to render instructions as comprehensible as possible.

As students reported later, this is very important when talking about successful instructions and so the sequence provided the opportunity to consider the importance of seeing both categories – instructions and body language – together, even if only one of them was tagged in the observation process. This, however, can only become obvious if students watch and reflect upon such an incident afterwards and discuss the findings – if possible – with a fellow student or mentor.

Excerpt 2: lesson 1, tagging No. 9, tag: 'L2 students'

Learners have studied certain toys one might get for Christmas during the first part of the lesson. Now the teacher is trying to elicit student utterances by asking what they actually would like to have for Christmas:

01   T: [tag 9] (name of S5)- (–)
          ((teacher is bowing down to pupil))
02   what would ↑YOU like for christmas- (-)
03   S5:   a game,
04   T: say- (–)
05   <<rhythmically>> i would like- a GAme for christmas;(-)>
06   S5:   i would like (.) a ↓game-
07   T: yes; (.) I- (.) would ↑LIKE-

08	S5:	I would ↑like-
09	T:	<<accelerated>> a GAME> for christmas
10	S5:	a GAme for christmas.
11	T:	o:h- (.) VERY good; (.)
12		you would like a GAme for christmas; (–)

Pupils in this class have studied English for less than eighteen months and most of the time they received language input; that is, they heard the teacher using the target language. When asked for language output, though, we often see learners come up with prefabricated utterances (Haudeck and Schwab 2011). This is to some extent also the case here as they have to use a given chunk ('I would like') plus a noun phrase dealing with games and toys. Although there is a row of similar teacher-pupil interactions in this phase of the lesson, not all sequences were tagged by the observer. This question-answer sequence nevertheless helps prospective teachers to reflect upon what learners of this age might be able to produce – on their own (here: a noun phrase) and with the help of others (here: a chunk) (e.g. van Lier 1996; Seedhouse 2007).

From a methodological point of view, it reveals what teachers typically ask for, namely a certain grammatical structure (e.g. Jäkel 2010). This also includes a shift from a meaning-and-fluency context ('what would ↑YOU like for christmas'-) to a form-and-accuracy focus ('say-') as the teacher is practising the linguistic construction of the item to be learned (lines 04–11). As these dimensions were not part of the tag set, such analysis could only be done in retrospect. Nonetheless, video recordings with smaller tag sets may offer more opportunities for reflection, as larger tag sets could be used for a more thorough analysis.

A sequence like this, for example, may help to reflect upon whether such a shift may facilitate language learning and in what way it is successful or not (Sert 2015). Moreover, it can raise the query of how much teachers are aware of such a move and how they can become more reflective on the underlying intention of one's question or instruction. It again puts emphasis on the fact that an in-depth reflection of one's teaching activities is very important with regard to raising awareness of the different dimensions involved. Unfortunately, these students were not given enough time to do this on a regular basis. Additionally, we suggest that at certain points the whole procedure may benefit from including more advanced teachers or lecturers to point out the various aspects of the video and thus help to deepen the reflection process. This could also include transcribing some instances as preparation for the reflection meeting (Schwab 2014).

Scenario 2 – Using VEO for Student Research Projects

As the VEO app can be used in teacher training in various ways, we encouraged students to apply it in a more autonomous way and to make use of it in their own research activities. Thus, a number of students did empirical research on and with VEO for their final thesis projects. In the second case study, we will take a closer look at one of these thesis projects, where the app was employed to investigate interaction processes in a bilingual primary classroom. The school where the study took place offers an English immersion programme, which means that the pupils get the chance to acquire the target language in the context of a particular content subject (maths, arts, PE, etc.). Every year, two classes are taught in this programme. Pupils also learn German as they have German as a separate subject. Thus, the school practises what is called 'Early Partial Immersion' (Mehisto, Marsh and Frigols 2008). Furthermore, teachers oversee their classes in teams; two teachers are responsible for one class, sometimes even being present at the same time.

At the onset of the project, the student attended the introductory VEO workshop to get a first glimpse of the app. Afterwards, she went to observe a number of lessons of a second-year bilingual group of twenty-four learners, using again an iPad mini supplied by the university. The two teachers involved in the study also contacted us and were provided with further information on the app via telephone and email. In the middle of her filming, the trainee teacher attended the second VEO workshop with the university, as well as a discussion group with other teachers who were involved in the VEO project. She then finished her observation and used the data for her academic paper focusing on teacher feedback in order to answer her research question: how do teachers provide feedback in the early English classroom and how can this be observed using VEO?

The tag set developed for this observation is depicted in Figure 5.3.

Figure 5.3 VEO tag set, taken from Treetzen (2016, p. 63).

Based on Nickerson (1998) and Hattie (2012), the following tags of providing feedback by the teacher were developed: (to the left) 'disconfirmation positive', 'disconfirmation negative' and 'confirmation'. 'Disconfirmation positive' provides the opportunity for student self-correction, whereas 'disconfirmation negative' implies that learners may not get such an opportunity. Included in disconfirmation positive are the subcategories 'clarification request' and 'repetition', and in 'disconfirmation negative' are 'explicit correction', 'recast' and 'negative feedback'. 'Confirmation' only includes the subcategory 'positive feedback'. 'Summative feedback' does not have any sub-division.

To the right, there are the tags mainly related to pupils' reactions. However, first there is 'praise', a tag which was added right after the first day of observation. Because it is provided directly by the teacher, it should go in the left-hand margin. VEO currently only allows four tags on each side, so this tag had to go to the right (cf. Treetzen 2016, 64). 'Praise' is followed by 'uptake', including the subtags 'repair' and 'need-repair'. Below there is 'reaction to feedback' with the subcategories 'degree of comprehension' (±/?), indicating whether the learner might have understood the feedback or not. The last tag is a so-called quick tag which is an open or undefined category that can be used when something occurs which is of additional interest. The three possession tags in the middle, 'individual', 'group' and 'class', were not used during the recording.

Although the trainee student conducted nineteen recordings in general, only seven distinct extracts were transcribed and analysed (see Figure 5.4) as the focus was on the use of the app and not the interaction as such. For a more in-depth and extended analysis of the data set in general, see Schwab (2020b).

In the following analysis, we will take a closer look the findings, show one example of a tagged sequence and draw conclusions for further research in this field. Table 5.1

Table 5.1 Tally of taggings, taken from Treetzen (2016, p. 68)

	PH_S_01a	PH_S_01b	PH_S_02	PH_S_03	PH_S_04	PH_S_05	PH_S_06	Total
Topic	**drama**	drama	drama	**drama**	maths	maths	**maths**	
Duration	**11 min 23 sec**	05 min 38 sec	09 min 26 sec	**13 min 02 sec**	05 min 19 sec	08 min 54 sec	**07 min 53 sec**	71 min 35 sec
Repetition	-	-	1	-	-	1	-	2
Clarification request	4	2	1	1	-	2	1	11
Explicit correction	-	1	4	9	6	1	1	22
Recast	13	3	4	2	-	-	-	22
Negative feedback	-	-	1	-	-	2	2	5
Positive feedback	3	2	-	1	4	3	15	28
Praise	4	1	1	2	1	2	2	13
Total	24	9	12	15	11	10	21	103

76 *Video Enhanced Observation for Language Teaching*

provides a summary of all the sequences transcribed and the tags used during this time of recording, with a tally of 103.

As we can see, almost all of the categories were tagged, although with varying frequency. The category most often used was 'positive feedback', the least common 'repetition'. Excerpt 3 shows a sample sequence of another tag with high frequency, especially in this lesson. It focuses on 'explicit correction', a category that has been quite controversial in the literature (e.g. Oliver 2000; Lyster 2007).

Excerpt 3: bilingual lesson PH_S_03, tagging No. 9, tag: 'explicit correction'

This sequence is part of a drama lesson. Pupils are asked to act out short role plays with animal hand puppets ('crocodile' and 'lamb') in front of the others. The two children talk about their (puppet's) names, where they live and their favourite food. After each dialogue, the pupils and the teacher comment on the performance – only the teacher speaks in English.

```
584 T: i really like how c. talks (.)
585     she's really good at english (.)
586     i think (.) she really has good ideas (.)
587     she did not have to think about it (-)
588     [tag9] the only thing also (.) the two before (.)
        |_____
              |
```

the teacher stands up from her desk and approaches the two and then turns to the class while standing next to the performers

```
589     you said what's your ↑favourite- (.) FRUI:T (.)
590     it's FOOD (-) FRUIT (.) is something else (.)
591     fruit is apple banana strawberry (.)
592     FOOD is food (.) okay? (-)
593     don't mix these two up they sound a little similar (.)
```

After the appraisal of the student performance by some of the learners, the teacher points out a flaw in the utterance as one pupil mixed up the two terms fruit and food, at least with regard to their pronunciation. In order to emphasize her point, the teacher turns to the class while standing next to the two learners. This obviously makes the sequence a clear and explicit (other-initiated other) correction.

However, we can also see that there is more to this sequence than is revealed in the tagging. Just before the actual tag (line 588), the teacher praises C extensively (lines 584–7), which was not rated by the observer, neither with 'praise' nor 'positive feedback'. Since the student did not mention it in her thesis either, we cannot say why there is no further tagging here. However, as for the first cohort, the observer did not receive extensive training on tagging and rating procedures before the study. In the workshop, she only received information about the features and possibilities of the app. Therefore, exact rating figures, where all incidents are tagged, could hardly be expected.

Thus, we should re-evaluate this sequence in more depth here: when looking beyond the actual tagging in the sample, that is, the interaction right before the 'explicit correction' (line 588), it becomes clear that the teacher lays the ground for the correction by praising the student's achievement before she actually points out the deficits. 'Praise', as the student realized in the course of the study, plays an important role in programmes for young learners of English (even if there are just two incidents of praise tagged here). This seems to be especially true in bilingual settings where learners are encouraged to use the target language as much as possible and the linguistic output is significantly higher than in regular classes such as in the first case study (Elsner and Keßler 2013).

Even if the overall tagging only shows a selection of all the incidents indicating a feedback move by the teacher (here: fifteen taggings in a thirteen-minute sequence), the study revealed the variety and complexity of teacher-provided feedback in this class and what feedback in a bilingual setting like this can look like.

In contrast to the group of teacher trainees discussed in the first scenario, this student followed a deductive approach and conducted an intensive study of the categories she was going to use for her observation. Based on that, a detailed tag set was developed comprising a variety of feedback options teachers can use in classroom interaction. She also altered the set during her observation process as she came across an additional practice ('praise') that seemed to be important in these lessons as it obviously is an important interactional feature of the primary classroom and its learners (Burnett and Mendel 2010). However, none of the lessons were shown to the teachers afterwards nor were any of the findings discussed with the instructors involved as this was not part of the research design of the thesis. In this study, the focus was on a general overview of feedback practices with an emphasis on the distribution of the tags. A detailed analysis was done later in Schwab (2020b), based on the recording but independent of the categories and foci.

VEO can thus be used in settings where observers are intended to scrutinize certain practices of classroom interaction without the individual reflection processes that followed in the first case study. Nonetheless, a detailed analysis of certain sequences, neatly transcribed, revealed a much more complex outline of the ongoing interaction than was originally tagged by the observer. Thus, we see great potential in more reflective practices that are done in joint reflection meetings and, if possible, enhanced by detailed transcriptions.

In line with such an approach is also the notion of tagging in retrospect (Batlle Rodríguez and Miller 2017), when trainees are exposed to a given recording and do the tagging while watching. Thus, the reflection process is done from a different angle and the endeavour becomes more comparative as a number of trainees watch the same video.

Discussion

In this section, we draw attention to a number of aspects that either impact or result from the use of video such as the VEO app at our institution. We discuss these aspects based on the idea that VEO can be used effectively in a German teacher education programme.

Generally, our data supports the pertinent literature which indicates that videotaping can be an effective tool to show the impact of one's teaching behaviour and what it looks like *in situ*, that is, in concrete situations (e.g. Blomberg et al. 2013). Nearly all students reported that it was a highly beneficial experience and that they would recommend using videography in more courses of their programme. As Tripp and Rich (2012) describe, videos can be seen as a powerful tool where teachers can actually review their own practice.

In regard to the VEO app, our analyses suggest that the instrument has a number of potential benefits for teacher education. For example, it can be a facilitator to develop a shared language and helps to lay a common ground from which one can develop professionally. The students in the first case study who decided to develop a joint tag set for all recordings had to develop a common understanding of the various tags they chose and take part in processes of negotiation and exchange. Based on this, we argue that VEO can be used to promote spoken reflection (Mann and Walsh 2017) not only after, but also before the observation through pre-observation tasks such as developing a tag set. Although some students said that there was not enough time for dialogic reflection after the lessons, one student claimed that there was a more intensive exchange among the group members which helped to reflect on the tags and their foci in a better way. Nevertheless, we suggest integrating dialogic and video-based reflection more systematically in teacher training programmes, providing more time to do so, and also including mentors and other experts when possible.

Many authors also suggest multiple procedures for how video can be used to promote not only spoken but also written reflection (Tripp and Rich 2012; Baecher et al. 2013; Mann and Walsh 2017). In the first scenario, students should have been provided with more time to talk about their videos afterwards, as most of them only watched the recording at home and did not talk about it in more detail right after the lesson. However, this depends a great deal on the school and the particular time management of the internship. In reference to having students use VEO as a research instrument, it is clear that this also requires more coaching and support, as all students commented on the importance of clearly defining and discussing the categories and 'what actually is meant by it'. Thus, our findings suggest making processes of reflection more transparent and integrating them systematically into our programme. Simply having the students use the VEO app does not seem to be enough; they need to be guided and given time and incentives by the lecturer to engage in reflective practices.

Time also plays a decisive role when looking at the technical aspects of the VEO app. Despite the fact that VEO intends to be less time-consuming, as watchers can jump from one tagged sequence to another and focus on selected episodes, preparing and planning individual video observation means an additional time commitment. This concerns not only the student teachers, but also the teacher educators who have to plan their seminars or sessions more carefully and make sure that video-based reflection becomes a genuine part of their course work.

A major advantage of the VEO app lies in its conceptualization. Through specific design, pre-service teachers can learn how to reflect in a scaffolded setting and become agents of their own development. An evidence-based application such as VEO can facilitate a focused and more systematic observation. In other words, student teachers can learn how to identify and 'select' critical moments in someone's teaching practice (Mann and Walsh 2017: 119). This helps future teachers become more sensitive to certain aspects of their professional practices. However, some students reported that using VEO can be rather challenging. Students from both case studies seemed to have problems with exact tagging due to some vagueness in the chosen categories. VEO is intended for spontaneous ad hoc use which might cause such problems. That said, defining the categories can also be seen as a chance for professional development, as we pointed out above. Many students did not apply the 'possession tags' in their customized tag sets, nor did they include the engagement bar as a way to make tagging easier. However, as Cavar (2020) showed in her study, a visual summary provided by the app, based on statistical data, can pave the way for a discussion on the lesson and may help to overcome a certain initial reluctance of the observee to deal with his or her teaching. Furthermore, the ± judgement in a tag set is not always easy to achieve and sometimes difficult to handle. Therefore, students often chose the ? symbol as they do not seem to be sure whether the observed behaviour was positive or negative and thus leave this decision for the discussion afterwards.

Looking at the teacher educators, our data hints that in order to scaffold processes of reflection and development using innovative video software, more support and training need to be provided. Usually, teacher trainers base their (oral and/or written) feedback on the immediate observation of classroom activities without using any technical devices. Thus, we argue that teacher educators should be trained in how to integrate new approaches such as videography – especially innovative videography – effectively. Moreover, they need to be given time and space for reflection, and further familiarize themselves with new video software such as the VEO app.

Our second case leads us to suggest using VEO not only as an instrument for professional development but also as an innovative research instrument. The data that VEO generates is both quantitative and qualitative in nature. Thus, it can be used for various research purposes. This, for instance, could include studies with an elaborated quantitative conceptualization where observers are trained in rating procedures. Furthermore, Schwab (2020b) suggests that VEO can be combined with an ethnomethodological stance, an approach he has coined *VEO for CA*.

Next to these aspects, there were some technical issues that caused problems for all students. First, participants reported on the poor video and audio quality of the iPad mini that they used. Fortunately, newer versions of the tablet provide much better quality. Second, the fact that no zooming and selective blurring features exist seemed to hinder them. Here, further improvement of the software is necessary. A third major issue in our context was the ethics of data protection and the concern that many parents have regarding their children being filmed, and also of some teachers regarding themselves being filed (which was especially the case at primary schools). This is a crucial problem for classroom research in general and needs further discussion (McDonagh et al. 2019).

Conclusions

The two scenarios examined in this chapter illustrate two possible models of how the VEO app can be used in a German context in teacher education by both researchers and practitioners. One crucial finding emerging from our research conducted in the VEO project is the value of video-based observation and thus scaffolded reflection in teacher training programmes. However, in order to implement VEO more effectively, clear procedures and models will have to be developed and integrated into the teacher training curriculum. The same applies to using VEO as a research instrument.

Based on our findings, we have developed two models for implementing VEO more effectively in teacher education programmes in Germany. Model A, illustrated in Figure 5.4, is based on our first case study and illustrates how VEO can be used as an instrument to scaffold processes of reflection among pre-service teachers:

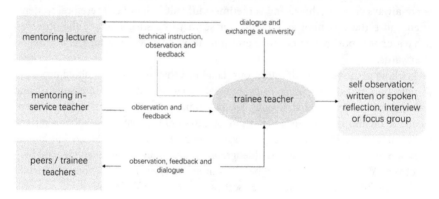

Figure 5.4 Model A.

Model B, illustrated in Figure 5.5, presents the second case study, which shows VEO being used by a student teacher as a research instrument to collect data for her final thesis:

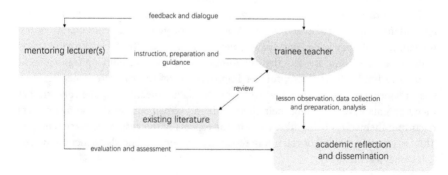

Figure 5.5 Model B.

Looking at the data we collected, it is clear that the app can provide pre-structured and detailed data. However, to ensure that the data is collected and used in a theory-based and well-structured way, it would help to develop and test a number of innovative research designs, such as the one in this study.

Through the VEO project, we have seen that much depends on those responsible for teaching the next generation of teachers, which is why we argue that it is essential to support and train teacher educators more systematically in this field. Furthermore, we found that VEO – if integrated systematically – can be a strong option to bridge the gap between theory, research and practice, and thus to promote professional development of pre-service teachers. Finally, we see great potential in developing connections between teacher education and companies that develop digital educational tools. We consider it crucial that professionals working in both fields inform each other's practices.

6

VEO as Part of Reflective Practice in the Primary Teacher Education Programme in Finland

Minna Körkkö, Outi Kyrö-Ämmälä and Tuija Turunen
University of Lapland, Finland

Introduction

VEO has been part of reflective practice in the primary school teacher education programme at the University of Lapland (UoL) Finland since 2016, when the first VEO trials were conducted (Körkkö, Morales-Rios and Kyrö-Ämmälä 2019). Currently, VEO is used for self-directed, peer- and supervisor-assisted individual and collaborative reflection. Research has focused on promoting student teachers' reflection skills through video-based reflection and developing supervision methods where the VEO app is utilized (Körkkö 2020).

By using a case study approach, this chapter presents the findings from a VEO trial carried out in spring 2017. Twenty student teachers and eleven university supervisors participated in the Advanced Practicum (teaching practice) in which they followed a video-enhanced reflection procedure during a five-week period. Two student teachers were selected for further analysis in this chapter, which discusses how the student teachers experienced VEO as a reflection tool and how it might have benefited their professional development.

In Finland, all primary and secondary school teachers complete a master's degree: primary school teachers in education and secondary school teachers' in their subjects. Teacher education programmes are located at universities, are research-based and take approximately five years to complete. During their studies, student teachers complete two pieces of empirical research, the first at the bachelor's and the second at the master's level. Teacher education includes theoretical studies and practical experiences at schools, underlining the connections between theory, practice and research (Kyrö-Ämmälä 2019).

Theoretical Insights

According to previous literature, learning is regarded as a reflective process of knowledge construction and the result of previous experiences (Schön 1987; Jay and Johnson 2002; Korthagen 2004, 2017). Reflection is defined as a cognitive process where student teachers focus on their own experiences, the context in which they are acting and other people in that context. Reflection can be self-reflection or collaborative reflection carried out with others. The assumption is that reflection changes student teachers' ways of thinking and can also affect their future actions.

Reflection can occur at many levels and focus on various themes. It can be descriptive, analytical or critical in nature (Schön 1987; Jay and Johnson 2002). Descriptive reflection describes what is happening in the situation. Comparative reflection takes a more analytical stance where the details of the situation are reframed in light of alternative views and perspectives. In critical reflection, one establishes a renewed perspective that includes making a judgement so that historical, socio-political and moral contexts are also considered. Critical reflection is a prerequisite for understanding the meaning of the situation, which enables one to gain new insights and develop new ways of acting.

Student teachers' learning is multidimensional and includes cognitive, emotional and motivational aspects (Korthagen 2004, 2017). Learning is seen as multilevel, which means that in order to understand it, teacher identity, persona, and strengths and weaknesses also need to be addressed. The definition of critical reflection includes questioning what kind of teacher one is and wants to become and what kind of ideals one possesses (Korthagen 2004). In this study, the analysis uses the onion model of reflection, which presents the six layers of learning: *environment, behaviour, competencies, beliefs, identity* and *mission* (Korthagen 2004).

In addition, the analysis exploits the ideas of Blömeke, Gustafsson and Shavelson (2015) concerning teacher competence as a continuum. Their model includes characteristics similar to Korthagen's holistic approach (2004, 2017). According to the model, teacher competence consists of three elements: visible observable behaviour, situation-specific skills (perception, interpretation and decision-making) and dispositions (cognitive and affective-motivational). Behaviour is dictated by latent dispositions, which transfer to behaviour through perception, interpretation and decision-making.

Student teachers' videos of their lessons reveal their behaviour, and reflection on their teaching reveals the thinking processes and interpretations behind their behaviour. Thus, reflection on videos offers insight into student teachers' pedagogical thinking, that is, thinking relating to teaching, and the practical theories that guide their work; supervisory discussions shed light on supervisors' pedagogical thinking as well (Kansanen 1993).

Student Teacher's Learning through Video-based Reflection

This study builds on previous studies on reflective practice, which have reported student teachers' difficulties in learning critical reflection skills and highlighted the role of guiding frameworks and knowledgeable others in promoting individual and collaborative reflection (Harford and MacRuairc 2008; Körkkö, Kyrö-Ämmälä and Turunen 2016). Specifically, the study draws upon previous research on video-based reflection in teacher education, which has yielded promising results (Borko et al. 2008; Snoeyink 2010; Gröschner et al. 2018).

Video-based reflection affects student teacher learning and professional development in many ways. Video viewing seems to increase teachers' intrinsic motivations and strengthens self-efficacy (Sherin 2004). It can also increase the sense of teacher autonomy and the sense of being able to make changes (Gröschner et al. 2014). Through video viewing, student teachers can develop their selective attention, that is, their ability to recognize relevant issues and events in their practice. This is because videos enable them to watch teaching from a perspective that they cannot otherwise access and thus help them to shift their focus from themselves to their pupils and their pupils' learning (Snoeyink 2010). Videos promote a shift from descriptive reflection to a more focused and interpretive one and enhance knowledge-based reasoning, that is, the ability to interpret reasons for and consequences of their decisions (Borko et al. 2008; Santagata and Guarino 2011). Video viewing can also encourage student teachers to question their beliefs and values about teaching and learning; they can identify contradictions between their image of teaching and actual teaching practices (Bryan and Recesso 2006).

It is important to note that other factors also simultaneously affect teaching along with video-based reflection, such as discussions with peers and facilitators and previous experiences (Christ, Arya and Chiu 2014). Through the study presented in this chapter, it was possible to examine how video-based reflection affected student teachers' cognition, but not to what extent their teaching was actually developed through the use of videos.

One disadvantage of VEO is that the video view is limited, which affects student teachers' opportunities to assess their classroom practices and pupils' learning (Bryan and Recesso 2006). Technical problems may also decrease the quality of the recordings. In addition, videos can offer too much information all at once and cause cognitive overload (Goldman et al. 2007). Therefore, it is necessary to complement video recordings with other contextual information and documentation, such as pupil work samples or lesson plans, to gain a better understanding of what is actually happening in the classroom (Sherin 2004).

Moreover, student teachers sometimes resist sharing videos with others (Borko et al. 2008). They may struggle with watching the videos of their own teaching and fear that others will judge their teaching if they see the video (Bryan and Recesso 2006; Snoeyink 2010). Therefore, it is important to build a supportive and trusting communal environment where student teachers are encouraged to show their videos to others. To reduce resistance, it may be useful to incorporate video technology in teacher education programmes as early as possible (Fadde and Sullivan 2013).

Student teachers are not automatically able to notice integral aspects of teaching and learning in videos; instead, they might concentrate on superficial issues, such as their appearance and their behaviour (Snoeyink 2010). These difficulties are related to their level of professional development and are the result of a lack of knowledge regarding the teaching profession and subject-specific knowledge (Blomberg, Sturmer and Seidel 2011). Finally, even though watching videos of one's own teaching can be encouraging and motivating, student teachers can find it difficult to criticize their own or their peers' teaching, which may hinder a deeper discussion of their developmental needs (Ellis et al. 2015).

VEO Trials at UoL

At UoL, teacher education is research-based; the study courses are integrated with research, and student teachers independently complete empirical research. The primary school teacher education programme lasts five years, and student teachers complete a master's degree in education studies, which includes both academic studies and practical professional development in a primary school (called the teaching practicum). Pedagogical and methodological studies are interconnected with the teaching practicum both chronologically and by content. Figure 6.1 illustrates the model of the teacher education programme at UoL.

As demonstrated in Figure 6.1, each practicum is connected to course work and research methods and includes a pedagogical seminar in which the student teachers reflect on their classroom experiences and enquiries during the teaching practicum. In addition, the student teachers construct a portfolio during their studies in order to document and reflect upon their personal pedagogical practical theories.

At UoL, VEO has been used as part of reflective practice since 2016 in the Advanced Practicum, which during the research was the final practicum before graduation. It runs for five weeks, the first of which is scheduled for planning and class observation. Student teachers teach in pairs in the same classroom where they carry out professional practices both individually and collaboratively. The Advanced Practicum

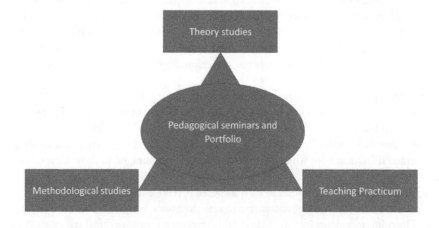

Figure 6.1 Integration of theory studies, methodological studies and teaching practicum in teacher education (Kyrö-Ämmälä 2019).

is composed of two teaching and two observation periods for each student teacher. During the practicum, student teachers are guided to construct their teacher identities and their personal practical theories. They are supervised by mentors at school and university lecturers from the faculty of education. In this chapter, 'supervision' refers to supervision which is carried out by university lecturers.

During the first trial in the autumn of 2016, supervision was based on videos recorded by student teachers through an app. During the five-week practicum period, each student teacher had two teaching and two observation periods. Each period lasted one week. Student teachers who observed the classrooms made six videos with the app. They were guided to record and tag two lessons, or part of them, using the VEO app and three ready-made tag sets: 'Communication', 'Classroom Atmosphere' and 'Motivation and Evaluation', each including two subtags. Tag sets were based on the aims of the Advanced Practicum and created as a result of communal discussion with teacher educators from UoL. Two of the videos were nearly twenty-five minutes long. The remaining four videos were short clips of from ten to fifteen minutes each. After recording, the videos were uploaded to the online portal. The student teachers watched their own videos via the portal at the end of the school day and were able to add comments and/or tags to their videos. The supervisors did not attend the lessons. Instead, the student teachers shared their videos with their supervisors through the VEO portal. Supervision included watching and commenting on videos and giving feedback via the online portal, as well as face-to-face, or during online meetings before, during and after the practicum.

According to the results from the first trial (Körkkö, Morales-Rios and Kyrö-Ämmälä 2019), student teachers found the app useful, but the impact of video-based reflection on their professional development was limited. Videos offered only a narrow view of classroom practice, which made it difficult for student teachers to reflect on their teaching and for supervisors to guide their practice. The findings indicated that videos might exclude essential aspects of the classroom environment and culture. Individual video-based reflection and supervisory discussions were not structured, which may also have limited the benefits. Moreover, student teachers and some of the supervisors were reluctant to use the app. Video-based reflection seemed to change the aims of supervision and the roles of the supervisors and student teachers. The results indicated that, because of technical limitations, video cannot be used as an exclusive tool for lesson observation. The results showed that it was necessary to provide student teachers with a strong external reflection guide to support their video analysis and to connect individual video-based reflection to collaborative video-based reflection with their peers and supervisors in supervisory processes (cf. Bryan and Recesso 2006).

Based on these results, the implementation of VEO was changed for the second trial in the spring of 2017, in which VEO was used for both self-reflection and reflective discussions with peers and as a tool for supervision. Student teachers followed the procedure of guided reflection, which aimed to bridge the gap between theory and practice by supporting student teachers in developing knowledge based on their practical experiences (Husu, Toom and Patrikainen 2008). The procedure was modified to the context of UoL and VEO by the authors and included the following four stages (Figure 6.2).

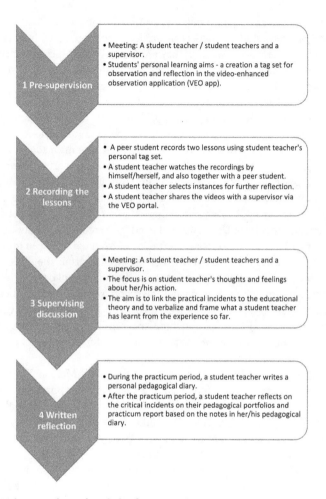

Figure 6.2 The procedure of guided reflection with VEO.

As illustrated in Figure 6.2, the procedure included the creation of an individual tag set based on personal learning goals, authentic lesson observation and feedback discussion (optional), selection of a lesson for recording, recording and watching the video, a supervisory discussion and written reflection. In this procedure, individual video-based reflections were connected to the process of supervision (Körkkö 2019).

The procedure also included guidance for individual and peer reflection and for supervisory discussion. The student teachers met their supervisors during the first week of the practicum face-to-face or online to discuss practical issues. The student teachers thought about what they wanted to achieve during the Advanced Practicum and formed two tags and possible subtags based on these personal learning goals. The supervisors advised them during the creation of tag sets, but the tag sets were not based on specific theoretical insights. During each teaching period, the student teachers selected a lesson for which they wanted their tag sets to be applied, and the peer students did the recording. The total number of recorded videos per student teacher was two. After the recording, student teachers discussed their lessons with their peers, and the videos were uploaded to the VEO portal. The student teachers recorded the videos without their supervisors' help. They were guided to record the entire forty-five-minute lesson or part of it. After recording, the student teachers watched and discussed the videos together at the convenient time to do so, and then uploaded the videos to the online portal where they could watch the videos of their teaching and reflect on their experiences, as well as choose two critical incidents for further discussion. The first incident was a positive one where the student teachers had experienced success, and the second was one which the student teachers had found challenging.

The student teachers shared all their videos with their supervisors on the online portal. The supervisors also had a chance to visit student teachers' lessons at school. The supervisory meetings were held at the end of the practicum period, usually during the final week, because it was the optimal time for discussing the whole period and everything that the student teachers had learnt. In that discussion, the practicum period was reflected on, and the student teachers' videos were watched focusing on the critical incidents chosen by the student teachers. Participants could use guiding questions, such as: 'What is happening in the situation?', 'Is there a relationship between what a student teacher is doing and what pupils are doing?', 'Is there something that cannot be seen in the videos?', 'How does the incident relate to theory?' and 'Which teacher role does the incident relate to?' During the practicum, student teachers were guided to reflect on their experiences in their individual pedagogical diaries. Afterwards, they explored their experiences when writing their final practicum report. They were guided to further reflect on their video-based experiences by using questions similar to the ones used in the final discussion with their supervisors.

Research Design

For the study reported in this chapter, two of twenty student teachers were selected for closer examination because, for these students, the use of the VEO app seemed to promote reflection most clearly during the practicum. Moreover, both students showed positive attitudes towards the VEO app. Student teacher 1 (ST1) was a male and practised in a general education year-five classroom with approximately twenty pupils. During the practicum, he taught several subjects, such as mathematics, Finnish language and religion.[1] His customized tag set included two tags. The first tag was 'deviation from a lesson plan', which included three subtags: 'a creative solution', 'a situation continues naturally' and 'a deviation is necessary'. The second tag was 'information technology', which included two subtags: 'increases interaction' and 'improves learning'.

Student teacher 2 (ST2), a female, carried out the practicum in a special education context with pupils from years one to three. The number of pupils varied from lesson to lesson. She taught several subjects, such as mathematics, Finnish language and geography.[2] Her customized tag set included two tags. The first tag was 'a student' which included two subtags: 'joy of learning' and 'a trigger'. The second was 'a teacher' which included two subtags: 'support' and 'individual'.

Both supervisors were females with teacher qualifications and doctorates in educational sciences. They had no previous experience supervising student teachers, but had many years of teaching and researching experience in higher education institutions.

Data Collection and Analysis

The two cases presented in this chapter are part of a bigger study reported in Körkkö 2020. The data for this bigger study were collected by the first author of this chapter and included separate focus group interviews with student teachers (n=10) and supervisors (n=9), as well as audio recordings from the supervisory discussions (n=4). ST1 and ST 2 participated in different focus groups – ST1 before attending his final supervisory discussion, and ST2 after finishing the supervision process. The interviews were semi-structured, including questions on particular themes, such as the functionality of a personal tag set, VEO in student teachers' self- and peer reflection, supervision and the guided reflection procedure, overview and evaluation of the supervision process, as well as suggestions for the future use of VEO as part of reflective practice. Supervisors' interviews were not used in this chapter.

The audio recordings from the supervisory discussions were used to study the contents of the discussions and to probe deeper into the participants' perceptions and experiences. ST1 and ST2 participated in different supervision discussions. The discussions, each lasting from one to one and one-half hours, were authentic situations where the researcher was not present. The supervisors delivered the audio recordings to the researcher.

The interviews were analysed through the qualitative data-driven thematic method to explore ST1 and ST2's perception and experiences on using VEO app as a supervision tool (Mayring 2014). During the analysis of the supervisory discussions, special attention was paid on the student teacher's reflections on their identity. The analysis was based on Korthhagen's (2017) onion model and combined data- and theory-driven thematic analysis (see Körkkö 2020).

The results are presented in two sub-chapters. The first one focuses on the interview data with students' perceptions and experiences, and the second sub-chapter discusses the VEO app as a tool to access deeper level of reflections (Jay and Johnson 2002).

Results: Focus Group Interviews

Video App in Self- and Peer Reflection and Supervision

Both student teachers found that working with VEO benefited their reflection and made them realize issues that they had not noticed while teaching. ST1 had noticed aspects of his behaviour in front of the classroom: 'I feel that I picked up lot of issues, like my fast speech. It was not in my tags, but I have gotten feedback on it earlier. Another thing I realized on video, which was not in my tag either, is that I was wandering back and forth and looked very restless.'

ST1 was not totally satisfied with his tag set because he found that the tag set did not serve him in the best possible way. ST1 thought that it might have been difficult for a peer student to tag instances during his lessons. He stated that, when watching videos, tags were located in self-evident places and they did not offer much new information to him. He suggested that it might be ideal to create a tag set a few weeks after the practicum period has begun when the student teachers have already become familiarized with their classrooms: 'I feel that my tag set could have been much better ... I do not know if it would be better if tag sets were created in a later phase of practice.'

ST2 found that her inner feelings during the lesson were not visible in the video. This strengthened her self-confidence and encouraged her. She said:

> I looked more confident outside than I felt in my mind. There was a hustle in my head, about what I can do, but then when I saw the video, I looked quite peaceful and confident. It encouraged me somehow, but, of course, I was able to criticise my own actions. Our working was very reflective; we discussed much, and the video helped with that as well.

ST2 seemed to be happy with her personal tag set. She found that her tags helped her focus on certain targets in her teaching: 'Tags promoted reflection, or made it easier, when you think about passing of time. Teacher resources are limited. It is easier when you can pick up pointers.'

Many previous studies have reported similar findings of video offering possibilities to look at one's professional practice from a new perspective (Snoeyink 2010). The motivational effects of video viewing have been recognized, as well (Sherin 2004; Goldman et al. 2007). In this study, both student teachers paid particular attention to their behaviour, which seems to be common for student teachers generally (Snoeyink 2010).

Besides self-reflection, student teachers found video-based peer reflection helpful. ST1 had discussed one video of his teaching with a peer, and he had noticed issues on video that the peer had not tagged. He said: '[Y]es, we discussed why you have tagged this, and thought ... some tags were quite self-evident, why she had tagged them, but then I was thinking why she had not tagged some instances.'

ST1's experience reveals that a recorder's observations can differ from those of the teacher who is observed, which can promote discussions about teaching and help student teachers look at their teaching from a different angle (Christ, Arya and Chiu 2014).

Also, ST2 had discussed two of her videos with a peer. For her, the most productive discussion was the final one when she watched her videos collaboratively and received feedback from a peer and the supervisor. She said: 'We had selected instances that we watched, both challenging and something that we need to develop, and then we discussed them.'

Both student teachers were happy with their interactions with their supervisors. Supervisors had offered them a new, more theoretical view of their teaching, which they appreciated. ST1 said: 'I think that she [the supervisor] had a researcher viewpoint; she sounded very scientific in her speech, whereas I had been thinking it very much from a practical point of view, it is difficult to explain, and perhaps she watched it from a different world.'

ST2 said: 'She brought research into this. She was able to bring it in a funny way, into our reflection and discussions. She did not review us, but she asked questions ... [and] brought it to a deeper level and asked about theories.'

The student teachers' experiences suggest that their supervisors aimed to promote the integration of student teachers' practice with theory through questions and challenged student teachers to widen their thinking beyond teaching situations. Therefore, it can be said that supervision included aspects of the reflective approach.

Results: Supervisory Discussions

Supervisory discussions included reflection on all layers of the onion model. Guided by the reflection procedure, most reflection focused on environmental aspects. Behaviour was the second, identity the third, competencies the fourth and mission was the fifth most common content of reflection. There were all types of reflection; sometimes teachers and supervisors described student teachers or their pupils' behaviour, but there was also more analytical reflection where student teachers looked at their teaching from different perspectives, such as those of the pupils, and linked their teaching to theory with the help of the supervisors' questions and comments. A minor part of the reflection included aspects of the critique. Thus, analysis of supervisory discussions strengthens the findings from focus-group interviews.

Reaching Meaning-oriented Reflection

The supervisors asked student teachers reflective questions and made comments that guided student teachers to concentrate on key episodes of the recorded lessons and expanded discussion beyond the videos. Student teachers not only looked back on their actions, they became aware of the essential aspects of those instances. Thus, supervisors encouraged meaning-oriented reflection that promotes professional development in the long run (Korthagen et al. 2001).

The following extracts illustrate a supervisory discussion between ST1 and his supervisor. The topic of discussion is activation of the pupils' advanced knowledge during a religion lesson that addressed worship service.

Supervisor: In your opinion, how did you succeed in activating pupils' advanced knowledge and comprehension?

ST1: I said that, even today, people go to services, and it comes from history. Then, I asked pupils if they had ever been in worship service.

Supervisor: You activated advanced knowledge at the beginning, but you do it throughout the lesson as well. If you watch your video, you see that you ask questions when you activate their advanced knowledge; have you realized that?

ST1: I have not realized it. I have to watch that video again.

The supervisor helped ST1 to realize ways of activation of advanced knowledge during teaching which guided his reflection towards more analytical reasoning (Jay and Johnson 2002). By doing so, the supervisor expressed her practical knowledge when she prompted ST1 to think about his lesson and encouraged him to watch the video again (Zanting, Verloop and Vermunt 2003). The discussion with the supervisor revealed how ST1 had planned the lesson and provided insights into his thinking, which could be seen in his decision-making and actions while teaching (Blömeke, Gustafsson and Shavelson 2015).

In the next extract, the supervisor and ST2 are watching the first recorded lesson where ST2 faces a conflict with a pupil. ST2 tries to make a pupil do an assignment, but he is not willing to do it. Instead, the pupil asks ST2 about her favourite TV programme, but ST2 asks him to complete the assignment and promises to tell the answer when he is finished with it.

Supervisor: What did you think about the situation, when he asked you a question? That it was a trigger and he started to work?

ST2: He [the pupil] asks much and guides the lesson in a direction he wants by asking questions so that he does not have to do assignments.

Supervisor: Could it be, when you were interested in tagging triggers, can it be a trigger? That question, that he gets an answer after he is finished, that it is a trigger?

ST2: I think that a trigger is in another place, where we play an old game, and it is very motivating. I answered his question and said, 'Let's do this. Here is a timer'

The supervisor guided ST2 to think about interaction between her and the pupil by asking about learning triggers that she had used to motivate him, thus encouraging her to think about the recorded situation more from the pupil's point of view. The supervisor offered an alternative view of the trigger, but ST2 did not accept it. The teaching situation had been challenging and stressful for ST2. Reflecting on the situation revealed emotions that related to the situation (Blömeke, Gustafsson and Shavelson 2015; Korthagen 2017).

Theorizing Teaching and Learning

Supervisors not only supported the use of meaning-oriented reflection, but also guided student teachers to theorize about their professional practice. Discussions addressed

94   *Video Enhanced Observation for Language Teaching*

student teachers' visible behaviour and competencies that they showed in videos, as well as student teachers' expectations and interpretations during lessons.

In the next extract, the supervisor asks ST1 his opinion of the amount and quality of interaction during a religion lesson.

> **Supervisor:** You can evaluate how much interaction there was between the pupils and how much between the pupils and you as a teacher. What part of the interaction included feedback that promoted pupils' learning? How do you evaluate the amount and quality of the interactions in these situations or in some other lesson?
>
> **ST1:** I saw that they worked in a very task-oriented way because they had to, because I gave them a schedule … pupils had their presentations, and then I gave them very simple feedback.
>
> **Supervisor:** When a teacher plans teaching, just planning is not enough … but a teacher needs to justify, give reasons for acting like this. What is it that leads to increased interaction, learning and interest, and better understanding?
>
> **ST1:** I understand it better now. Doing a creative production was one of the learning tasks in the second lesson. Group work supported this task. Learning happened during the lesson because the schedule was strict, and they needed to finish it. We practiced handling pressure; it was one of aims that pupils are able to follow the schedule.

At first, ST1 was unable to answer the supervisor's questions. In his answer, he described the actions in the classroom. After the supervisors' clarifying comment, ST1 was able to justify his actions, thus showing his ability to reflect in a more analytical and productive way (Jay and Johnson 2002).

In the following discussion, the supervisor guides ST2 to think about items of her practical theory from a theoretical point of view.

> **Supervisor:** There is a model … created by Professor Pertti Kansanen … we have a meta-level of thinking as teachers. Then we have a practical theory, how we act in practice, and that is the intended interaction. Before the interaction, we think about issues and plan them, then there is an event in classroom and, after that, a teacher evaluates it. Their pedagogical thinking is continuous reflection. Then practical theory means all those theories that determine your choices, what you do, that you are aware of them. They are perhaps those values in meta-level.
>
> **ST2:** I think about writing something about the proximal zone of development, working in the pupils' zone of proximal development.

In this extract, the supervisor referred to the literature on teacher pedagogical thinking and gave ST2 theoretical concepts to think about herself as a teacher on different levels of conceptualization.

Discussion and Conclusions

According to the results of the study reported in this chapter, both student teachers found that using the video app promoted self- and peer reflection. The videos offered them a different perspective on their teaching. Peer reflection enabled student teachers to compare and contrast their thinking to that of their peers. These findings are in line with the results from previous studies that have shown the positive influences of video viewing on self- and peer reflection in teacher education (Snoeyink 2010; Santagata and Guarino 2011). The VEO app contributed positively to the student teachers' reflection skills, especially because the student teachers were motivated to use the app for their learning from video. The personalized tag sets promoted student teachers' ability to notice issues in their own and their peers' teaching. Videos recorded by VEO served as essential springboards for discussions with supervisors. These findings highlight the importance of the supervisor's role in guiding the construction of tag sets and challenging student teachers to give their peer students constructive feedback, which includes developmental suggestions. Creating tags that are easily observable can be challenging and require practice.

The nature of student teachers' reflections can be partly explained through the video-enhanced reflection procedure, which concentrated on actual behaviour and theorizing that behaviour. Analysis of the supervisory discussions confirmed the student teachers' experiences of supervision and showed that the supervisors played an integral role in guiding reflection. Without that, the student teachers would not have reached a deeper level of thinking. Supervisors challenged student teachers to justify their actions, think about consequences and ponder teaching from a theoretical point of view. This occurred by applying principles of guiding student teachers to adopt a reflective approach through questions, comments and suggesting alternative perspectives, which revealed student teachers' cognitive processes and their decision-making during teaching (Blömeke, Gustafsson and Shavelson 2015). As previous research has suggested, it seems beneficial to connect an explicit guiding procedure with video-elicited reflection and supervision (Borko et al. 2008; Harford and MacRuairc 2008). This allows personal variation and modifications of the procedure.

Even though supervisory discussions expanded beyond the environment to consider other aspects, reflection on personal strengths and developmental suggestions were scarce. Moreover, student teachers seldom criticized their own or their peers' practices. Therefore, in the future, to increase the amount of reflection on identity and to develop a more critical attitude, it may be beneficial to pay more attention to the characteristics of the reflection procedure. Different analysis frameworks result in different kinds of reflections (Santagata and Angelici 2010). The reflection guide could include more questions regarding personal strengths and developmental needs, as well as feelings and motivation, which also play an integral role in learning to become a teacher (Korthagen 2017).

In the future, there is a need to study the learning process of student teachers during the practicum more thoroughly, focusing on what student teachers actually learn from videos when they reflect on their teaching and how this learning is applied in teaching, if at all. Peer reflection through a video app requires further research to find the best ways of implementation. Finally, it is essential to further investigate the role of the supervisor in promoting student teachers' learning of reflection skills, especially how supervisors can guide student teachers towards developing a more a critical approach in respect to their teaching.

The benefits of our reflection procedure with VEO include that it highlights student-centredness, supports student teachers' self-enquiry and provides external guidance for individual and collaborative reflection. Our model enables variations, and we believe that it would be adaptable to other contexts, as well.

7

VEO-integrated IMDAT in Pre-service Language Teacher Education: A Focus on Change in Teacher Questioning Practices

Merve Bozbıyık
Middle East Technical University, Turkey
Olcay Sert
Mälardalen University, Sweden
Kadriye Dilek Bacanak
Gazi University, Turkey

Introduction

What counts as evidence of development in (language) teacher education research is not an easy question to tackle. Researchers who follow a qualitative paradigm use data collection tools like interviews and observations (e.g. Appleton and Kindt 2002), and focus on a variety of objects of development, for example, development in the practical knowledge of designing and using tasks and activities (Wyatt and Borg 2011). Looking into the reflective practices of teachers and what teachers think they do in classrooms has been one of the common ways to investigate teacher development (e.g. Wyatt 2010). There may, however, be a gap between what teachers *think* they do and what they actually do in classrooms (Li 2017, 2020). Therefore, combining (1) analyses of actual teaching practices (e.g. by using discursive methods like conversation analysis) and (2) reflection and feedback practices that are stimulated by recorded videos can bring data-based evidence to development, and at the same time be the drive behind development. Such an approach to investigating teacher development (over time) has recently been undertaken using reflective and evidence-based teacher education frameworks like IMDAT (Sert 2015, 2019). IMDAT initially (2015) combined video-recordings and teachers' reflections to document change in teaching practices that are locally situated in classroom interactions. Integrating a mobile video-tagging tool like VEO (see Chapter 3) into the IMDAT teacher education framework can create affordances for evidence-based reflections and feedback that draw on tagged lesson videos.

In this chapter, we draw on data collected as part of the VEO Europa project. VEO has been integrated into a pre-service language (i.e. English) teacher education programme that follows the IMDAT teacher education framework. IMDAT includes an initial training on classroom interaction practices, followed by lessons taught by candidate teachers. Post-observation feedback sessions between experts and novices (e.g. trainer-trainee, mentor-student teacher) are conducted after these lessons, which are then followed by written reflections of the student teachers (STs). The framework includes another round of teaching, this time observed by another peer – which is then followed by another post-observation feedback session and a process of critical reflective writing. This chapter reports findings based on one pre-service teacher's video-recorded lessons that are analysed using conversation analysis (CA) methodology. Conversation analytic findings from classroom videos are complemented with audio-recorded feedback sessions as well as written reflections. By focusing on one interactional phenomenon, namely teacher questioning practices, we demonstrate how the focal teacher changes her questioning practices in the classroom over time, as she teaches, gets feedback from an expert and a peer, and reflects on her teaching practices. The findings have implications for (mobile) teacher education, as well as for situated and longitudinal research on classroom discourse that employs conversation analysis and other discursive methodologies.

Review of Literature

In this section, we will first review recent research on the place of classroom interaction in teacher education, with an emphasis on data-based reflection. We will then provide a brief background on the interactional phenomenon under focus, namely teacher questioning practices.

Classroom Interaction and Teacher Education

Teacher development, at all levels, is a collaborative process that requires a teacher's engagement in her teaching and learning practices coupled with a continuous process of balancing reflection and feedback. Some researchers (Walsh 2006; Seedhouse 2008; Sert 2015) have argued that when teachers become more aware of the interactional dynamics of their own classrooms, they can develop skills to make better decisions in classrooms to enhance student participation. This line of research has resulted in teacher education frameworks like SETT (Walsh 2006, 2011), IMDAT (Sert 2015, 2019, 2021) and SWEAR (Waring 2021) that put classroom interaction at the heart of teacher development.

Walsh's Self Evaluation of Teacher Talk (SETT) framework (see Chapter 11, this volume) has been one of the most influential attempts to help teachers reflect on their own classroom interactional practices for developmental purposes. Walsh (2006, 2011, 2013) encouraged teachers to identify features of their own classroom interactions (e.g. clarification requests, corrective repair) and align them to pedagogical goals (e.g. to clarify when necessary, to evaluate student contributions) in one of the four classroom 'modes' (managerial mode, materials mode, skills and systems mode, classroom context mode) at a given time (see Walsh 2011: 113). The SETT framework has been adopted in a number of contexts as Walsh (2006) made SETT procedures (p. 166), the observation instrument (pp. 167–8), and workshop materials (pp. 169–70) available for researchers and teacher educators. In one recent study, for example, Aşık and Kuru Gönen (2016) explored Turkish pre-service teachers' perceptions of the use of SETT and their development, revealing positive outcomes. The framework has also been adopted as a research tool, for example by Baumgart (2019), as she carried out a critical-reflective analysis of a teacher's classroom discourse in Ireland.

SETT is intertwined with a construct known as Classroom Interactional Competence (CIC), defined as teachers' and learners' ability 'to use interaction as a tool for mediating and assisting learning' (Walsh 2011: 158). CIC includes use of language convergent to the pedagogical goals of the moment, shaping learner contributions (seeking clarification, scaffolding, modelling or repairing learner input) and effective use of eliciting. Sert (2015) described new features of CIC that include the ways teachers (1) manage interactional troubles, (2) deploy and manage multilingual and multimodal resources (e.g. gestures) and (3) display awareness of students' unwillingness to participate. Research on CIC also included tracking how a teacher creates learning opportunities (Sert 2017), bringing empirical evidence to language learning in a lesson of a teacher who has gone through the IMDAT teacher education framework (see Section 3). For more research findings in relation to CIC, see Sert (2019, 2021) and Walsh and Sert (2019).

The reflective IMDAT framework was shown to develop teachers' classroom interactional competence at secondary school level with adolescent students (Sert 2015), and was adopted in training teachers of very young learners of English (Balaman 2018). Recently, Sert (2019, 2021) argued for the integration of mobile video-tagging tools into the IMDAT framework that focuses on the development of teachers' CIC through evidence-based and data-led (Mann and Walsh 2015, 2017) reflection and feedback practices. The use of mobile video-tagging tools, like VEO, was found to facilitate reflection and peer feedback (Çelik et al. 2018) practices, as many chapters in this book as well as recent research in teacher education contexts show (e.g. Körkkö et al. 2019). A mobile video-tagging tool like VEO allows focused observations on various aspects of classroom interaction, ranging from the types of teacher questions to the correction practices. In the present paper, one of the observation tags included the types of questions asked by the teacher, and this became the focus of analysis first by the participants themselves, and then by the authors of this chapter. The following section will, therefore, briefly introduce teacher questioning practices.

Teacher Questioning Practices

Despite recent attempts to create pedagogical settings where students become agents of their own learning by initiating sequences of interactions, classroom interaction research thus far has shown that most of the interactions in classrooms are teacher-initiated. These initiations predominantly include questioning practices by teachers who aim at eliciting responses from students for a number of reasons, for instance for checking understanding (Waring 2012), or expanding student turns (Walsh 2006; Svennevig 2013). Since the beginning of research on classroom interaction in the twentieth century, researchers have repeatedly found evidence for a triadic pattern in whole-class interactions, typically involving a teacher (I)nitiation with a question followed by a student (R)esponse, which is then (F)ollowed up in some way, for instance by (F)eedback or (E)valuation (Initiation-Response-Feedback/Evaluation (IRF/E)) (Sinclair and Coulthard 1975). Although research on student initiations (Jacknick 2011; Waring 2011) has successfully documented that the teacher-initiated triadic dialogue is not necessarily the norm, teacher questions still play a crucial role for us to understand the dynamics of teaching and learning in instructed learning settings.

Since the 1960s, different question types have been classified in classroom discourse research: exam questions vs. real questions (Searle 1969), known-information questions vs. information-seeking questions (Mehan 1979) and display questions vs. referential questions (Long and Sato 1983). Teachers initiate known-information questions (also called exam questions, and display questions) that may facilitate students' demonstration of their knowledge (e.g. Willemsen et al. 2018). Teachers may also formulate information-seeking questions (also known as real, and referential questions) to help students share their thoughts, among other things. In what follows, we will present a very brief account of question types in pedagogical interactions, as space precludes a full account.

Using conversation analysis, Koshik (2002a, b, 2003, 2005, 2010) investigated question types in L2 settings, and categorized questioning practices as Designedly Incomplete Utterances (DIUs), Reversed Polarity Questions (RPQs), Wh- as challenges, Alternative Questions and Questions that animate the voice of an abstract audience. Each of these has particular functions and features with regards to their forms, sequential positions and the response types they project. DIUs are 'grammatically incomplete sentences, phrases, or words to be continued, but not necessarily completed, by the student' (Koshik 2002a: 288). (Embodied) DIUs can be initiated in order to elicit a response from students (aus der Wieschen and Sert 2021) or to provide a hint (Sert and Walsh 2013). They may also direct students to interactional and linguistic trouble sources for self-correction as an alternative to provide explicit corrective feedback (e.g. Lyster and Ranta 1997). As a kind of assistance question (Tharp and Gallimore 1988), a DIU may promote participation and learning opportunities (e.g. Waring 2008).

Reversed polarity questions (RPQs) are identified as yes/no interrogatives (YNIs) to bring adverse assertion to students' problematic utterances (Koshik 2002b). Such questions seem to prefer simple type-conforming responses including 'yes', 'no' or equivalent tokens such as 'yeah' and 'huh uh', accompanied by mutual gaze and head movements (nodding or shaking) (Raymond 2003; Kärkkäinen and Thompson 2018). Overuse or repeated use of such questions, then, would receive only 'short answers', and in language classrooms, this may not be ideal as teachers want students to talk and present ideas. This may also be why they are called closed questions as opposed to open questions (see Dalton-Puffer 2006), which are also known as wh- questions. Using wh- questions, teachers may request elaboration or clarification in response to learners' prior turns or provide open invitations to students. To illustrate, teachers may ask questions like 'How was your weekend?' and its variations, and thus help students socialize using more extended turns of casual chat practices (Waring 2013).

In sum, teachers use a variety of questioning practices in line with (or not) their intended pedagogical purposes. The choice of the question type may become a factor in creating opportunities for student participation. Therefore, broader question categories, like open and closed questions, generally become focal reflection and feedback points for teachers in training. In this study, we will show how a pre-service teacher changes her questioning practices to promote extended learner contributions, bringing us evidence of her development of teacher language awareness and CIC over time as part of her training within the IMDAT framework.

Data and Method

Data and Context

The broader data set of this study includes (1) video recordings of twenty-two EFL lessons (seventeen hours in total) which were taught by eleven pre-service teachers (PSTs) at a secondary school in Turkey. The data set also includes (2) six-hours of twenty-two audio-recorded post-observation feedback sessions and (3) twenty-two written critical self-reflections. For the purposes of the current study, we focus on one pre-service teacher, Belma (pseudonym), as a single case. The data for the present chapter consists of forty-five-minute (each) video recordings of two English lessons within the 8th grade at a secondary school in central Turkey, two audio-recorded post-observation sessions (one with a university supervisor (US) and one with a peer teacher candidate), and two written critical self-reflections. During the data collection in 2016 Spring, Belma was placed in a practicum school where she was supported by a mentor, and spent two semesters (thirty weeks) in a classroom with thirty language learners whose age ranged from fourteen to sixteen.

During the final year of their undergraduate studies, language teacher candidates in Turkish universities take two practicum courses. During the first course they only observe lessons and write observation reports, while in the second course, they teach under the mentorship of a school teacher, examined by a US. During the second course, which is the focus of this study, the US observes and evaluates at least one lesson (in the case of this study, two lessons were observed in two different times, first by a US and the second by a peer student teacher). As part of the IMDAT teacher education framework (Sert 2015), VEO-integrated IMDAT (Sert 2019) has been put into practice as part of the student teachers' practicum studies (see Figure 7.1).

The implementation of IMDAT included an initial workshop (Step 1) on English language classroom interaction and the use of the VEO app (Chapters 3 and 4). The workshop included hands-on activities with student teachers (STs) for demonstrating aspects of classroom interaction, including question types, feedback, language choice, classroom management and multimodality. These aspects were aligned with the components of Classroom Interactional Competence, reviewed in the previous section. These were illustrated to STs using real classroom videos (see Sert 2019 for details on such materials), transcriptions of which appeared in publications like Sert (2013, 2015, 2017) and Sert and Walsh (2013). A tag set in VEO (Figure 7.2), which was developed by the second author of this article[1], was introduced to STs during the workshop, and video-tagging tasks based on the tag set were carried out with selected videos until STs were able to identify and tag the said aspects individually and in pairs.

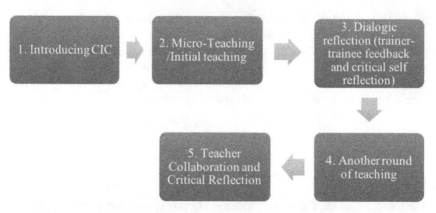

Figure 7.1 IMDAT: A classroom interaction-driven, technology-enhanced and reflective teacher education framework (Sert 2019: 223).

After this initial stage of **IMDAT**, **(I)**ntroducing CIC, the **(M)**icro-teaching/initial teaching phase followed, which required Belma and her peers to prepare a lesson observed by the US and tagged using VEO (the US used a tag set focusing on the teacher (Appendix 1), and a project assistant used the learner tag set (Appendix 2), both of which were adapted from the tag set given in Figure 7.2). The third phase of

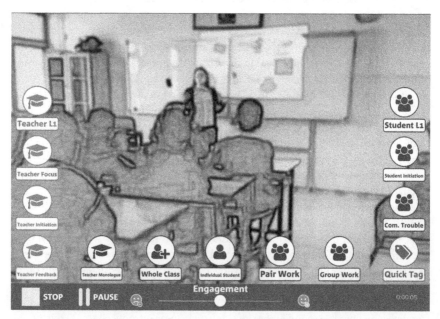

Figure 7.2 The first version of the 'Language Learning and Teaching Tagset' used in this study.

IMDAT was a (**D**)ialogic reflection/feedback session between the US and Belma, which included feedback based on the observation carried out with VEO. This was followed by a critical self-reflection by Belma to be written and delivered in written form before another round of teaching started. Belma's first lesson aimed at reviewing vocabulary on chores. After six weeks Belma then designed and delivered (**A**)nother round of teaching, observed and tagged by a peer. This (**T**)eacher collaboration is the last phase of IMDAT, which included the two peers having a post-observation feedback session together, following which Belma wrote another critical self-reflection. More details on the steps of IMDAT can be found in Sert (2019: 224–9), including samples guidelines provided to the STs (pp. 237–8).

Written consent from the participants was received prior to data collection and permissions were granted from the ethics committee. All names used in this study are pseudonyms. The VEO app was installed to a tablet computer, which enabled the US to tag moments in the first lesson that were perceived to be important for reflection and feedback. The subsequent post-observation feedback session and the peer-feedback session after the second lesson were audio-recorded. The post-observation feedback sessions in a way afforded stimulated recall, as visual evidence was used to 'provoke reflective thinking' (Kim and Silver 2016). The reflective writing documents also included an element of stimulated recall, as the student teachers could view and review their lessons both on a tablet computer (see Figure 7.3) and on the VEO portal while writing their reflections.

Figure 7.3 A sample tagged lesson on a tablet computer.

Method

In this study, we used conversation analysis (CA) (Sacks, Schegloff and Jefferson 1974) to investigate interactions in the video-recorded classrooms. Using transcription conventions (Jefferson 2004; Mondada 2018) that pay close attention to prosodic (e.g. intonation), temporal (e.g. silences) and visual aspects of interaction (e.g. gazing behaviours, gestures, body positioning and orientations to materials), we conducted a line-by-line, sequential analysis focusing turn taking, sequence organization, repair and preference organization. The initial, open-ended, 'unmotivated looking' (ten Have 2017) stage that includes 'an iterative cycle typical of CA' (Kim and Silver 2016: 207) led to a broader collection of actions that facilitate learner contributions in classroom interaction, with a focus on teacher questioning practices. The audio-recorded post-observation feedback sessions after the lessons were also systematically analysed and helped us to identify and track the participants' own orientations (emic perspective on data, see Markee 2013) to moments in recorded interactions that were talked into being. Complementary evidence to the CA analysis was also sought after, when participants specifically referred to the focal interactional episodes (e.g. how teachers facilitate or hinder student participation through different question types). This enabled us to track changes in practices over time (i.e. changes in teacher questioning practices from the first lesson to the second lesson). Such an approach that includes participants' stimulated recall of interactional events is warranted by Pomerantz (2005):

> in some circumstances, using participants' comments in conjunction with recordings of interactions provides the potential for enhancing one's analytic claims and/or for opening up avenues for investigation that otherwise might go unnoticed.
>
> (p. 93)

The IMDAT framework has worked hand in hand with the methodological approach we took in this study, in that the participants talked interactional and pedagogical events into being after reviewing lesson videos and engaging in reflective dialogues. This afforded us to take a chronological approach, allowing observations at situated, (micro)longitudinal and retrospective levels (see Markee 2008; Jakonen 2018; Pekarek Doehler 2018).

After building a collection of teacher questioning practices using CA, for this chapter, we particularly focused on the VEO-recorded lessons of a single teacher, starting with a single case analysis of an episode (in Time 1) that represents her use of questions in an 8th grade English as a foreign language classroom. We then analysed the post-observation feedback session in which the participants talked this episode (extract 1 in the analysis) into being (extract 2), which was then reflected upon in written form (extract 3). We then tracked Belma's questioning practices in the following lesson she taught (Time 2, extract 4), and further investigated the audio-recorded post-observation peer-feedback session (extract 5) and the final written reflective document (extract 6). With the analysis of this single case, we hope

VEO-integrated IMDAT   105

to provide evidence of a developmental trajectory in pre-service teacher education afforded by the VEO-integrated IMDAT framework, with an emphasis on the value of teacher language awareness and classroom interactional competence (Walsh 2006) in teacher development.

Findings

Using two classroom interaction extracts from two different points in time, two excerpts from post-observation feedback sessions (one with a university supervisor and one with a peer), and two written critical self-reflection extracts, this section will demonstrate the ways the focal ST, Belma, changed her questioning practices from Time 1 to Time 2.

Time 1 (March, 2016)

The extract that follows comes from the beginning of the revision lesson in Belma's (T) first classroom teaching performance. In this part of the lesson, Belma points at the pictures of chores on the slide, and asks whether the students do these chores. She also puts a tick or a cross on the pictures following the students' responses.

Extract 1: Classroom Interaction: chores, 28_3_16_8[th]_11-45

```
01   T:    oka::y +don't you go to the (.) grocery?+ (0.8) +for shoppi:ng?+
     t              +--------points at the slide----+       +------1--------+
                                             1: opens her hands to both sides
02   S1:   ay::h (0.6) hiç yapamam
           hu::h         i can never do
03   S4:   [y↑e:s]
04   T:    [fo::r] (.) buying brea:d?
05   S4:   ye:s
06   S2:   ye::s
07   T:    yes +(0.8) you do:+
     t          +-----2-------+
                    2: puts a tick under the picture about 'going shopping'
08         +(1.3)+
     t     +-3---+  3: looks at the pictures on the slide
09         a:nd +don't you help your mum setting the table?+
     t          +-------------------4---------------------+
                    4: points to the picture about 'set the table'
10   S1:   >bak, onu yaparım<
           oh   i do it
11   S2:   y↑e:s
12   T:    goo:d
13   S5:   yes
14   T:    +do you empty the dishwasher?
     t     +------------------5---------> line 18
                    5: points at the picture with the relevant picture
15   S3:   n↑o:
16   Ss:   no:: (.) no: no
17   T:    you need to do:+
           -------------->+
18         (1.7)+
     t     --6-->
                    6: put a cross on the picture about 'empty the dishwasher'
19   S1:   it's bo:ring+
     t     ------------+
20   T:    but mums +do tha::t+
     t              +-----7---+       7: opens her hands to both sides
21   Ss:   ye:ah
```

106 *Video Enhanced Observation for Language Teaching*

In line 01, T initiates a reversed polarity question asking whether the students go to the grocery, waits for (0.8) seconds and completes her turn with an increment (for shoppi:ng?+). After S1 states he can never go to the grocery in Turkish (02), T formulates another question which projects a short yes/no response (for buying bread?) (Raymond 2003) (04) in overlap with S4's positive response (03). In lines 5 and 6, S4 and S2 provide their confirmation, respectively, and T accepts these short responses and embodies her response by putting a tick under the picture (07). After 1.3 seconds of silence, T asks whether they help their mothers set the table through another reversed polarity question (Koshik 2002b) in line 9. S1 states he does this chore in his L1 (i.e. Turkish), which is followed by S2's confirmation, T's positive assessment (good) and S5's confirmation from lines 10 to 13. T then shows another picture that captures the action of 'emptying a dishwasher'. While doing so, she formulates a yes/no interrogative (do you empty the dishwasher?) in line 14, which receives a minimal but type-confirming response from S3 (no), followed by a choral, elongated and repetitive 'no' by other students in line 16. T responds to the students with a comment on their answer in line 17, and puts a cross on the picture in line 18. Finally, S1 provides an account for her action with the statement that emptying the dishwasher is boring (19), to which T responds with a but-prefaced counter argument (20), followed by the choral confirmation produced by other students (21).

Extract 1 has demonstrated the student-teacher formulated questions in Yes/ No interrogative and reversed polarity format to elicit students' responses, which demonstrably projected short answers from the students. Such questions tend to receive 'yes' or 'no' responses (Koshik 2010), and they may not lead to sequence expansions (Heritage 2012). In addition, the extract has also shown that T moved on to the next pictures on the slide after students' short responses, rather than eliciting follow-up responses from the students, thereby missing opportunities to enhance student participation.

Immediately after the lesson is over, US, who had been tagging Belma's lesson, and Belma meet for a post-observation feedback session in the school premises. The following extract showcases how US and the ST co-construct in interaction the need to focus on question types, by viewing the episode in extract 1. Using the tagged video, US tries to elicit Belma's (T in extract 2) intended pedagogical purposes, and gives some suggestions based on the activity to develop Belma's awareness of her own teaching performance.

The participants initially view the tagged episode that includes extract 1 for 14.6 seconds (line 03), after US's comment on how VEO tags show question types and T's acknowledgement token in lines 01 and 02. In lines 04 and 05, US quotes T's question formats first (don't you help (.) don't you go:) and goes on to ask her about her intended pedagogical goals (from lines 07 to 09) when she had been planning the activity. US formulates this reflection question first by asking what T intended to do, and then reformulated his question by referring to the pupils in line 11 (what did you want from the students). Therefore, it can be noted that the US intends to elicit the 'planned' pedagogical agenda of T, while also trying to elicit the intended consequences of the pedagogy in the form of student participation. Starting her response by stating what she 'was going to' do, using 'in fact' (tr: aslında) in line 13, T claims that she was firstly going to ask each student individually to describe the action on the picture (line 18).

VEO-integrated IMDAT

Extract 2: Post-Observation Feedback Session 1. Question types

```
01   US:   şimdi soru tiplerine odaklanıyo burda:
           now the focus is on the question types here
02   T:    °hnm:°
03         (14.6) ((they watch the episode given in extract 1 on VEO))
04   US:   don't you he:lp (0.4) don't you go: (0.3) don't you: ↑ask
05         [°(inaudible voices)°
06   T:    [°yea:h°
07   US:   >şimdi< sen bu aktivitede normalde
           now, what did you want
08         ne istiyodun bundan önce:? (0.8) yani: (.) dersten önce
           in this activity (0.8) i mean (.) when you had planned
09         planladığında bunu [burda
           this before the lesson
10   T:                        [.hhh
11   US:   öğrencilerden ne isti[yodu:n?]
           what did you want from the students (here)?
12   T:                         [ eve:t]
                                 yes
13         aslında: (0.3) şey yapcaktım: onlara sorcaktım işte: (0.7) hani:
           in fact (0.3) well, i would do i was going to ask them(0.7)i mean
14   US:   [↑ve onlar resimdeki eylemi söyliyceklerdi: ]
           and they were going to tell the action on the picture
15   T:    [göstercektim resimlerini (0.3) sen hangisini]
           i would show the pictures, i was going to ask
16         yapıyosu:n falan diye: .hh
           like which one do you do
17   US:   [hı: hı:h
           huh hu:h
18   T:    [önce bireysel olarak sorcaktım (0.3)[↓aslında:
           first i would ask individually        actually
19   US:                                         [bireysel olarak sorucaktın
                                                  you would ask individually
20   T:    eve:t
           yes
21   US:   peki öyle gitti mi:?
           well, did it go that way?
22   T:    hayır ↓gitmedi:
           no it didn't
23   US:   gitmedi: (.) neden öyle gitmemiş olabilir? (.) ↓diye:
           it didn't (.) why do you think that it didn't
24         düşünüyos:un yani: (0.6).hh e::r bu: neyle alakalı olabilir?
           go well? .hh e::r what could be the reason?
25         (0.7)
26   T:    bilmiyorum hocamı (.) yani aslında öyle yapabilirdim hani öyle
           i don't know sir (.) well actually i could have done it so
```

108 *Video Enhanced Observation for Language Teaching*

```
27          yapmamam için bi: .hhh durum yoktu [ama:
            there was no reason for me not to do it that way but
28   US:                                       [hı: hı:h
                                                huh hu:h
29          (0.6)
30   T:     [öyle olması lazı:m
            it should be that way
31   US:    [ama onu bir sorun olarak gördün şu an >di:mi yani?<=
            but now you see it as a problem, don't you?
32   T:     =evet evet
            yes yes
33   US:    yani ordaki: (0.4) eylemi söyle[meleri]
            i mean that they (the students) tell the action there
34   T:                                    [eve:t]
                                            yes
35   T:     [benim amaçladığım da böyle bi şey di:ldi zate:n
            this is not what i was aiming for anyway
36   US:    [o öyle onu onaylayı:p devam etmeleri:, ama o şekilde gitmedi:
            they confirm and continue, but it didn't go on in that way
37   T:     [eve:t]
            yes
38   US:    [ordaki soru tiplerine: (0.3) ben sana videoyu gönderince bir bak
            when i send the video to you, have a look at the question types
39          yine: sen: n:- ne sorup ne göstermişsin? onla:r nasıl cevap
            there what did you ask, what did you show? how did they
40          vermi:ş? .hhh çünkü belki de sadece yes ve no demelerini
            respond? because you might be asking questions that only
41          gerektiren (.) soru soruyorsundur (0.3) öyle bir durum var[dı::r]
            lead to yes and no, maybe it is like that
42   T:                                                              [eve:t]
                                                                      yes
```

---

[1] Hocam is a honorific term commonly used in addressing university teachers.

Her response overlaps the US's collaborative completions, displaying the ongoing alignment work during the session. In line 19, US requests confirmation in declarative format, which functions as a pre-expansion to the forthcoming elaboration questions that elicit further reflection regarding her intended aims with this activity (line 21, *well, did it go that way?*). Following T's response (*no it didn't*), US elicits further reflection on whether T knows the reason why (23, 24) the activity did not go as planned. From lines 26 to 30, T first uses an epistemic hedge (Weatherall 2011) and claims insufficient knowledge of the reasons why it did not go as planned. In line 31, US asks if T now sees this as a problem, finishing his turn with a tag question, which receives a positive response (*yes yes*) from T in line 32. In line 35, T explicitly restates that this was not her intended pedagogical goal. In what follows, from lines 38 to 41, US recommends T to examine her questions and students' responses by viewing the video, and goes on to suggest that this situation may be about the yes/no type questions.

VEO-integrated IMDAT   109

Extract 3: Written Critical Self-Reflection on lesson 1. Close-ended questions

01 T: *I observed myself critically and* **realized** *some problematic points. One of them is related*

02   *to* **question types**. *Actually, the problem stemmed from withdrawing from my plan. For*

03   *example, in warm-up part I initiated with open ended questions. (00:20-00:34) I*

04   *thought to take answers from students. Unfortunately, they didn't want to share their*

05   *weekend activities except from one student. So, without noticing, I jumped to the close*

06   *ended questions. (01:08-01:11) My simultaneous objective was to take a reaction from*

07   *the students. But, it wasn't appropriate to my aims. I had wanted to make them speak.*

08   **Taking yes or no answers to my close ended questions didn't suit my aims**. *Instead of*

09   *close ended ones, I might have* **asked** *some different open-ended questions... In the*

10   *presentation part also,* **I had a problem with question types**. *Actually, as I had planned*

11   *before, I was going to ask them about the chores like "Do you do how much of them?".*

12   *Then I would have asked personally about which chores s/he does. By the way I would*

13   *have made them* **speak and use** *the vocabulary.* **But the task got away from my plan**

14   **and also objectives** *because I got the idea that they know the vocabularies. So, my*

15   *activities changed a bit simultaneously.* **I found myself while asking close ended**

16   **questions** *and* **ticking up the chores** *based on their yes or no answers. (10:37-10:45),*

17   *(11:35-11:46).*

In this extract, we have shown how video-tagged lesson observation (1) afforded a joint focus on the teacher's questioning practices, (2) facilitated reflection on the intended pedagogical goals and actual classroom practices and (3) established the beginning of a shared understanding on how certain type of questions may or may not facilitate student participation and engagement.

As part of the IMDAT teacher education framework in this study, the student teachers are encouraged to write critical reflections on their teaching practices. In her written critical self-reflection, T specifically referred to this episode and how she elicited short responses following her questions:

Although T had initially planned to increase student participation with what she calls open questions (i.e. questions that project elaborate answers), she mostly produced closed questions, which indicates a divergence between her pedagogical aims and classroom performance. T refers to particular moments in the warm-up phase and vocabulary presentation phase of her lesson on the VEO portal, including the sequence in extract 1. In this critical self-reflection, she writes that she 'realized some problematic points' including 'question types' (lines 1 and 2). In line 3, she argues that she first started with 'open-ended questions' but jumped to 'the closed questions' (line 5 and 6) as she did not receive many answers from the students. By referring to specific points in the video, she writes that receiving 'yes or no answers to [her] close ended questions didn't suit [her] aims' (lines 7 and 8). She then refers to the vocabulary

110 *Video Enhanced Observation for Language Teaching*

presentation phase of her lesson, writing that she 'had a problem with question types' (line 10). She finally goes on to reflecting on the episode in extract 1, which was talked into being in extract 2 during the post-observation feedback session: 'I found myself while asking close ended questions and ticking up the chores based on their yes or no answers' (lines 15 and 16).

Summary of Time 1

Based on our collection from the first lesson, the analysis of extract 1 has documented Belma's (T) questioning practices that include yes/no interrogatives and negative polarity questions, which received limited responses from the students. In the post-observation feedback session, the US and Belma viewed this particular episode that includes her questioning practices (extract 2), and talked Belma's intended pedagogical goals into being, which resulted in her further examination of her questioning practices (extract 3) as part of her critical self-reflection. Belma reported that she had some difficulties in using different varieties of questions that can elicit more elaborate student answers, which, according to her, led to a mismatch between her pedagogical aims and classroom practices.

Six weeks after the lesson captured in extract 1, in Time 2, Belma taught another lesson and held another post-observation feedback session, this time with a fellow student-teacher, a peer she had been collaborating with in the same school. The extracts will demonstrate how Belma produced diverse questioning practices to facilitate learner contributions, and how she and her peer reflected on this change over time, evidencing increased teacher language awareness and, we argue, the development of Classroom Interactional Competence.

Time 2 (May 2016)

Six weeks later, Belma conducted another lesson with the same students, while her peer recorded and tagged her teaching performance using VEO. In contrast to her questioning practices analysed in extract 1, extract 4 will illustrate how Belma promoted learner participation by extending students' utterances, using diverse questioning practices. Extract 4 is representative of Belma's (T) questioning practices in this lesson, while the lesson as a whole is also comparable as it is a revision lesson like the first one conducted in March 2016 (extract 1). The theme of the lesson is the differences between invention and discovery, and the extract comes from the first phase of the lesson, similar to the episode in extract 1.

The extract starts with T's information seeking question in lines 01–03, asking the students about their weekend, specifically referring to what they did after the *TEOG*[2] exam. This open question is followed by a hesitation marker and a vocalizer by S1. Receiving no response to her question, T, in line 5, repeats the first part of her question with the same interrogative format and smiley voice (*$eh: what did you do:?$*). In line 06, S2 translates (into Turkish) the teacher's question to her peers publicly, which is responded to by S1 as he corrects the translation by S2, adding a detail on the time with

VEO-integrated IMDAT

Extract 4: Classroom Interaction, lesson 2: after teog, 2_5_16_8[th]_00-39

```
01    T:      a::nd what did you do: at the weekend?
02    S1:     +[er::
03    T:      +[after teo:g+
      t       +------1-----+
              1: opens her hands to both sides
04    S1:     ehe
05    T:      $eh: what did you do:?$=
06    S2:     =teog nasıldı diyo
              "how was teog" she says
07    S1:     ↑teog'dan %sonra% na:ptınız diyo:
              "what did you after teog?" she says
      s1          %--1--%    1: shows his hand to s2
08    S3:     playing ga:mes
09    T:      which ga:mes?
10            (1.8)
11    S3:     [e::r
12    T:      [online ga:mes
13    S1:     (inaudible voices) provoca attack
14    T:      +ye:s+
      t       +-2--+    2: nods her head
15    S1:     digital (pirates)
16    T:      +ye:s+
      t       +-3--+    3: nods her head
17    S1:     (inaudible voices)
18    S4:     ↑my friends
19    S1:     my friends
20    Ss:     +[eheh heh
21    T:      +[did you come together+ o:r (0.4) +online games?
      t       +---------4-------------+    +------5------> line 26
22    S1:     ye:s
23    T:      onli:ne?
24    S1:     ye:s
25    T:      ↑what (0.3) the name of ↓the ga:me
26    S1:     (witch of the hateness)+
      t       ---------------------->+
27    S2:     (witch of the lo:ve)
28    Ss:     +eheh heh+
      t       +---6----+    6: smile
```

reference to the teacher's increment in line 03 (*'what did you after teog?' she said*). The open question asked by the teacher and (possibly) the peer support provided through translation and repair (see aus der Wieschen and Sert 2021 on how such translations can establish intersubjectivity) elicits a response from another student (S3 in line 08) as he provides a candidate answer (*playing ga:mes*). This response functions as the second-pair part of the question-answer adjacency pair. T then expands on this answer with an elaboration question in line 09 (*which ga:mes?*), waits for almost 2 seconds, and provides space for S1 to provide the names of two computer games in lines 13 and 15, minimally acknowledging these responses in line 16. S1 and S4 go on to contribute to the interaction with grammatically incomplete utterances in lines 18 and 19. T subsequently orients to these turns from the students by asking an alternative question in line 21, which is possibly not taken up by S1 (or other students) as S1 provides a confirming response twice, which violates type-conformity. Possibly avoiding insisting on a problem of intersubjectivity, T formulates another question in line 25, asking for the name of the game, receiving responses from two different students. The diversification of question types and facilitating student participation become two important points for reflection in the post-observation session held right after the lesson between Belma (T) and her peer (P) who observed the lesson.

112 *Video Enhanced Observation for Language Teaching*

Extract 5: Post-Observation Feedback Session 2, peer-feedback. Student responses

```
01   P:   öğrenci cevapları nasıldı:? (0.3) sana göre
          in your opinion, how were the students' responses?
02   T:   öğrenci cevapları: (0.8) ↑iyiydi: (.) mesela (0.3) e:r ben yine
          students' responses (0.8) were good (.) for example (0.3) e:r again
03        geçen dersteki gibi e::r hani haftasonunda na:ptınız falan diye
          like the previous lesson, i started the lesson by asking `what
04        başladım derse: (.) >işte< teogda na:ptıklarını (.) >işte< teog
          did you do during the weekend'(.) >well< I asked what they did
05        sonrası falan filan onları sordu:m (.) .hh yine cevap aldım
          during teog and after teog, etc. .hh i received a response again
06        geçen[(.)ki dersten]
          i received more responses
07   P:        [evet iyiydi: ]
                yeah it was good
08   T:                     daha çok [cevap aldım]
                            compared to the previous lesson
09   P:                              [ hıh hı::h ]
                                      huh hu:h
10   T:   .hh hani geçenkinde biraz sıkıntı çekmiştim hani sadece:
          well during the previous one i had some troubles i mean
11        b:- bi öğrenci falan cevap vermişti am↑a: .hh (0.3) bunda hani
          only one student gave a response but in this lesson well
12        biraz daha: (.) .hh katılımda bulunmaya çalıştıla:r (.) daha çok
          they tried to participate slightly more so i received more

13        cevap aldım ya:ni (0.6) öğrenci cevabı olarak (0.3) işte
          responses (0.6) student response(s) (0.3) well
14        reading comprehension sorularında biraz sıkıntı çektik
          we had some difficulties in reading comprehension questions
15        (0.4) ondan sonra [hani]
          (0.4) after that [well]
16   P:                     [orda] okumadıkları için
                            because they had not read (there)
17   T:   evet muhtemelen
          yes possibly
18   P:   eve:t
          yes
19        (0.4)
20   T:   ondan oldu sonra listening'te yine e:r işte onlara
          it was because of that, in the listening again e:r
21        iki kez dinlettim yap- yapabildiler, yapamadılar
          i made them listen to it twice again, they could- couldn't do
22        sonra arkadaşları cevaplayınca: .hh buldular fala:n (0.8) öyle yani:
          then they found it after their friends provided responses
23        (0.3) öğrenci cevaplarından da memnundum (0.3) katıldılar
          (0.3) so i was also pleased with student answers (0.3) they participated
24   P:   °evet°
          yes
```

VEO-integrated IMDAT 113

In the post-observation feedback session, after the peers watch the relevant episode together, P in line 01 asks Belma's (T's) opinion about the students' responses. In line 02, T starts her turn with a positive assessment (were good, tr: iyiydi). In lines 06 and 08, she states that she elicited more student responses compared to the first lesson, comparing her performance in two different lessons. Meanwhile, in line 07, P displays alignment and first produces a confirmation followed by a second-assessment (**yeah it was good**), mirroring the same adjective (good) that T used. T then engages is an extended turn between lines 10 and 15, and first refers to the trouble in the first lesson in line 10, followed by her claim about the increase in the number of students and answers in the second lesson. Following an elaboration on the reading activity, the sequence ends by T's self-assessment of the student responses as well as participation of the learners in line 23 (**so i was also pleased with student answers (0.3) they participated**), which is joined by P in line 24. The analysis of extract 5 clearly shows that it is not only the types of questions that change from lesson 1 to 2, but also the self-assessment of T and the peer-assessment in the post-observation feedback sessions, which was facilitated by the use of VEO in observation, feedback and reflection. Towards the end of the semester, after a week following the post-observation feedback session represented in extract 5, T writes another critical self-reflection on various aspects of her teaching performance.

T writes in her reflection that she was more relaxed and confident in the second lesson (line 1). She refers to the episode in extract 4, and states that, compared to the limited answers she received in the first lesson, this time she received more answers to her questions with a reference to a particular moment from extract 4 (line 4). Although she first seems to justify this by the examples she provided, she also refers to the question types at the end of extract 6, claiming that her closed type questions (see extracts 1 and 2) had not served the purpose of getting the students to speak (lines 9 and 10). She therefore builds a link between question types and speaking/participation opportunities provided to students.

Extract 6: Written Critical Self-Reflection 2. Speaking

01   *From the beginning of the lesson I was more relaxed and confident than my previous*

02   *lesson. At the end of the lesson, I left the class happily.Like my previous lesson I initiated*

03   *the lesson with speaking about their weekends. In my first lesson, I had nearly just one*

04   *answer, but in the 2ⁿᵈ lesson the numbers of the answers increased. (00:45-01:09),*

05   *(01:55-02:34), (02:35-02:54). In this lesson they weren't ashamed to speak and give*

06   *answers. My warm and cheerful attitude might have decreased their anxiety level. When*

07   *I watched my lesson I realized that my examples gave them idea and they found*

08   *something to share. For example, I gave an example as watching television then a*

09   *student said "Yeah!" and shared his idea. (01:50-02:34). **In previous lessons, my closed***

10   ***type questions didn't serve the purpose**, but in this lesson my examples were enough*

11   *to **make them speak**.*

Summary of Time 2

In sum, in Time 2, Belma (T) elicited more student responses by diversifying her questions and extending students' utterances during her second teaching performance. In the post-observation feedback session, she then talks this into being together with her peer. They jointly co-construct positive assessment of T's performance with regards to increased student participation enabled through teacher questioning practices in classroom interaction (extract 5). Finally, in her critical self-reflection in extract 6, she compares the closed type questions requiring short answers in her first teaching performance to her performance in the second lesson. Therefore, the findings coming from six different discourse events over time reveal that T diversified her questioning practices to facilitate more learner contributions, and developed her awareness about her classroom practices and student participation by getting engaged with the VEO-integrated IMDAT framework.

Discussion and Conclusions

In this chapter, we have shown that the focal student teacher, Belma, diversified her questioning practices to facilitate learner contributions, and developed awareness of her interactional and pedagogical practices afforded by the VEO-integrated IMDAT framework. In the analysis of the first phase of IMDAT, extract 1 has demonstrated that Belma initiated more yes/no interrogatives and reversed polarity questions (RPQs), which elicited limited answers from the students. Such questioning practices required either 'yes' or 'no' in initial position as type-conforming responses (Raymond 2003, 2013). These findings are also in line with Kärkkäinen and Thompson (2018)'s results, in that their findings also displayed that such polar questions in positive or negative format projected simple type-conforming responses (yes, no or equivalent tokens). As we have shown in extracts 2 and 3, the ST oriented to these questioning practices as problematic, and the post-observation feedback session and the critical reflective writing process embedded in IMDAT made discursive co-construction of this reflection possible. In the next round of teaching, exemplified by extract 4, we have shown that ST received more student responses in response to her questioning practices that involve open questions that elicited more than a 'yes' or a 'no' (Waring 2013), in line with findings of researchers like Willemsen et al. (2018). Such questioning practices played a significant role in expanding student contributions in the classroom interaction, and therefore one can argue that such changes in teacher questioning practices may indicate the development of classroom interactional competence. This development over time has been afforded by VEO-integrated IMDAT, which shows that data-led and evidence-based reflective practices as well as dialogic feedback create opportunities for noticing troubles and taking initiative for their resolutions. The developmental aspect of this research through the use of multiple data sources, as well as using participants' emic perspectives, has proven to be fruitful in generating important research findings.

Case studies are powerful ways to document teacher development in great depth, and they have also been very useful in showing the affordances of different technological tools, including VEO, in researching teacher development. Çelik et al. (2018), for instance, focused on peer-observation and feedback practices and recommended the use of mobile and video-based observation tools for teacher development. In this chapter, we have also shown the added value of peer-feedback (also see Sert and Aşık 2020 for a quantitative study of peer-feedback practices) and peer-observation practices. We argue that a teacher education model like IMDAT which first starts with expert (mentor/supervisor)-novice feedback sessions and gradually moves into peer-feedback practices, especially when evidence of teaching performance is made visual with VEO or a similar tool, can have many benefits. In our research, STs have developed their teacher language awareness and classroom interactional competence, and in the case of Belma, their teacher questioning practices. However, they also engaged in receiving and giving feedback based on visual evidence and in a dialogic format, which has an added value to their development.

It should be noted that this was one way of integrating VEO into teacher education. If the aim is sustainable development for teachers, we then need to make sure that projects like this one are taken up and maintained by practitioners for years to come. In some countries, university supervisors play a more major role in examining candidates (e.g. in Turkey) than mentors in schools (Sweden, for instance, is an example where school-based mentorship is primary). The use of mobile tools then needs to be organically tied into context-specific teacher education curricula to create sustainable change, rather than being used only in temporary try-outs. For instance, VEO is now being piloted in a project called Digi-REFLECT in Sweden (Sert et al. 2020). In this case, rather than employing a framework like IMDAT, the digitalized reflection and feedback processes are being integrated into the learning objectives of the local teacher education curriculum, resulting in a unique tag set. Each context is specific, as this book successfully shows, and digitalization in teacher education requires a context sensitive approach that considers the curriculum at the same time as the needs of the teachers and learners. Being context-specific also requires an increased interest in local classroom interactional practices in situ, and this is why a conversation analysis-integrated teacher education curriculum (e.g. see a proposal by Sert 2010) can be beneficial for teacher candidates to develop an analytic eye for understanding and managing classroom interaction. As the review of literature in Section 2 has shown, classroom interaction practices should be at the heart of teacher development, and thus learning from relevant micro-analytic teacher development research (Seedhouse 2008; Walsh 2011, 2013; Sert 2019, 2021; Waring 2021) may prepare us better for the digital future. Classrooms are taking different forms, but social interaction in these physical and digital settings will always be central to (language) learning and teacher development.

Acknowledgements

The use of VEO in this chapter was possible thanks to the VEO Europa Project (PI, Paul Seedhouse). The extracts used in the analysis come from the MA thesis of the first author (Bozbıyık 2017), co-supervised by the second and the third authors. We would like to thank the student teachers who participated in this study.

Appendix

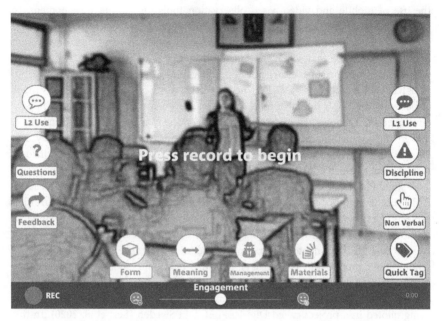

Appendix I: The tag set that focuses on the teacher: 'L2 Teacher – Hacettepe University'.

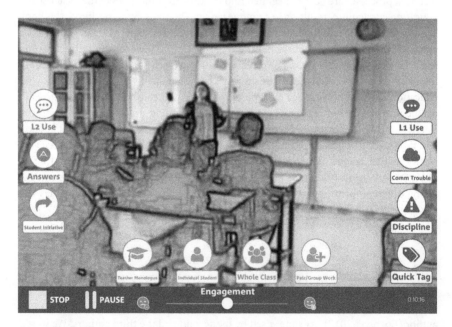

Appendix II: The tag set that focuses on the learners: 'L2 Learner – Hacettepe University'.

8

Integrating the Video Enhanced Observation (VEO) App in Peer Observation Feedback Interaction

Jaume Batlle Rodríguez
University of Barcelona, Spain
Paul Seedhouse
Newcastle University, UK

Introduction

Observation of teaching has been widely used in many different countries and contexts in many ways and for very diverse reasons. From evaluative purposes to Continuing Professional Development (CPD), observation has become a powerful tool because, among other reasons, it enables reflective practice about what is going on in the classroom (Mann and Walsh 2017). That is why observation has aroused such interest: it becomes a relevant tool to understand the learning-teaching process, as well as how teachers can develop professionally. The aim of the observation determines, to a certain extent, the way it is carried out, and this applies especially to the post-lesson feedback given by the observer. For example, a one-way evaluative observation (such as the one commonly used in the UK OFSTED inspections) does not imply a priori any two-way discussion about what was going on. Rather, the evaluator/observer delivers evaluation and advice to the teacher (O'Leary 2014: 19–26), in a performance in which 'the observer is commonly perceived as possessing greater power' and 'is legitimized by organisational arrangements' (Cockburn 2005: 384). For that reason, observation practices are seen by many teachers as an inspection or one-way evaluation (O'Leary 2014: 69) and they are reluctant to allow anyone into their classroom to observe them (Richards 2005: 85). However, there is an increasing demand for a different type of observation, that is, one whose focus is on CPD (O'Leary 2014, 2017) and which involves teachers' perspectives in the process.

Peer observation has been recognized as an effective tool for teachers' CPD (McMahon, Barrett and O'Neill 2007; O'Leary and Price 2017) due to its collaborative nature, and because it is based on mutual comprehension, a more equal relationship and two-way interaction. With peer observation, participants are not obliged to provide an assessment of the teachers' performance and it can be carried out to generate critical reflections about teaching experiences, professional development and teaching practices (Bell 2001). Reflective practice is designed to deliver these, and to help teachers grasp the complexities of teaching processes, which are made up of 'different elements (e.g. students, teachers, resources, environment, etc.) that are largely defined by their iterative connections' (O'Leary 2017: 5). Reflective practice is mainly carried out in post-observation feedback, which is the focus of this chapter.

Reflective practice (Schön 1983; Kolb 1984; Schön 1987; Mann and Walsh 2017) has the objective of enhancing teachers' abilities and practices through sharing methods, techniques and ideas. Teachers, through reflective practice, analyse and discuss their own teaching experiences to learn from them. Reflective practice involves a complex understanding of teacher's performance, taking into account their attitudes, representations and beliefs about what does it mean to be a teacher (O'Leary 2014: 113). Traditionally, CPD development through reflective practice has been researched through self-report, using written texts (portfolios) or semi-structured interviews. However, Mann and Walsh (2017; see also Mann and Walsh 2013; Walsh and Mann 2015) promote data-led and evidence-based reflection with the aim of producing a more concrete and empirical description of reflective practice. This is intended to provide teachers and teacher trainers with a more complete description of how reflective practice is carried out.

We follow this approach in this chapter by analysing the interaction between observer and observee in post-lesson feedback. This study aims (a) to understand how a technological innovation (the VEO app) becomes integrated into peer observation feedback interaction, (b) how it is used by the participants, (c) what value (if any) is added by this innovation. In consequence, this study seeks to reveal how VEO-related artefacts are employed when participants are carrying out post-observation feedback interaction. In this way we will show how the VEO app becomes integrated into the process of feedback interaction and determine whether this adds any value to the process.

Using a multimodal conversation analysis approach, this study is focused on the analysis of how, why and when VEO-related artefacts such as tablets and computers come into play during the feedback sequences. By 'VEO-related artefact', we mean any digital device which is used to capture and/or display videos of a lesson or other screens related to the VEO app. The reason we refer to these as 'artefacts' in this chapter is that this is the term widely used in multimodal CA to refer to objects which are handled or oriented to in some way by interactants. The argument will be that the VEO app becomes central to the process of peer observation feedback interaction as (a) it provides video data, lesson and observation notes as a basis for the interaction and (b) the VEO-related artefacts become centrally implicated as a focus of the interaction. Multimodal CA analysis is necessary to portray exactly how this happens. We therefore refer to VEO in two different (but related) ways in this chapter. As in the other chapters, VEO is an app which is being used for teacher development. Additionally, in this chapter only, a 'VEO-related artefact' will be described as the focus of interactional attention in detailed multimodal analyses of interaction.

Background

Peer observation is mainly intended to promote CPD through reflective practice (Gosling 2002; Hammersley-Fletcher and Orsmond 2005; O'Leary 2014; Sachs and Parsell 2014; Mann and Walsh 2017; O'Leary and Price 2017, among others). Defined as 'peers observing each other's teaching to enhance teaching quality through reflective practice, thereby aiding professional development' (Shortland 2004: 220), this activity implies a formative purpose. Both the observer and the observee, but mainly the first one, come to some decisions about what the observation should focus on and how it should proceed. In this way, the teacher being observed becomes responsible for their own CPD. Once these decisions have been taken, the observer watches and monitors the lesson in relation to the agreed focus of observation (Richards 2005: 85). However, it is by nature a collaborative activity and both the observer and the observee contribute to the discussion in a post-observation feedback session (Gosling 2002). Peer observation, therefore, aims to promote reflective discussion between an observee and an observer, in a post-observation feedback session.

Interaction in the post-observation feedback session (feedback interaction) is therefore a key source of data for analysis if we wish to understand how CPD develops through peer observation. It can be understood as a constructive dialogue (Kohut, Burnap and Yon 2007), as the focus of discussion is, generally speaking, on the strengths and weaknesses of the observee's performance and how to improve his/her teaching actions. The observer specifies what he or she thinks and feels about the observee's performance, with a view to improving it. Therefore, the observer leads the feedback discussion for the benefit of the observee's professional development. However, although the effectiveness of feedback interaction for CPD has been specified (Shortland 2010), few studies have studied the precise nature of feedback interaction to understand the developmental processes involved. Most studies have focused on the characteristics of post-observation feedback, but for another kind of observation, namely tutor-tutee or trainer-trainee. Regarding the latter, for example, Copland (2010) specifies how the feedback session can be disappointing for trainees if they do not align with the trainer's position and do not accept the assumed asymmetry between participants. Dobrowolska and Balslev (2017) reveal the discursive strategies developed by the observer during mentoring observation feedback, while Farr (2003) quantifies how minimal response tokens, overlaps and interruptions are carried out by speakers in a trainer-trainee post-observation feedback interaction. On the other hand, following a socio-cultural perspective, Engin (2015) focused on how trainers scaffold trainees' participation, while Lange and Wittek (2018) analyse how exploratory talk is developed from the pre-observation meeting to the post-observation feedback interaction, finding that reflective practice is sometimes developed with some kind of trouble to become an effective tool for CPD. However, these studies do not involve microanalysis of the interactional processes involved in peer observation feedback interaction.

There have been some studies of feedback interaction. Strong and Baron (2004) focus their attention on the suggestions trainers gave to trainees, while Phillips (1999) approaches the Second Language Teachers Training context, studying the relationship between in-service teachers and participants in pre-service teacher training as institutional interactions. Phillips found that the asymmetrical relationship is significant for the development of the interaction, due to the observer taking the role of an expert by managing and developing the agenda, asking questions to the observee and giving feedback actions. Farr's (2011) study of teaching practice feedback uses a corpus linguistics as an approach to the study of feedback interaction. In her work, Farr characterizes the discourse of teaching practice feedback according to the specific actions to be developed (reflection, direction, evaluation, and relational and cathartic talk), but as a frame to analyse the corpus linguistics data.

The studies reviewed above analysed feedback interaction in which observation sheets or diaries were used to manage the feedback. However, VEO, as an ICT tool for classroom observation and reflective practice (Körkkö, Morales and Kyrö-Ämmälä 2019; Körkkö, Kyrö-Ämmälä and Turunen, Chapter 6), is considered in this chapter as an artefact that changes the way feedback interaction is carried out to a great extent. It has been shown that mobile digital technology can mediate and direct interaction between participants in a physical world (Thorne et al. 2015). In this way, our aim is to uncover participants' sense making when they use mobile technologies in talk-in-interaction (Thorne et al. 2015: 260). As objects or artefacts, mobile devices can be understood as resources for the organization of social interaction. Objects are not considered as external to the interaction, but rather as meaningful resources if and when the participants orient to them during their action construction (Streeck 1996; Nevile et al. 2014a). Materiality, as Mondada (2019: 4) states, is instrumental 'to the meaningful accomplishment of action' as well as the target of sensorial access. Artefacts, as interactional accomplishments, can be used by participants to manage topical talk and transition between speakers, elicit talk, secure interactional progressivity and perform particular actions such as explanations (Nielsen 2012, Mikkola and Lehtinen 2014). Interactants, as Jakonen (2015: 101) argues, 'do indeed mobilize different kinds of objects within the material environment to construct action'. Artefacts can be at the centre of the collective attention (Mondada 2007: 198) if interactants are talking about something related to the specific object. In the case of VEO, interactants may also be watching and listening to videos produced by the devices and reading notes made on them.

In activities created for learning or constructing knowledge, artefacts may be intimately related with the social actions carried out to manage and develop this knowledge. Therefore, it is expected that, in peer observation feedback, tablets and computers using the VEO app could be significant artefacts for action construction. VEO is designed not only to be able to play back videos of the lesson, but to show tags inserted by the observer at precise points in the video. It may well be that tablets and computers can be understood as situated resources (Nevile et al. 2014b), because they will be involved and enabled in the interactional processes that the participants will be carrying out. In CA, however, we must look for evidence of what the participants are actually orienting to, rather than making prior assumptions, so we will be analysing the data in section below.

There are very few studies of what actually happens during peer observation feedback interaction. This study is original in showing in detail how a technological innovation is integrated into both the interactional and the peer feedback processes.

Method

Our data set consists of a total of eight hours and nineteen minutes in fifteen video-recorded peer observation feedback interactions in Spanish carried out by eight Spanish as a Foreign Language experienced teachers (two male and six female) grouped in four pairs. This took place between February and March 2017 as part of an internal training program in a private Spanish as a Foreign Language School located in Barcelona (Spain). This CPD programme had already been running for four years prior to the introduction of VEO. Peer observation activity proceeded as follows: First of all, the participants established a pre-observation meeting to discuss what they were going to observe and divided up in pairs. In this specific case, as it was the first time VEO was used for peer observation and internal training, it was decided to focus on general teaching, instead of focusing on some specific aspect of teachers' performance; a specific focus might have caused more difficulties in carrying out the task and managing VEO and its tag set. Moreover, it was decided that each teacher should observe his/her peer two times. After each performance, the observers shared the recording and the notes made using the VEO app so the observee could take these into account during the feedback interaction. Moreover, it should be noted that all the staff could watch and write comments on all of the videos. However, they only did so after the pair feedback session had taken place, so any comments written by the rest of the teachers did not have any effect on the post-observation feedback. Each pair carried out the post-observation feedback, discussing with the help of VEO any points they wished to make, so the post-observation feedback was always carried out whilst using a computer or a tablet. In some cases, after the first post-observation feedback, teachers agreed that they would focus the second observation practice on a specific aspect of teacher's performance. Finally, once all peers had carried out their whole observation practices, all the teachers met up in a final meeting to assess the activity and reflect about how to proceed in the next internal training cycle.

We analyse the recorded data using a multimodal CA approach (Mortensen 2012; Mondada 2018). This approach hinges on how participants in social interaction produce meaning through the analysis of all the semiotic resources at their disposal. From this perspective, researchers assume an emic perspective on the basis of analysis is carried out. Multimodal analysis is necessary because we aim to analyse how, why and when VEO-related artefacts such as tablets and computers come into play during the feedback sequences and become integrated into the activity. Transcripts are presented together with photographs of the interaction to show features such as gaze and movement. Because if this, the relationship between participants, body movement and artefacts can be observed and analysed.

Results

Activity Shift

As stated above, peer observation feedback interaction is an institutional variety of interaction generally characterized by an asymmetrical relationship between an observer and an observee. Commonly, the observer leads the sequence, providing his/her thoughts about the lesson, to which the observee generally provides a response. In our study, an innovation has been introduced for the first time to a peer observation system which had already been running for four years. VEO is a system that permits (a) video recording of the lessons, (b) the observer to add notes to be shared by the participants in the peer observation activity and (c) recording of the results of the peer interaction by means of further notes and/or recording. In the results below, we show how exactly the VEO-related artefacts become central tools for the development of the feedback interaction. Participants create new multimodal speech exchange systems and feedback interaction procedures as an adaptation to the new artefact.

As we can see in extract 1, the VEO-related artefact (tablet) becomes integrated into the sequential development of the feedback interaction. Fra (the observee) and Alb (the observer) are developing the feedback interaction around their usage of the VEO-related artefact. They are talking about the acquisition of habits and routines by the students and how this impacts on classroom management. When Alb (the observer) is developing this topic, the participants are looking at each other, not the VEO-related artefact (lines 1–5, Figure 8.1). However, in line 5 Alb initiates a turn expansion to explain the reasons to support her feedback argument. Typically, this is closing-implicative, since in the data observers tend to provide justifications at the end of their feedback delivery. Fra leans forward and, at the same time, shifts his gaze to the VEO-related artefact and Alb follows Fra by changing his gaze to the artefact (line 5, Figure 8.2). Their body movements establish the artefact as the central focus of the scene. Gazing to the tablet is used as a sign for topic shift (Goodwin and Goodwin 1987; Rossano 2010). As soon as their attention is focused on the VEO-related artefact, the observer is in a position to change the topic of discussion (line 6). After a brief pause, the observer introduces the new topic of 'positive things' that she has noticed about the observee's performance (line 6).

Extract 1: JBR_EF_F&A_1:1,6:36

```
01   Alb: +no eso es cierto* +o sea cuando u:n- un grupo se acostumbra
          no that's true I mean when a- a group is already used
          +looks at the tablet
                    -> +looks up———————————->
        Fra: >>looks at Alb—>
02        ya: a un profesor +y a los *hábitos y a las rutinas
          to a teacher and to the habits and to the routines
                              ->+ looks at Fra
03        pues (.) evidentemente
          so evidently
04   Fra: [luego (va más fluido)
          then it goes more smoothly
05   Alb: [es mucho más #fácil porque lue*+go% ya #(.) se entra con
          it is much easier because then you just slip into
```

```
Fra:                          *leans fwd
Fra:                          +looks at the tablet
Alb:                                    ->%looks at the tablet->
```

Figure 8.1 Alb looking at Fra.   **Figure 8.2** Alb looking at the tablet.

```
06      esas dinámi*ca#s (.) luego cosas que me parecieron muy positivas
        this dynamic. Further on things that struck me as very positive
        Alb.           *touches and scrolls down the tablet
```

Figure 8.3 Alb touching and scrolling down the tablet.

```
07      por ejemplo es eh la::: (.) ay ahora no sé dón#de lo marqué
        for example is eh the ah now I don't know where I tagged it
```

Figure 8.4 Alb touching and scrolling down the tablet.

```
08  Fra:   *no importa *
           never mind
09  Alb    pero era: >bueno< (1.0) cuando- en el momento +en el que
           but it was, well, when at the moment in which
    Alb.                                          ->+ .... …..
```

```
10      utili#za+bais (.)* en el que utilizaron la lengua materna
        you used in which they used the mother language
Alb:.   ............+looks at Fra->>
Fra:                *looks at Alb->>
```

Figure 8.5 Alb looking at Fra.

As we see in extract 1, the VEO-related artefact is central for the development of the interaction. In many cases in our data, topic shift involves a change in bodily movements in relation to the VEO-related artefact, which becomes a significant object in relation to sequential development. Shifting gaze to the artefact implies that topic is about to shift (Goodwin and Goodwin 1987; Rossano 2010). In a similar way, intonation, topic shift markers and idioms may also be used to indicate that topic shift is imminent (García García 2016).

Moreover, we can see that the VEO-related artefact was used as a resource to develop the topic of discussion in lines 6–10. The observer uses VEO-related information on the VEO-related artefact to manage the feedback process (Hazel 2014). Topics and arguments are developed in line with how information is presented on the VEO app. When Alb tries to keep talking about positive aspects of the performance, she looks at the VEO information, touching and scrolling down the screen (line 6) with the aim of finding more interesting information to comment on. She continues looking for positive aspects of the performance and trying to find some specific information (line 7). Once the observer has chosen (line 9) a new topic to develop (related with the use of the students' L1 to compare grammar structures between languages (data not shown)), the participants stop looking at the VEO-related artefact while they develop the topic of discussion (line 10).

Topic change in peer feedback interaction is managed in our data by integrating the artefact in the social actions carried out for that purpose. However, topic change is not always carried out successfully. In some cases, joint attention is not maintained by participants. In the next extract, Jul (the observer) is discussing how the students read the lesson aims. Unlike the former example, feedback interaction is developed through the use of the computer as a VEO-related artefact, rather than a tablet. It is therefore necessary to take into account some differences in the spatial configuration: the VEO-related artefact in extract 1 was next to the observer, whereas in extract 2, the computer is between the two speakers. However, the mouse is controlled by the observer, who is the person who manages the VEO-related information on the computer and who leads the feedback. Moreover, in extract 2, we see the participants looking at the screen while they are developing a specific topic, namely how the teacher instructs the students to read the lesson aims.

Extract 2: JBR_EF_R&J_2:1,4:14

```
01  Jul:  #em: me gustó mu+#cho que por ejemplo: +les hicieras le*e:r los
             em I liked a lot that for example you made them read the
    Jul.  >>looks at the screen->
                        +points out the screen
                                             +points out the screen
    Rog.  >>looks at the screen->
```

Figure 8.6 Jul and Rog looking at the screen.   **Figure 8.7** Jul and Rog looking at the screen, and Jul pointing the screen.

```
02  objetivos >o sea me parece una buena forma de explicarles< que
    aims I mean it seems to me a good way to explain them that
03  todos tienen que estar atentos y* todos quieras o no# (.)
    everyone has to be attentive and everyone, whether you want it
    Rog.                              ->*looks at Jul->
```

Figure 8.8 Rog looking at Jul.

```
04  registran *lo# que van a hacer en la clase* (1.5)*# (1.0)
    or not, notice what they are going to do in class
    Rog.   ->*looks at the screen->
    Jul.                                          *looks at the
      screen
```

Figure 8.9 Rog looking at the screen.   **Figure 8.10** Jul looking at the screen.

```
05      [o sea]: a- me lo apunté para m+í ta#mb+ién*
        I mean a- I noted down for myself too
Jul.                            + … ….+picks up the mouse->>
Rog.                                      ->*looks at the
  screen->
```

Figure 8.11 Rog looking at Jul; Jul looking at the screen and putting her hand on the mouse.

```
06  Rog:   [*mhm]
           ->*looks at Jul->
07         (1.5)
08  Rog:   sí: (1.0) +*sí °eso #es° (1.0) es verdad que: en todas las clases
           yes:   yes indeed it's true that in all the classes
    Rog:          *nods
    Jul:   +looks at Rog->>
```

Figure 8.12 Jul looking at Rog; Rog looking at the screen.

```
09      creo que es hhh. complicado ponerlo pero si podemos
        I think that it is complicated to write it down but if we can
```

While Jul is assessing the observee's performance, she points (Mondada 2007) at the screen (line 1, Figure 8.7). Jul is basing her assessment on a note she wrote earlier on the VEO-related artefact, which is read by them both on the screen. Rog is looking at the screen (line 1, Figure 8.7), although sometimes he switches gaze to the observer (line 3, Figure 8.8), whereas Jul looks at the screen while pointing (line 1, Figure 8.7), but quickly changes gaze to the observee (line 4, Figure 8.9). Once her assessment has been delivered (line 4), Jul starts looking again at the screen (line 4, Figure 8.10), just before adding a closing post-expansion of her arguments (line 5). As a closing, she specifies that she has noted this activity to implement it in her own lessons. At that moment, Jul picks up the mouse as a sign to start on the next note and therefore to shift topic to comment on another specific performance item. Rog directs his gaze to Jul (line 5, Figure 8.11), but immediately shifts his gaze to the screen (line 8, Figure 8.12) and adds new information, thus extending the former assessment talk. With this action, Rog is developing the former assessment topic further. As Rog is taking the floor and continuing to develop the topic, Jul lets go of the mouse and focuses her gaze on Rog (line 8, Figure 8.12), postponing her topic shift. In this case, releasing the mouse is related to postponing the topic shift.

In extract 2, we have shown that the relationship between social actions and VEO-related artefacts in peer observation feedback interaction depends on joint attention and joint accomplishment. When the observer, who manages the feedback interaction, wants to proceed to the next topic, he or she takes a pre-figuring action, namely shifting gaze to the computer screen and taking hold of the mouse. Bodily movements made by the observer in relation to the computer or VEO-related artefact anticipate and prepare for the coming verbal topic change. However, we see in Figure 8.11 that Rog does not follow Jul in looking at the computer screen, but rather shifts gaze to Jul and takes a turn to develop the previous topic further. In peer feedback sequences, although the observer has the overall lead, the observee has the right to respond. In some cases in the data (not shown), the observer paused and asked if the observee wished to respond before moving to the next point. Although that does not happen in this extract, we can see that this is a transition relevance point as Rog is able to take a turn without any interactional perturbation occurring. Therefore, joint attention to the artefact is a pre-condition to the observer changing topic for feedback development. If this does not happen, attention to the artefact has to be declined and the observer has to focus his/her attention to the recipient.

The preceding analyses have shown how the VEO-related artefact (the tablet or the computer) is inextricably entwined with the social actions that are carried out by the participants. We have seen that participants focus their attention on the artefact when they change the topic. Joint attention to the artefact is a pre-condition for topic change. The observer leads the management of the artefact, as the notes and videos about the lesson are available through the artefact and it is by reference to the notes and videos that he or she delivers the feedback. The observer has the duty to manage the information and, in consequence, change topic, due to the asymmetrical relationship between participants. If joint attention to the artefact is not accomplished, topic is not changed, even if the observer has carried out an action involving the object to signal impending topic shift.

Signalling the Artefact

As has been stated, the VEO-related artefacts (computers and tablets) are meaningfully integrated with social actions and activity shift. Participants commonly look at the screen while assessing performance. The screen plays a central role in the development of feedback interaction: it provides information in the form of the notes written by the observer and also the videos recorded of the lessons. Participants have the possibility to orient to this information when delivering their comments and assessments, and often a pointing gesture (Mondada 2007) is used to signal the artefact, which focuses attention on the screen and the information provided there. When this happens, the artefact becomes consequential for interactional development.

Notes

Notes are one resource commonly used to develop peer observation feedback interaction. Typically, the observer takes brief notes during the lesson (generally on paper), which are subsequently used to analyse and evaluate what was seen in the classroom during the feedback session. In our data, notes were written using VEO on a tablet or computer. In extract 3, we see how the feedback discussion is based on the information in the notes the observer has written on the VEO-related artefact. At the beginning of one feedback interaction between Alb (the observer) and Fra (as observee), the participants are negotiating the way they will organize the feedback. Alb proposes following the notes added to VEO (lines 1–3), which is accepted by Fra in an overlapping turn (line 2). Then, once the procedure for organizing the feedback has been agreed, Alb explains that she didn't add notes for all the aspects which she tagged (lines 4–5).

Extract 3: JBR_EF_F&A_1:1,0:23

```
1   Alb:   ok empezamos a comentar *o ºbueno (.) quiere-º (0.3)*
                 ok we start to comment or well do you wan-
    Alb:   >>looks the tablet      *looks at Fra.      *looks at
                 tablet
    Fra:   >>looks the tablet->>
2   Fra:   tú misma
                 it's up to you
3   Alb:   co%mentamos ya direct#amente *aqu#í: el:+: *sí? vale (.) entonces
                 we comment directly here the:: Yes? ok then
                 %points to the tablet and scrolls down
                                            *looks at Fra
                                                 *looks at the tablet
```

Figure 8.13 Alb and Fra looking at the tablet.   **Figure 8.14** Alb looking at Fra.

```
4      e:h tam%poco he ido- no he puesto notas e#n tod&as todas las
       either I haven't gone I haven't made notes in all the
Alb:      %touches the tablet and scrolls down->
```

Figure 8.15 Alb touching the tablet and scrolling down.

```
5         etiquetas solo en algunas
              tags only in some of them
6    Fra:    mh[m
7    Alb:    [vale?% al principio bueno- (.) comenté esto de otros que
              ok? at the beginning well I commented that of another that
              ->%
8         era lo de pasar +lista# %vale? que lo hizo u#na
              it was that thing about roll call right? That it was made by an
Alb:                      +looks at Fra
Alb:                           %looks at the tablet->>
```

Figure 8.16 Alb looking at Fra.   **Figure 8.17** Fra and Alb looking at the tablet.

```
9    estudiante y ya he comentado bueno
     student and already I have commented, well
```

As we can see in extract 3, the VEO-related artefact is a focal point in the interaction. Although the artefact is close to Alb and she is in charge of its use, both participants turn their gaze to the artefact (line 3, Figure 8.13). Alb uses the notes to explain what she considers positive or negative performance (line 4). At that moment, the artefact and its information are the focus of gaze and posture (Figure 8.15). Not only the participants look at the screen, but the observer points to it to specify that this particular note is relevant for her assessment. Pointing selects the specific information to be used as evidence in the interaction.

Video

VEO also displays video data of the lesson that can come into play during the assessment.

Extract 4: JBR_EF_R&J_2:1,9:50

1 Jul: **con otro tipo de grupo seguramente [que sí que hubiera surgido**
    with another type of group certainly yes it had taken
  Rog: >>looks at the screen->
  Jul: >>looks at the screen->
2 Rog: [°no no sí:°
                                              no no yes
3 Jul: **efecto sabes? pero con ellos (1.5) +y luego por ejemplo+ #aquí**
    effect you know? But with them and then for example here
  Jul: +…. …. …. … ….+signs

Figure 8.18 Jul signing the screen.

4 **que:: les estabas pidiendo no? que marcaran dónde# estaban las**
    that you were asking them weren't you? to mark where were
  the screen->

Figure 8.19 Jul signing the screen.

5   **estructuras para pedir consejo (.) o dónde estaba #el consejo en**
    the structures to seek advice or where was the advice in

Figure 8.20 Jul and Rog looking at the screen.

6   **sí (1.0) al principio les hiciste hacerlo a ellos**
    yes at the beginning you pushed to them to do it
7   [***pero luego lo& hacías tú::**
    but then you did it
   Jul: *looks at Rog
   Jul: &stops pointing at the screen
8 Rog: [***sí y luego lo marco yo*: +pero es lo q- %°sí sí:°**
          yes and then I did it but that's wh- yes yes
   Rog: *looks fwd   *looks at Jul
   Rog: +looks at the screen–>>
   Jul: %looks at the screen–>>
9 Jul: % (0.8)%**pero también es verdad q#ue con este tipo de grupos**
          but also it is true that with this type of group
   Jul: % ….. %puts hand on the mouse–>>

Figure 8.21 Jul putting her hand on the mouse.

In extract 4, Jul and Rog are talking about the characteristics of Rog's groups and his difficulties in managing his performance with these students. Jul (as observer) suggests that, although the activities proposed by Rog could have worked with another group (line 1), with this group they were not suitable due to their behaviour (data not shown). To support this claim, Jul gives the example of one activity where the students had to identify grammatical structures for the function of seeking advice (line 5). At first, the students started doing the activity, but, suddenly, they stopped doing the task (lines 6–7). She argues that the students didn't follow the instructions and Rog therefore had

132   *Video Enhanced Observation for Language Teaching*

to indicate where the advice was (line 7). Rog agrees with this appraisal (line 8) before Jul puts her hand on the mouse again and starts justifying the negative assessment (line 9). These two actions work together to close down the topic.

In extract 4, the assessment concentrates on the students' behaviour in carrying out an activity and the screen is showing the video of the lesson. Just after Jul starts to talk about the students in lines 3–6, she points to the screen. Specifically, she points at the spot on the screen where the students can be seen (line 4, Figure 8.18). She then points at the specific part of the screen where Rog and the board are located (lines 4–5, Figures 19–20). Finally, pointing comes to an end once she finishes the comment about what was going on (line 7). Rog then stops looking at the screen and focuses on what his recipient starts to say in line 8. Through pointing at the screen, the information provided on the VEO-related artefact is made relevant to the feedback process. The participants point at the screen to make relevant specific items of information that can be found there. Generally, it is the observer who does so due to his or her institutional role.

Written notes and video data play different roles in the feedback development cycle. Written notes are oriented to as text on the VEO-related artefact, are read by both participants and commented on by both. Video images, however, are pointed to as evidence to support an argument. The pointing specifies which part of the screen is providing the relevant evidence. Because written notes are already available to the observer to read silently, it is not necessary for the observer to add any specificity when both parties read the notes together. Rather, the observer 'adds value' by paraphrasing or adding supplementary verbal comments, as in extract 3. By contrast, when orienting to the screen video as data, there are many different potential points of interest which could be focused on for feedback purposes. Therefore, the non-verbal communication (pointing and gazing) is employed by the observer to make specific what exact object the observee should focus on whilst the observer delivers verbal feedback.

Conclusions

Although this was the first ever peer feedback session using the new VEO app for this group of eight teachers, they were able to creatively and actively integrate VEO into a central role within their practice. We can see above how the tablets/computers as VEO-related artefacts have become integrated both into the organization of the interaction (topic management) and into the activity of peer feedback as an evidence-provision tool (notes and video). The micro-analysis demonstrates that the teachers have developed multimodal speech exchange systems appropriate to the peer feedback task using VEO, in which verbal, non-verbal elements, artefacts and task-relevant actions are inextricably intertwined. Moreover, VEO is able to become the central organizing focus for their peer feedback CPD practice. There is no evidence in the corpus of interactional trouble related to the introduction of VEO, so we can assume the observation has been smoothly integrated into the existing professional activity. This study therefore provides clear evidence that it is possible (in this setting) for teachers to adapt the VEO app into their existing peer feedback practices without disruption.

It has been shown that the observer displays an orientation to the VEO-related artefact just when the current topic of assessment is coming to a close. In order to close down the topic, there must be alignment between observer and observee in terms of joint attention and actions. When the observer begins to show an orientation to the artefact (looking at it and taking hold of the mouse in case of the computers) the observee has to establish joint attention for the social action started by the observer to come to fruition. In our data, topic closure is marked mainly by silences and phonological markers (e.g. extract 2, line 7), while explicit markers like 'what else' -'*qué más*'- or discourse markers as 'well' -'*bueno*'- are less common. The VEO-related artefact is also integrated into the activity of assessment through gaze and pointing. Gaze is used to establish contact with the screen and the information provided there, but pointing at specific sections of the screen is used to establish a mutual focus on the specific information relevant to the evaluation. Pointing, then, becomes an embodied action which provides specificity in terms of the focus of the assessment.

In line with Thorne et al. (2015), one of our interests in this study has been to understand how participants in peer observation construct their feedback interaction when this is mediated by a specific digital technology such as VEO. The extracts analysed in this study show that computers and tablets becomes relevant artefacts for peer observation feedback interaction as co-present objects (Mondada 2019: 97–8). The artefact becomes integrated into the activity and is at the centre of the interaction. It comes into play to change topic and when the observer points the notes and the video provided by the object. Feedback interaction with VEO can therefore be categorized as an object-oriented activity (Mondada 2007; Mikkola and Lehtinen, 2014) in that computers and tablets become situated resource objects (Nevile et al. 2014b) which are relevant for the development of both the interaction and the professional activity.

We have seen that VEO has provided useful and meaningful information for peer observation feedback and, therefore, for reflective practice (Körkkö, Morales and Kyrö-Ämmälä 2019; Körkkö, Kyrö-Ämmälä and Turunen, Chapter 6). This specific mobile technology became relevant for both interactional and professional practice as participants oriented their actions to the VEO-related artefacts. Specific information about the lesson was provided on the screen, as the notes written down by the observer or the recorded video. This enabled both availability of the information for the interaction and joint attention by the participants. The information is therefore shared between participants and it is not only available for the observer. VEO, in this way, allows the observee to have direct access to the information rather than through the filter of the observer, unlike PO without the use of the app (Phillips 1999). Peer observation without VEO was carried out by an observer, who had in his or her possession the information about what had to be commented. However, thanks to the integration of the VEO-related artefacts into the feedback interaction and to the participants' joint orientation to them, the interaction becomes more shared and less asymmetrical, so all participants have access to the information – the notes and the video – on the screen.

9

Improving Discipline and Classroom Management Using VEO in a Turkish University Pre-service Context

Saziye Tasdemir and Paul Seedhouse
Newcastle University, UK

Introduction

English is the main foreign language in Turkey. It has a huge role, with it being taught from the second grade (age seven) in state schools and as early as kindergarten in some private schools (Özen et al. 2013). Since English is a part of the curriculum from primary school to high school (twelve years), there is a large number of English language teaching departments in Turkish universities (seventy-eight) (Yüksek Öğretim Program Atlası 2020). Despite Turkish students being taught English for an estimated 1000+ hours (Özen et al. 2013), the language proficiency levels show that there is need of improvement in teaching, with the EF English Proficiency Index (2019) ranking Turkey 79 out of 100 countries/regions, with a very low proficiency score (Education First 2019). These numbers underline the need to focus on English language teacher education in Turkey. In one of the most extensive studies investigating the state of English language teaching in Turkey, British Council and TEPAV (Özen et al. 2013) identified one of the contributing factors as the teachers' failure to adopt communicative teaching practices and provide space for students to practice the language. Identifying this as a classroom management issue, the report stated that in the observed classes almost all of the communication was teacher led and that this showed a discrepancy between what is taught in teacher education programmes and what is practiced.

Good classroom management skills are an essential part of effective teaching. Evertson and Weinstein define classroom management as 'the actions teachers take to create an environment that supports and facilitates both academic and social-emotional learning' (2011: 4). Because of the complex nature of teaching, any moment in the classroom involves a range of possible decisions and actions (Scrivener 2005). In fact Kyriacou (2018) likens the act of teaching to a person spinning plates, placing emphasis on the many actions the teacher needs to be balancing by successfully switching their attention from one action to another.

Beginning teachers frequently identify student discipline and classroom management as one of the biggest challenges they face (Evertson and Weinstein 2011; Alpan et al. 2014; Saraç, Zorba and Arikan 2015). Despite classroom management being such a common concern, the focus allocated to it in teacher education programs remains minimal (Evertson and Weinstein 2011; Todorova and Ivanova 2020). A common theme emerging from Jones's (2011) review of the literature shows that teachers are overwhelmingly dissatisfied with the focus given to classroom management in their training programs. The situation does not appear to be any better in the field of language teacher education, with Wright describing the state of classroom management as 'an insignificant sideshow to the main events of methodological training and the development of linguistic knowledge' (2006: 81). Coskun and Daloglu's (2010) analysis of the course content of an English Language Teacher education program in Turkey displays a similar trend, as they discovered that only 1 per cent of the courses related to classroom management.

Another factor contributing to pre-service teachers' struggles with classroom management is the number and quality of teaching practices they carry out within their teacher training programs (Jones 2011). It is widely accepted that the practicum component of English language teacher education plays a vital role in student teachers' professional development (Gebhard 2009; Tülüce and Çeçen 2016). Opportunities to observe and teach during training are also indispensable for developing classroom management skills, as Wright (2006: 82) suggests they are 'learned in context'. However supporting the findings of Jones (2011), studies evaluating the ELT programmes in the Turkish context (Coskun and Daloglu 2010; Celen and Akcan 2017) state that while student teachers agree on the importance of the practicum, they believe the current number of opportunities they have to observe and teach is not sufficient.

Since the seminal work of Dewey (1933) the importance of consciously thinking about one's practice and working on areas of development has been widely accepted across various professional fields for decades. Following Schön's (1983) reminder of the value of linking theory and practice, the objective of creating reflective practitioners has become central to teacher education programs (Loughran 2002). Following the general educational trend, reflective practice began to gain importance in the field of TESOL in the early 1990s (Farrell 2018).

Defining reflective practice as the basis of professional competence, Larrivee (2011: 983) underlines its importance and argues that reflection is 'the most promising path to developing effective management strategies'. Supporting this position, Scrivener (2012) draws attention to the unique nature of any individual classroom context. While there are a variety of management techniques that can be applicable to any kind of teaching context, there are also numerous factors influencing the individual context, making reflecting on one's practice a valuable tool for developing classroom management skills (Scrivener 2012).

From the literature, it is evident that increasing the number and quality of teaching experience sessions in the practicum courses is a way forward to addressing pre-service teachers' concerns surrounding classroom management, as well as supporting their overall professional development. Since an increase of teaching experience hours would require a system wide change, a relatively minor step that can be taken is to make the most of the teaching practices through the incorporation of reflection.

Reflection can be carried out in a number of ways: writing journals, completing checklists and surveys, doing audio and video recordings of lessons (Richards and Lockhart 1996). With the development of technology, there has been an increase in using videos for reflection in teacher education (Gaudin and Chaliès 2015). Watching videos of their own practice allows student teachers to examine their teaching in more detail (Richards and Lockhart 1996) and can lead to greater understandings (Richards and Nunan 1990). Several studies confirm the benefits of video-based reflection compared to memory-based reflection, stating that it allows for a deeper level of reflection (Kong 2010), improvement in the ability to reflect (Welsch and Devlin 2007) and it provides an objective account of the teaching practice (Akcan 2010). Despite its affordances, video recording does not come without drawbacks. Setting up video cameras in the classroom can be technically challenging (Lofthouse and Birmingham 2010) and the presence of the camera in the classroom can become obtrusive (Çelik, Baran and Sert 2018). The process of watching the recorded videos also comes with challenges including the difficulty in sharing large video files (Lofthouse and Birmingham 2010) and the time it takes to either watch the whole video or edit it for a more focused reflection (Rich and Hannafin 2009; Çelik, Baran and Sert 2018). The incorporation of video annotation tools for reflection has been able to address some of these drawbacks. Video annotation tools make reflection more accessible and allow users to redirect the time spent on video editing into the reflective process (Rich and Hannafin 2009). They can also guide reflection by providing an analytical framework, resulting in a higher ability to focus on significant instances (Sherin and Van Es 2005).

VEO is a video observation tool that incorporates the affordances of video annotation and takes it a step further with a focus on mobility, intuitive use, flexibility and accessibility (Haines and Miller 2017). Early research incorporating VEO looks into its use in comparison to traditional observation techniques in a Turkish in-service EFL context (Çelik, Baran and Sert 2018), for peer observation with Spanish as a Foreign Language teachers (Batlle and Miller 2017), as a data source to promote reflexive school leadership (Hidson 2018) and a reflective tool in pre-service primary school teachers' practicum (Körkkö, Morales Rios and Kyrö-Ämmälä 2019). This chapter aims to expand this body of research, while also addressing the call of Mann and Walsh (2017) for more data led reflection and a better understanding of how reflection is carried out in the field of TESOL.

Practicum Courses in English Language Teaching (ELT) Programs in Turkey

Undergraduate ELT programmes in Turkey are four years long and consist of eight semesters (Celen and Akcan 2017). The students take various modules focusing on the English language, language teaching methods and pedagogy. The final year of the programme has two practicum courses: School Experience (7th semester) and Teaching Practice (8th semester) (Sert 2010). During the School Experience course, pre-service teachers observe lessons of an experienced teacher in their assigned school for more than twelve weeks. They are then expected to write observation reports for the course assessment. For the Teaching Practice course pre-service teachers get the opportunity to teach several classes. At least one of these lessons is observed by their practicum supervisor and they receive a grade based on their lesson planning and teaching performance (Sert 2010).

At the start of senior year, the whole practicum is divided into groups and assigned to a lecturer within the department to be their practicum supervisor. Up until 2018, the number of students assigned to a supervisor was capped at fifteen according to the guidelines provided by the Ministry of National Education, new guidelines introduced in 2018 lowered this number to eight (MEB 1998, 2018). The students are then put into pairs with their chosen peer to be peer buddies throughout the final year. The practicum groups are assigned to a school where they will be carrying out their observations and teaching throughout the year. Within the school each student is paired with a cooperating teacher whose classes they will be observing.

The structure outlined here is the base structure for ELT courses; specifics such as the number of lessons students teach, the number of lessons observed by the supervisor, the structure of observations and course requirements vary in different universities.

The Context of the Case Study

This chapter looks at the two lessons undertaken by one specific student: Lale, who was a senior year student of an English Language Teaching programme in a Turkish university in the academic year 2016–17. The English Language Teaching programme cohort of 2016–17 had approximately 200 students and this was divided into ten practicum groups. Each supervisor was assigned a group of twenty students completely at random. The base task of the practicum supervisors was to observe a minimum of one of the student-teacher's lessons and provide feedback. Lale's practicum supervisor decided to incorporate VEO into the practicum observations. The practicum guidelines did not have a technological element required for the observations, so the incorporation of VEO was an innovation added by the supervisor for his own group with the aim of facilitating reflection and improving professional development. As using video was not a mandatory element of the practicum, the students assigned to this supervisor were given the choice to switch groups if they had any objections to being recorded during their teaching or to the use of VEO. Despite the freedom to opt out, all twenty students decided to remain in their originally assigned practicum group.

Within the practicum module, the students are required to teach two full length English classes at the school they are assigned to. At least one (ideally both) of the lessons is observed by their supervisor and then they are provided with feedback. When interviewed, the supervisor emphasized the difficulty of having to manage and observe twenty students during their practicum module, especially due to time restraints. As it was practically impossible for him to balance his workload of teaching while also observing forty classes over the course of a couple months, he decided to incorporate a peer observation and feedback element into the practicum. The structure of the practicum consisted of two teaching cycles (see Figures 9.1 and 9.2) which were usually two months apart. The first lesson was observed/recorded on VEO by

Figure 9.1 Practicum structure.

the supervisor and this was followed up by a feedback meeting. For the second cycle, the same structure was followed, with a peer instead of the practicum supervisor. For both lessons the students were required to prepare a detailed lesson plan beforehand and write a report after. They also had the option of volunteering to write a reflective essay on their teaching which was not a course requisite and was not included in the marking process.

The VEO Story

The incorporation of VEO into the language teacher practicum was its first use in Turkey. As a lecturer in an ELT department the practicum supervisor was interested in ways to improve the practicum process. In an interview, he mentioned having previously incorporated video into various elements of his teaching, mainly to record micro-teaching sessions within certain modules. The supervisor also attempted incorporating video into the practicum teaching sessions and, while the benefits of using video were apparent, there were also several drawbacks, such as the difficulty of setting up a video camera in the classroom and the size of video files hindering and limiting the sharing process.

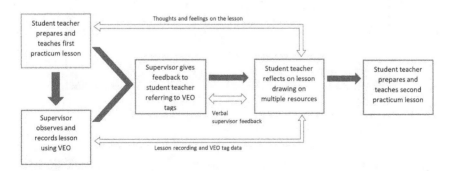

Figure 9.2 Detailed practicum structure using VEO.

With these past experiences, the supervisor was keen on using VEO as a video observation tool for the practicum course within the VEO Europa project. VEO was first used this way with the 2015–16 cohort of the same department and university as a pilot study.

For the pilot study, the Language Learning and Teaching Tag Set (see Figure 9.3) was used. This tag set was developed within the VEO Europa project by a group of language education researchers to be used in language teaching classrooms. It was designed as a holistic language teaching tag set and incorporated both teacher-focused and student-focused tags, as well as tags to capture the general features of the lesson.

Having seen its implementation, the supervisor observed that the student teachers struggled with the use of the tag set. He attributed the difficulty to the number of tags involved in the tag set, which adds up to eight main and twenty subtags. Taking this into account for the main data collection, he chose to narrow down the Language Learning and Teaching Tag Set and create a new one that focused solely on the teacher, named the L2 Teacher Tag Set (see Figure 9.4). This consisted of seven main and thirteen subtags.

While the number of tags does not seem drastically lower than the main Language Learning and Teaching Tag Set, this change was seen as necessary by the supervisor. Apart from the number, some tags were retained in the new tag set, such as the focus on questions and feedback. The two newly added tags were 'L2 use' of the teacher and 'discipline'. The latter proved to be a significant addition to the tag set for this context, as the focus on classroom management and discipline emerged as the main problem and focus, both in the supervisor feedback interview and in the participant's own reflective essays.

Although a new tag set was created for this cohort, it was not set as the mandatory tag set. The participants were given an option to choose between the more general

Figure 9.3 Language Learning and Teaching Tag Set

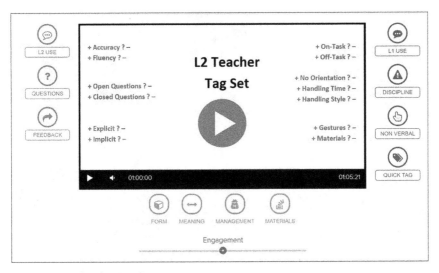

Figure 9.4 L2 Teacher Tag Set

Language Learning and Teaching Tag Set and the narrowed-down L2 Teacher Tag Set. Additionally, keeping in mind that the number of tags can be overwhelming for novice users of VEO, the supervisor advised the participants to narrow down their observation focus even further, and to pick five tags to focus on for each class. Allowing this flexibility in focus within the predetermined tag set is in line with literature. In their extensive literature review on studies looking at video self-analysis, Tripp and Rich (2012) found that while having a guided framework increased the quality of reflections, teachers wanted to be able to choose their own reflection focus.

Data Collection and Analysis

This research uses a case study methodology. Yin (2018) identifies case study as the preferred method when the research aims to answer 'how' and 'why' questions. Thus, case study was selected, as this research aims to gain in-depth understanding into how video enhanced observation (VEO) can be used to improve professional development in a specific setting. The case for this study is defined as the individual pre-service teacher. The major strength of the case study approach is that it can provide a convincing and accurate account of the research subject, drawing data from multiple sources (Yin 2018). With the multiple sources of evidence available, the researchers have had the opportunity to use triangulation, thus strengthen the validity of the case (Stake 1995; Yin 2018). In line with this, Figure 9.5 displays all the data collected for this case.

In order to understand the process of reflection, the analysis began by looking at the feedback interview data to see what the supervisor and trainee identified as important,

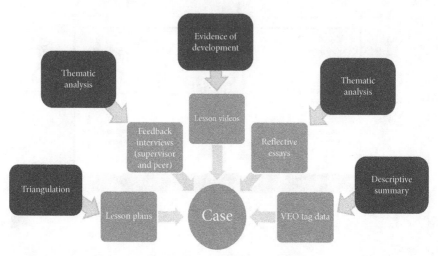

Figure 9.5 Data collection and analysis.

and what issues were underlined as an area of improvement. This was carried out employing a thematic analysis, following the steps identified by Braun and Clarke (2006). Following this, a data source triangulation was carried out by looking at the VEO tag data, to see whether or not the most frequently used tag data was in line with the thematic analysis of the interview (Yin 2018).

After the analysis of the data from the supervisor, the same thematic analysis procedure was carried out for the reflective essay of lesson one. This data was treated as the primary source; although reflective essays were not a required component of the course, this participant produced a rich account of her teaching in a nine-page long essay focusing on what went well, what could have been improved and what can be changed for future lessons.

The reflective essay was then used as a guideline to look into the classroom recording data. The most prominent theme was selected and instances that were treated as significant by the student teacher were transcribed in order to get an idea of what actually happened.

The same cycle was repeated for the second lesson. However, rather than looking at the second lesson data according to the most prominent theme of the second reflective essay, the focus was kept the same as the first lesson, in order to allow the researcher to look for evidence of change/improvement if present.

Evidence of Development

The chapter shows that the VEO app not only provides value, with its tagging feature making video viewing a smoother process, but also allows for detailed data-based reflection. The process of reflection which is sparked by the trainee watching videos of their lessons in conjunction with supervisor feedback has generated a very long and self-critical reflective essay by this participant. She would not have been able to produce a reflective document in such detail without having had access to classroom video recordings that are tagged, providing focus points as well as a framework for reflection.

In order to highlight the evidence of development, we will initially be looking at lesson 1 and then follow up with lesson 2. The data will be presented in the following order:

- Supervisor feedback from the supervisor/trainee feedback meeting
- VEO tag data of lesson one done by supervisor
- Trainee reflective essay and excerpts from lesson 1
- Plans for change for lesson 2
- Trainee reflective essay and excerpts from lesson 2
- General reflections from essay 2

The most prominent theme of the supervisor feedback meeting was classroom management/discipline. This is in line with the literature on beginning teachers' areas of struggle (see Evertson and Weinstein 2011; Jones 2011). Excerpts 1 and 2 below show instances where this was outlined as an area to focus on by both the supervisor and the trainee herself.

Excerpt 1: Supervisor feedback meeting

S: Supervisor
T: Trainee

1	S:	Let's see what do we have here?
2		*(they start to view a tagging)*
3		Here you're explaining something to this student, we lost the
4		students in the back.
5		The guys right now
6	T:	Yes they were-
7	S:	are talking loudly. The others can't even hear what this
8		student is saying err so it's no orientation, you're not
9		orienting to that side
10		*(viewing tagging)*
11		err
12		*(viewing tagging)*
13		here is the first time you're displaying orientation towards
14		the classroom management program err problem at the fourteenth
15		minute. I mean those ten- after the fifth minute in this six
16		minute long part the back of the class is a bit disrupted

Here we can see the supervisor focusing on an instance where the classroom management became an issue. This is done by incorporating the tagged VEO video into the feedback meeting and looking at instances tagged by the supervisor. In lines 7–8, the supervisor identifies the issue as the teacher showing no orientation towards the

144   *Video Enhanced Observation for Language Teaching*

students who are talking loudly and disrupting the class. He then pinpoints the exact moment the teacher displayed orientation in line 13 and summarizes in lines 15–16 that there was a six-minute long period of the class where management appeared to be an issue. Further into the interview, excerpt 2 comes where we can see the supervisor giving feedback on how to resolve classroom management issues (lines 7 to 10). The feedback is to start by using non-verbal actions such as gaze and proxemics, which are amongst the classroom management techniques termed as 'wordless interventions' by Scrivener (2012: 237) and 'signal and proximity interference' by Levin and Nolan (2014: 210). The supervisor offers a variety of options to take in a similar situation; this is important as Scrivener and Larrivee (2005, 2011) note that being an effective classroom manager comes from knowing the possible actions to take during any given classroom moment and being able to adapt according to the situation.

Towards the end of the feedback meeting, the supervisor advises the trainee to look at all of the instances where classroom management-related tags were used (lines 16 and 18). Following this in line 19 we see the trainee agreeing with the supervisor and identifying classroom management as her biggest issue.

Excerpt 2

1	S:	uh huh so at that point, somehow, before the 15th minute
2	T:	uh huh
3	S:	before you get to the point where you say guys, a slight
4		orientation towards him with body language, walking to that
5		side
6	T:	uh huh
7	S:	nonverbal at first, you can solve it with proxemics, with gaze
8		at first. Those are the first steps, if you notice those aren't
9		working you can adjust your voice a bit, slight raise of voice
10		while looking in their direction
11	T:	uh huh
12	S:	and it will most likely be resolved. In classes like these
13		it'll be resolved because once you engage them these kinds of
14		classes stay engaged and it mostly lasts until the end of the
15		class. We saw examples of it in previous lessons, so I'd say
16		check all of these parts
17	T:	yes
18	S:	related to classroom management
19	T:	that's my biggest issue

The summary of tag data produced by the VEO app is in line with the thematic analysis of the feedback meeting, showing the 'discipline' tag as the most frequently used tag.

Table 9.1 shows a more detailed breakdown of the lesson 1 tags and it can be seen that ten out of a total of nineteen tags are under the 'discipline' main tag; six instances were tagged with the 'no orientation' subtag and a further four with the 'handling style' subtag. This shows that the VEO tag data is in line with the verbal feedback given by the supervisor.

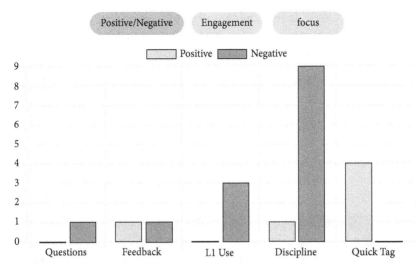

Figure 9.6 Lesson 1 VEO tag data.

Table 9.1 Lesson 1 VEO tag data break down

Tag	Subtag	#
Discipline	No orientation	6
	Handling style	4
Quick tag	–	3
L1 Use	On-task	3
Feedback	Explicit	2
Questions	Open questions	1

Lesson 1

The reflective essay written by Lale focused on multiple areas of her teaching; she divided the essay into different sections using the following headings:

1. Lesson plan and classroom procedure
2. The successful and engaging part of the lesson
3. The problematic and not engaging part of the lesson
4. Usage of L1 by students
5. Questions
6. Feedback
7. Communication problems
8 Classroom management
9. Next class

This choice of content and organization is worth focusing on, as these were decisions made by Lale herself, given that the reflective essay was not a mandatory

146   *Video Enhanced Observation for Language Teaching*

component of the course. Throughout the essay Lale had some general reflections on her performance, as well as very specific parts where she included the time stamp of the instance she was reflecting on.

The analysis of the reflective essay showed that classroom management was the most prominent theme of the essay:

> Unfortunately, my classroom management was bad. I could not handle the classroom well. Students started to talk with each other. When I watched the video, I realized that there were noises most of the time. This caused some problems. We could not understand each other. Because of this, they did not understood my instruction for the poster activity.
>
>   (Reflective essay data)

In the extract above we can see Lale identifying her classroom management as an issue and giving a general description of how the lesson went down in terms of management. She also mentions the realizations she had after watching herself teach. The affordances of reflecting via video are apparent in her writing, as she includes the exact timestamp of the instances she is referring to, a level of detail that would not be possible without video evidence, and extremely time-consuming to obtain without tags.

> I had to interrupt the lesson and say "Hush." or "Listen to me." all the time. I sometimes just said their names. When S1 was reading his sentences and S2 started to talk, I said "Hush."(23:14). When the guys at the back started to talk, I said "S1." with raising my voice (24:23). When posters were ready and a student from each group came to the board, there was noise (35:06). First I said "Guys." twice loudly. Then said "Listen, please." S1 was still talking so I said "S1, please."
>
>   (Reflective essay data)

In the extract below (see Table 9.2), we can see one of the instances Lale referred to in her essay, alongside the classroom data transcription of the same instance.

Lale refers to the same instance in two separate parts of her reflective essay. This is a part of the lesson where she decides to adapt her listening activity. In addition to playing the audio multiple times, she decides to read the audio text herself so the students have a chance to complete the activity, which is a fill-in-the-blank worksheet. In line 19 the lesson is interrupted by a student from another class asking for one of the students in the class, and the mispronunciation of the summoned student's name causes laughter in the classroom. The rest of the extract shows Lale's attempts at managing the class. In line 23 we see her first attempt at quieting the students down, which is followed by her continuing with the task – reading the listening text herself. This does not get the attention of those students who are still talking amongst themselves, which leads to Lale's second explicit attempt at managing the talk in line 30. It should be noted that, apart from two instances where she explicitly tries to quiet the students down, Lale's choice of action is not to orient to the talking students, but rather just to carry on with the task in hand. This results in Lale reading the text with no-one listening to her for

VEO in Turkish University Pre-service Context

Table 9.2 Lesson 1 classroom and reflective essay excerpt

		Classroom data transcript	Reflective essay excerpts
01	SS:	(unclear chatter)	
02	T:	okay (0.2) err it was sup-	
03		so fast [right?]	'I played the video but I got the feeling that
04	S:	[(inaudible)]	they still had some problems. I asked if it was
05	T:	yeah (1.1) it was fast	fast and they said "Yes." so I decided to read
06		right?	it myself (13:36). At this time, a student came
07	SS:	yes yes	to the class and asked for one of the students
08	T:	[now I will read more slowly	(14:00). she said the name wrong and students
09		so you can fill it okay?]	started to laugh and talk. I tried to handle it
10	SS:	[(*unclear chatter*)]	but it seems that I failed. I said **"Guys, please**
11	S:	ehem	**listen to me."** and started to read but students
12	T:	okay (1.5) parties can be a	still laughed and talked (14:12). At this part, I
13		lot of fun (0.4) people get	should have just be silent and wait until all of
14		invited to parties (0.5) you	them stopped talking.'
15		can have a party because it's	
16		a (0.2) special occasion (0.3)	
17		or just because	
18		(*Knock on the door*)	
19	X:	S burda mi?	
20		(*Is S here?*)	
21	SS:	hahahaha	'The student on duty came to class and
22	SS:	(unclear chatter)	called for someone. Because she said the
23	T:	**okay listen to me (0.2) guys**	name wrong, students started to laugh and
24	SS:	*chatter continues*	talk(14:10). First I said **"Okay, listen to me."**
25	T:	you can have a party because	and then **"Guys."** twice but they did not stop.
26		it's a special occasion	So I started to walk around and read it like
27	SS:	*chatter continues*	that. That brought some silence to the lesson.'
28	T:	or just because	
29	SS:	*chatter continues*	
30	T:	**guys (0.4) listen to me** (0.2)	
31		you also have a party	
32	SS:	*chatter continues*	
33	T:	sometimes people wear party	
34		hats at parties	
35	SS:	*chatter continues*	
36	T:	these are called party hats	
37	SS:	*chatter continues*	
38	T:	some people decorate with	
39		streamers and balloons	
40		*T begins to walk around the class while*	
41		*reading*	
42	SS:	*chatter continues*	
43	T:	at some parties there is a	
44		cake (0.6) sometimes there are	
45		just snacks and drinks	
46			

several lines. She describes these explicit management attempts as unsuccessful in her reflective essay, stating: 'I tried to handle it but it seems that I failed.' She then continues to reflect on both what seemed to work: 'So I started to walk around and read it like that. That brought some silence to the lesson.' and possible future actions to take in a similar situation: 'At this part, I should have just be silent and wait until all of them stopped talking.'

Reflecting on other possible actions to take in a certain situation is a step forward in becoming a more effective teacher (Scrivener 2005). In this instance, Lale hypothesizes that getting the students silent before carrying on with the activity would have delivered better results. Indeed, ensuring student engagement prior to starting an activity is advised by teacher educators. Scrivener underlines the importance of this by stating 'An instruction given over student chatter, or when students are looking the other way, stands little chance of working' (2005: 92).

Plans for Change

In addition to reflecting on her first teaching, Lale's reflective essay also included reflections on what kind of future action she could take in order to improve her practice.

> I realized so many mistakes I did during that lesson while I was watching the video. Actually, when I finished the lesson, I thought that lesson went well. After I had a small talk with my teacher, I understood that there was something that needs to be improved. This became more clear when I watched the video several times.
>
> The first thing that I wish I had done was to disband the guys that sit at the back. They talk with each other and they distracted one another's attention. The noise that they caused got other students' attention and they started to talk as well.
>
> The ongoing noise was my fault. At the beginning; they did not talk that much but because I did not interfere with their talking, they started to talk more and more. That was because I do not like to be a despotic teacher and also because they were middle schoolers and I did not want to break their hearts or make them sad.
>
> (Reflective essay data)

In the extract above, Lale mentions how the feedback meeting and watching herself on video contributed to her understanding of the areas of her teaching that needed improvement. She demonstrates the ability to step back and consider the possible reasons for the disruption and states that it was due to her lack of interference. She then explains her own reasoning for her choice of action. Nevertheless, the area of classroom management remains one to be improved upon for her future lessons.

Lesson 2

For her second lesson, Lale produced another long reflective essay (seven pages long) using the same headings as the first one. The thematic analysis of this essay showed that the most prominent theme had shifted from classroom management to questioning

VEO in Turkish University Pre-service Context 149

strategies, followed by feedback and correction as the second most important theme. This can be due to Lale seeing classroom management as an improved area of her practice, thus removing the need to reflect on it in the same length and depth as the first lesson.

As previously mentioned, in order to be able to look at any evidence of development, the focus will be kept the same as the first lesson, despite classroom management not being the primary theme of the second reflective essay.

In Table 9.3 we have a classroom management instance that Lale reflected on in two separate parts of her essay, and the transcript of the corresponding instance. In this extract Lale is trying to set up a task for which she has given the instructions, and as she moves on to distributing the worksheets, one student says they don't understand what is to be done.

Table 9.3 Lesson 2 classroom and reflective essay excerpt

		Classroom data transcript	Reflective essay excerpts
01	S3:	hocam ben anlamadım	After I gave the instructions, I
02		*(teacher I didn't understand)*	distributed the worksheets. One
03	T:	just a minute	of the students said 'Hocam, ben
04		*(T distributes worksheets)*	anlamadım!' (Teacher I didn't
05	S4:	dağıtıyım mı hocam?	understand) (22:04). I waited
06		*(should I pass them out teacher?)*	until all students got their papers
07	T:	to you- and you. You didn't	and clapped my hands and said
08		understand? Just wait just wait	'Everyone!' to get their attention
09	SS:	*(unclear chatter while receiving*	because they started to talk (22:34).
10		*worksheets)*	They did not stop talking so I said
11	T:	okay	one of the students' name so that
12	SS:	*(unclear chatter while receiving*	to stop them talking. I gave a task
13		*worksheets)*	to the student who seemed to talk
14	T:	guys	more. I said 'Murat, can you read
15	SS:	*(unclear chatter while receiving*	the example?' (23:33).
16		*worksheets)*	
17	T:	okay	
18	SS:	*(unclear chatter while receiving*	
19		*worksheets)*	My students did not understand
20	T:	*(claps her hands to get attention)*	from the first example so I tried
21	SS:	*(unclear chatter)*	to explain the second one (24:36).
22	T:	shhh Murat! Please. Berke can you	When some students understand
23		please go there?	but some did not I said 'You can
24	S5:	hocam gelmesin yapmayın ya	help your friends.' (26:58). Some
25		*(teacher don't make him come)*	noise occurred but it is okay since
26	S6:	zaten yeri orası hocam	this is a language classroom.
27		*(that's his seat anyway)*	
28	T:	shhh okay go there	
29	SS:	*(unclear chatter)*	
30	S:	please hold the line	
31	T:	yes please hold the line ay okay	
32		Berke quickly. Now guys look at your	
33		paper, look at your paper. Look at your paper.	
34		Look.	

35	S:	yes
36	T:	good now there are two sentences.
37		Like for every picture you will write
38		two sentences
39	S:	(unclear)
40	T:	yes you will write two sentences
41	S:	should shouldn't *(unclear chatter*
42		*continues)*
43	T:	yeah like er like in the first pi-
44		look at the example
45		please Murat can you read the
46		example? Read, read the example
47	M:	tamam hocam *(okay teacher)*
48		

In the essay extracts we see her reflecting on the instance by listing the different actions she took in order to manage the disruption. In contrast to the first lesson, where she continued with the task instructions despite the lack of engagement, in this lesson she takes the time to get the students' attention. At first, she uses verbal cues saying 'okay' and 'guys' to get them quiet (lines 11, 14, 18). Seeing this does not work, she resorts to using gestures and claps to get their attention. This also does not seem to quiet the students down, which then leads Lale to switch strategies and call out an individual student who is talking (line 23). Looking at the classroom extract, this seems to give her some space to continue with the task and repeat the instructions so everyone is clear on what to do. However, some level of chatter is still continuing (line 43) and this is when we see Lale appointing a student to read the example (lines 46–47). She describes this choice of action in her reflective essay by stating that 'I gave a task to the student who seemed to talk more. I said "Murat, can you read the example?" (23:33)'.

In the second essay extract, she elaborates on the various methods she employed to manage the class and the confusion relating to the instructions. These included verbal cues, gestures and giving a task to the disruptive student (Lewis 2002; Scrivener 2005). She concludes by showing an understanding of differentiating between types of student talk during the lesson, stating that 'Some noise occurred but it is okay since this is a language classroom.'

Reflections on Self-improvement

Lale reflects on the area she identified as the most problematic below:

My classroom management was better than the last time. I am pleased that it developed. The only part it get bad was the last part because of the instructions. Another minor mistake was that when I tried to open the slides, there was a silence (00:22). Maybe, I could have given them a small task or asked a question while I was doing that. Apart from these, the management was good.

While stating that her classroom management has improved, she mentions the above extract as the only instance where it did not go well. Despite being identified as a part that 'got bad', the lesson excerpts show Lale taking an active stance in classroom management by trying out several solutions to resolve the issue, in essence 'remaining fluid' as Larrivee (2011: 990) puts it.

Reflecting on the whole practicum process, Lale notes that VEO allowed her to notice 'minor' aspects of her teaching that would have otherwise gone unnoticed:

> After the lessons, I usually realize the huge mistakes I do. But minor mistakes always are overlooked. This opportunity helped me realize those and I actually tried to do my best for the second lesson. I tried to not do the same mistakes. It helped me to develop my classroom management which was bad during the first lesson.

She emphasizes the improvement in her classroom management skills and largely attributes this to the video reflection process underlining the replay affordance of video recordings:

> All in all, this lesson was more successful than the previous one. This was mostly because I wrote a reflection and watched my lesson again and again. I tried to be careful to not to make same mistakes and it actually worked. In the future, I will try to do this time to time to reflect upon my teaching. This way I can see the parts that is good and the parts that needs developing or fixing. I want to know how my skills are. I hope they will get better.

Possibly due to the effectiveness of this process, we see Lale viewing reflection as a window into her own practice and making plans to incorporate it in her professional development in the future.

Conclusions

This research set out to investigate how video observation with the VEO app is used for reflection and professional development in a practicum setting in the Turkish context.

The findings have shown that VEO facilitated professional development in a pre-service practicum in several ways. The tagging feature provided a framework for reflection and facilitated the video viewing process. This was apparent in the supervisor trainee feedback meeting where they used the tags to jump to significant instances. The supervisor was also able to guide the trainee's reflection by advising her to look at all of the 'discipline' tagged instances. The affordances of tags are also seen in the detailed reflective essays the participant produced, as she was able to reflect on her teaching at length and with great focus on detail, incorporating timestamps from the lessons. This is consistent with the study of Sherin and Van Es (2005), as they found that the use of a video annotation tool led to more organized and focused reflections.

The evidence from this study suggests that the incorporation of VEO in the practicum can help pre-service teachers improve classroom management skills through reflection. Through written reflective data and classroom data we see Lale become a more capable classroom manager, gaining the ability to notice her options in any given classroom instance and decide on an action accordingly (Scrivener 2012). This finding is promising as beginning teachers identify classroom management skills as their greatest challenge (Evertson and Weinstein 2011) and there is a lack of focus on the subject area in teacher education (Wright 2005). Increasing the quality of the practicum experiences of pre-service teachers with video self-reflection is of especial importance in contexts where organizational and institutional factors (such as the number of trainees per supervisor) limit developmental opportunities.

In summary, therefore, it seems that VEO provides a promising way forward in assisting pre-service teachers' professional development and creating reflective practitioners, provided the app is carefully integrated into all systems.

10

Video-enhanced Lesson Observation: Moving from Performance Management to Continuous Teacher Development

Elizabeth Hidson
University of Sunderland, UK

Introduction

This chapter focuses on an example of the innovative use of video-enhanced lesson observation in the annual cycle of teacher performance management: a mandatory appraisal process in English schools. It presents the case study of a pilot project developed and trialled at one English secondary school over the course of a school year. The use of the VEO app for video-enhanced lesson observation was introduced by the school as part of a change to their performance management process.

The chapter is structured in three parts. First, the background to the research contextualizes the shift away from standalone graded lesson observations in England and looks at the appraisal process and the place of lesson observation within it. It highlights that CPD is part of the policy intent but problematizes the emphasis on teacher performance and underperformance to the exclusion of the professional development necessary to secure it. Second, the VEO Europa project research framework is presented in order to situate this school case study within the larger-scale research project looking at VEO. The focus of the research questions of the VEO Europa project was on teacher professional development. This meant that this school's interest in the wider use of VEO became a relevant parallel case study. In this case, the focus was on the way that VEO was incorporated into the school's pre-existing vision for teacher development through better performance management processes, including the use of student voice. The third section presents the case study findings and the resulting model of video-enhanced teacher development for performance management. It offers a discussion of these, summarizing the implications for practice, with a move away from performance management processes often seen as a solely performative and stressful experience for teachers and towards one of continuous teacher development undertaken from more of a coaching and mentoring perspective.

154 *Video Enhanced Observation for Language Teaching*

The chapter concludes with advice for schools to consider when introducing VEO as an element in their wider approach to continuous teacher development.

Part One: Lesson Observations and Teacher Performance Management in England

Lesson Observation as Part of Teacher Education

Lesson observation is one of the main ways that we train teachers, what Shulman (2005) would call a 'signature pedagogy' of the teaching profession. Different professions educate their practitioners in ways that are most suited to the role that they will carry out. Novice teachers observe how expert teachers teach then reflect and develop their own practice. When novices teach, expert teachers observe and give feedback. From their first experiences of teacher education, teachers are used to frequent observation. In their early days, almost every lesson will be observed, whether formally or informally, followed up by written or verbal feedback on their developing skills in the classroom. Initially, and inevitably, feedback focuses on matters of classroom management and student behaviour, moving to more nuanced practice and issues of learning as time passes. The student teacher will usually show enormous growth over their first year and into their early career as they become familiar with the national Teachers' Standards (DfE 2011), good practice is established and experience gained. Once the teacher has completed their induction phase and moves on from being 'newly qualified', they will usually join their colleagues in their school's annual performance management cycle.

What Is Performance Management?

Annual appraisal of teachers has been a statutory requirement in England since 2002. The current legislation governing this process is The Education (School Teachers' Appraisal) (England) Regulations 2012 regulations (DfE 2012). Schools, trusts and local authorities may have different names for this process, but 'performance management' is a term that will be familiar to many and is used interchangeably in this chapter, not least because the regulations couch the outcomes of the appraisal process as relating to the judgement of performance or *under*performance against the Teachers' Standards. The model policy provided to schools by the Department for Education (DfE 2012), which was last updated in March 2019, has one section on appraisal (Part A) and another on formal capability procedures (Part B), making it clear what a high-stakes process this can be for teachers. Although the policy states that schools and teachers should see this as a 'supportive and developmental process' (p. 7), which informs continuing professional development (CPD), it is also used to determine decisions on pay progression and formal capability procedures. The breadth of detail around capability procedures compared to those around CPD means that it is difficult to see this policy in a supportive light. The outcome is that schools often see the two processes as separate, leading to them developing a separate bespoke policy for CPD divorced from the appraisal process.

Lesson Observation as Part of Performance Management

Lesson observation as part of performance management is built into the DfE (2012b) model policy as a mechanism for assessing teachers' performance. While there is no statutory minimum or maximum limit on the number of lesson observations that can be carried out in any one year, the discourse around the quantity of observations is that this should not be excessive. Previous performance management legislation had the number at three hours per year, which, although dropped in the 2012 legislation, is a figure that several teachers' unions have continued to promote as a maximum. Schools are signposted towards being specific about how observations will be conducted but left without guidance about how to judge the quality of lessons. For something so integral to the way that we train teachers, this has been an area of heated debate (Coe 2014; O'Leary 2016). The use of Office for Standards in Education (Ofsted)-inspired grading criteria, where observers make a judgement of 'outstanding', 'good', 'requires improvement' or 'unsatisfactory', has resulted in scoring systems and checklists that prompted the government department to issue clarification to schools to address the 'myth' that Ofsted expects teachers to be observed and graded by their schools (Ofsted 2019).

The official shift away from grading individual lessons began in 2014 with an announcement by Ofsted's National Director for schools about piloting a new approach to the recording of evidence about the quality of teaching in school inspections (Cladingbowl 2014). Despite this, many schools and training providers have seemingly been reluctant or unable to jettison graded lesson observations. This is perhaps symptomatic of the performativity culture prevalent in schools (Edgington 2016), where schools are resigned to being judged against externally imposed measures of practice and may fear deeper scrutiny if unable to provide statistics that demonstrate that they can measure teacher quality in a way that can be shared easily with inspectors.

What Counts as CPD?

This leaves the questions of how and what to assess in terms of teacher competence. A competent teacher is one who does their job well. Obviously, a large part of the teacher's role is the substantive classroom teaching – supporting learners to make progress and achieve in relation to their potential against the context of age range and subject area. Few in the teaching profession would argue against CPD as such, and most would welcome more opportunities for meaningful engagement with their own development. The crux of the issue with CPD is that the range of activities collated under that particular umbrella term can also have limited use and appeal. A feature of many schools' in-service training (INSET) is the whole-school training day, where various colleagues with teaching and learning responsibilities (TLRs) highlight the latest policy changes that staff need to be aware of. This experience has little to do with the strategic development of subject-specific pedagogy. Recent research by the Teacher Development Trust (2020) also has shown that teachers welcome having influence over their individual professional development goals. In this chapter we argue that we have at our disposal techniques and technologies that act as mechanisms to

156   *Video Enhanced Observation for Language Teaching*

re-align the performance management process as a form of teacher development rather than teacher management. This is a case of schools embracing the CPD element of the appraisal legislation and linking it to developments in teaching practice that are specific to the individual teacher.

Part Two: The VEO Europa Project: Video-enhanced Observation in Schools

This chapter provides one snapshot from the VEO Europa project. Previous chapters have outlined the research context behind using digital video for teacher development and explored the circumstances leading to the development of the VEO app. Chapter 4 offered a practical guide to using the VEO app (https://apple.co/2DMDh7t): a video-based observation app developed at Newcastle University by Jon Haines and Paul Miller. The VEO system allows users to create or select a set of tags to use as a reference framework for the observation. The tagging of key moments of teaching practice facilitates later reflection and dialogue through direct access to those tagged moments. The observer either can record the lesson and simultaneously tag key moments for later review, or can undertake the review retrospectively. Videos can be reviewed and optionally shared within the teacher's professional community. The aim is to facilitate teachers' reflective practices, including the 'noticing' (van Es and Sherin 2002; Rosaen et al. 2008) of aspects of their own work, enabling them to become active agents of their own CPD.

The VEO Europa project (www.veoeuropa.com) funded by Erasmus+ ran from 2015 to 2017, led by Paul Seedhouse at Newcastle University. Our project focused on the use of the VEO app to support professional practice through video-enhanced observation, involving over 400 teachers, teacher educators and trainee teachers in England, Germany, Finland, Turkey and Bulgaria. The research questions guiding the project team centred on exploring the different uses of the VEO app in a range of educational settings:

1. To what extent is professional development supported by VEO?
2. How do trainers and trainees use VEO in their work?
3. How do teachers use VEO to monitor and assess student learning?
4. To what extent does VEO help teachers improve their monitoring and assessment of student learning?

The Case Study School: 'School C'

One of the project's research questions asked how participants used VEO in their work, and another related explicitly to professional development. Knowing that teachers can be very creative in the way that they use and re-purpose tools and resources, we were open to exploring any aspect of the use of the VEO app that involved the video-enhanced lesson observation process that was the main focus of the project. We were very interested in the way that one of the schools in England had incorporated the video-enhanced lesson observation process into their annual cycle of teacher performance management.

The school was an above-average-sized mixed community secondary school with a sixth form. In a recent inspection report, the school had been praised by Ofsted for its commitment to continually improving and quality-assuring teaching and learning and its capacity for sustained improvements was judged to be strong.

Over the course of the school year, the research team visited the school and provided training on the VEO app to a group of staff who were interested in using it. The school had a form of research-focused CPD where staff could select a personal area of interest and carry out action research over the course of the academic year. The intention was for staff to be able to use VEO to support this element of their CPD. The wide-ranging topics, each selected by the teachers as a personal performance or development goal included many examples where video was a logical tool for either teaching (such as using video feedback with students) or as a tool to carry out the practitioner research. At various points across the year, we returned to the school to interview staff, observe how they had been using VEO and to gather data for the research project.

One of the senior leaders of the school opted to include VEO in a specific process that they were keen to develop – that of video-enhanced lesson observation as part of the annual performance management cycle. Set against this backdrop, in the next section we share the pilot process developed and trialled at the school over the course of the 2016–17 school year. The VEO app supplemented and enhanced the school's performance management process, which already incorporated three linked lesson observations as a key mechanism.

Part Three: Video-enhanced Lesson Observation for Continuous Teacher Development

Typical performance management at 'School C' followed a three-part cycle over the academic year. The performance manager (usually a more senior teacher and line manager) and the teacher in question would meet to agree the teachers' annual objectives at the start of the cycle. Historically, the annual objectives may have had little bearing on the lesson observation, leaving the observation to take a relatively minimal part other than to confirm that the teacher was capable of teaching a good lesson, as expected. More recently, the school had changed their approach to performance management, placing a greater emphasis on negotiating the goals of the teacher and embedding them into the process.

When describing the school's approach to teaching and learning, the deputy headteacher explained that they saw CPD as encircling the teaching processes. Keeping relationships at the core, the various methods for engaging and challenging students to make progress all offered opportunities for teacher development, and often formed the topic for the action research carried out by the teacher as part of their school-based CPD. This ring comprised the development of expert subject knowledge, personal

158   *Video Enhanced Observation for Language Teaching*

reflection, research, peer observations and feedback as well as seeking and acting on student feedback. This teaching philosophy meant that all lesson observations were carried out with the expectation that excellent teaching demonstrates strong relationships, challenge, excellent subject knowledge, strong explanations, questioning and feedback: a statement captured on the lesson observation form in Figure 10.1.

This lesson observation form demonstrates the connection between the performance management target and the lesson observation process. The top section of the form contains space to articulate the purpose, or the topic of the observation

Lesson Observation Feedback Form

Teacher:	Observer:
Subject:	Class:
Purpose:	

Primary focus of the observation: What are you developing in your own practice?

Lesson 1

Excellent teaching requires strong relationships, challenge, excellent subject knowledge, strong explanations, questioning and feedback.

What is happening?	What is the impact on learning?
-	How is this facilitating progress?
-	-
-	-
-	-

Lesson 2

Excellent teaching requires strong relationships, challenge, excellent subject knowledge, strong explanations, questioning and feedback.

What is happening?	What is the impact on learning?
-	How is this facilitating progress?
-	-
-	-
-	-

Lesson 3

Excellent teaching requires strong relationships, challenge, excellent subject knowledge, strong explanations, questioning and feedback.

What is happening?	What is the impact on learning?
-	How is this facilitating progress?
-	-
-	-
-	-

Post Cycle Reflections

What went well?

What could be improved?

What are the next steps to help improve?

Teacher signature:	Observer signature:

Figure 10.1 Example of a lesson observation form for recording outcomes and feedback.

cycle – what it is that the teacher wants to work on as their personal learning goal over the course of the year. This topic could be drawn from a range of action research topics (see, for example, the list of examples of teacher action research questions on p. 240 in Pine (2009)) but the key thing is that it is personal to the teacher. The teacher must be motivated to develop this aspect of their practice and think about what they will try out in the classroom that can be observed, with feedback provided on how that aspect impacted on learning and facilitated the students to make progress. The feedback form was designed to collect the observer's field notes and comments at three points across the year, culminating in post-cycle reflections between the observer and observee. As long as teaching was effective, the focus remained on the teachers' deeper development in relation to what they had negotiated as their target.

Enhancing the Process by Including the VEO App

The change involving the observation process being based on the teacher's negotiated personal target was positive, in that it moved away from standalone lesson observations (with or without a grade) towards a formative, iterative process leading to a 'summing up' via the post-cycle reflections. However, the potential of the VEO app meant that this entire process could be further enhanced, because of the way that VEO allows the lesson to be recorded and stored securely in the app for the observer and the observee to discuss, taking a dialogic approach to highlighting elements of practice. The diagram in Figure 10.2 illustrates the way that VEO was integrated into the performance management cycle in the case study school.

Using the VEO app, an observer can record the lesson via their tablet computer. An observer has the ability while observing to tag moments of particular interest

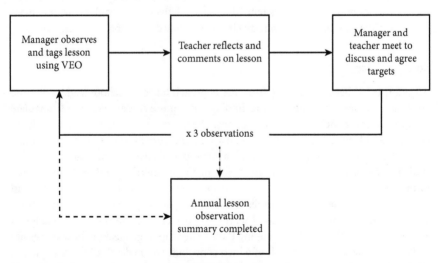

Figure 10.2 Lesson observation using VEO during the performance management cycle in the case study school.

in the lesson. If they note a particular example during the lesson, they are able to use the selected tag set to tag and timestamp the episode for later review, such as a positive moment of teacher-student interaction or an instance of a student's lack of understanding. If they note something that they feel falls outside of the parameters of the tag set, then they can use the 'quicktag' feature to signal that the timestamp relates to something of interest that requires later review. Alternatively, the observer could simply allow the recording to continue without continual tagging and return to the recording afterwards to do some additional tagging. In this way, the observer is not tied physically to one area of the classroom, but can, if they wish, move around the classroom to check what pupils are doing. Observers often ask questions about understanding, or have a look at students' task sheets, activities or exercise books to get a richer sense of the way that the lesson activities impact on learning and the way that students are making progress over time.

Other options for using VEO in the observation include moving the tablet around the teaching space while the recording continues or pausing the recording until the observer wishes to capture some of this additional lesson activity. The app is able to pause and continue, with the only caveat being that the timestamp feature will then relate to the location of the tag within the recording, rather than to the chronological time during the lesson. In addition, with the demands on staff time, if a scheduled observation was not possible, then the teacher could simply place the tablet in a suitable area of the classroom and leave it recording, with the option for the observer to view it later. If the tablet is moved during recording, then there may be a reduction in the quality of the recording as it will suffer from shaky camera movements. Whilst the app itself is intuitive, as is modern video-recording technology generally, it is worth considering the way that the camera can be used to best effect when recording in classrooms. Relevant work on the use of cameras in the classroom has been done by the National Centre for Research Methods (see, for example, Kilburn 2014), although the VEO Europa researchers found that observers tended to have relatively few problems with camera work, usually using the camera intuitively and sensibly during observations.

Student Voice

An unexpected benefit resulting from the approach taken by school leaders was the attendant use of the mobile video technology to capture student voice to triangulate with the observer and observee's reflections. The use of student voice, where students' opinions and feedback are sought, can be a valid measure of teacher assessment (Coe et al. 2014). Student voice can give a valuable perspective on the extent to which students are either meta-cognitively aware of the teachers' intentions with regards to their learning, or even just how they responded to a particular activity, which in itself can provide the teacher with feedback for the planning process. During a lesson observation, it is common for an observer to move around the room and engage to some extent with the students, gauging their understanding, checking how things are usually done by this teacher – all of which contribute to the depth of the assessment. Sometimes, student feedback may be noted on an observation form, but often it may go un-recorded but be part of the anecdotal feedback, so the intentional capture of student voice during lesson observation was interesting in this school. Cremin et al. (2011) highlighted that students' views must be taken into account during Ofsted inspections, so the chance to involve the students as a trusted part of an authentic process (Czerniawski 2014) is very much in keeping with the school's teaching and learning philosophy of keeping relationships at the core.

In the case study school, the students' comments were routinely recorded by the observer as part of the live observation: as responses to questions asked as the app was recording, for example. As well as this, one practice that was shared with the research team was where the observer invited a small group of students to assemble outside of the lesson and give some comments about how they had found the lesson, while being recorded separately. In one example shared, a small sixth-form group discussed the different revision strategies the teacher had given them to prepare for a forthcoming exam and how the students planned to use them. The teacher's reflections on the use of student voice are presented later in this section.

Insights from the Case Study School

The aim of this chapter is to provide insight into the practicalities of using VEO as part of the process of performance management. These insights were gained through interviews with three staff in the school: a senior leader (a deputy headteacher), a line manager (an assistant headteacher) doing observations as part of the appraisal process and one experienced teacher who was observed using VEO throughout the performance management cycle during the school year.

The Senior Leader

The senior leader outlined his feelings about this change of direction for the school, describing it as taking a 'brave step' by deviating from the way that many schools interpreted the kind of evidence they needed to provide for Ofsted inspections. He highlighted that, as their recent Ofsted inspection had been positive, they now felt that they had the 'luxury of time' to continue to develop their teaching, learning and professional development, secure in the knowledge that they had been commended for their approach. Key to this process was redesigning the lesson observation proforma: in his words, 'doing away with tick boxes' as an approach. The benefits to the school were that the whole process of performance management, tied now to what the teacher wanted to develop in their own practice, was felt to be increasingly valuable. The school, he felt, had taken steps towards becoming more reflective and collaborative. Teachers' own judgements about their developmental needs and goals were being seen as important and this meant that teachers were able to make more rapid development. By linking the lesson observations to the goal that was set, progress towards the goal could be seen from one lesson to the next. The way that student voice was being used was also felt to be powerful. From the senior leader's perspective, video allowed for a better professional dialogue between the observer and observee.

The Line Manager

The line manager had opted to pilot and research the new performance management process by including VEO at each stage. He was allocated several members of staff for performance management and felt that the first element to focus on was the change in the way that lesson observation itself was being used as part of the process. He described this process of change as:

> a real cultural shift in the way you do lesson observation because rather than just a teacher putting on a performance which is: "I'll wheel out my greatest-ever lesson and do it three times a year" … you can't do that anymore with this because you actually say to the teacher "what am I going to focus on?" and suddenly the ownership's on the teacher rather than the observer.

In this extract, the line manager highlighted several of the problems with lesson observations. One is the sense that a lesson observation requires an all-singing, all-dancing showcase lesson. Various authors have reported on teachers swapping out the lesson they would have taught because it would not be 'exciting' enough for an 'outstanding' lesson observation (Webb 2006; Dixie 2011) as well as anecdotes about teachers refusing to 'play this game', preferring to teach as they normally would, regardless of what they perceived the consequences of this strategy might be. The line manager in the case study school has suggested that by incorporating the development goal into the observation process, the focus shifts to the aims and objectives of the lesson, and the changes in practice that the teacher seeks to make. Another issue alluded to is the validity of the one-off or standalone lesson as a snapshot of that teacher's usual practice (Coe 2014; O'Leary 2016). A full-time classroom teacher will teach hundreds of hours of lessons across a school year involving different subjects at primary school level and different year groups at secondary level, so the extent to which any isolated lesson is a reliable indicator of teaching quality has been a matter of much debate.

A Lesson Observation

One lesson observation recorded by the line manager in the middle of the performance management cycle, involved him sitting initially in the back corner of the classroom at an empty desk and using his tablet computer to pan and track the teacher's movements, and to focus occasionally on what nearby individuals and pairs of students were doing. At times during the lesson he would stand up and continue to record as he moved around the classroom. He used the pause facility to stop and start the recording. Early in the lesson video, the line manager can be heard asking a pair of students to talk him through the way they are responding to the set task. One of the students is hesitant about his response as he is not sure of the answer. In another, he asks a student to let him film the work the student has done so that he can share it with the teacher. In another segment, when students had moved into groups, the line manager visits each group and occasionally pans the room to gain an overview of what is happening. In another episode, he asks a group of students how they are finding the group work, eliciting a comment from one boy that he feels quite responsible as the spokesperson for the presentation put together by his group. Towards the end of the lesson, the line manager checks back with the student who had been unsure about his answer, to find that the student was now confident with his understanding.

The Teacher

Following on from the observation, the teacher was able to review the lesson video and reflect on how he felt the lesson had gone. He was able to see and hear his own input and actions, as well as to hear the comments from the students, and compare those to his own memory of the lesson and the students' outcomes from the lesson. He explained that it had taken him some time initially to move away from noticing his own actions in the lesson and begin to focus on the lesson itself and the students' learning, a common theme in using video for teacher learning (van Es and Sherin 2002; van Es 2012):

> What I found when I'd done it before is that I was just constantly looking at myself, picking out faults and working out what I would say too often: where I would stand, or how I would look. I started looking at how I viewed the lesson slightly differently as the project went on and viewed it more about how pupils were demonstrating their learning rather than what could I criticise about myself.

Using video in this way is an example of the teacher developing a more professional vision (Hidson 2019) as they learn to move beyond the initial self-consciousness and into the realm of evaluating what they can see of their practice. In this case, the teacher was able to assimilate the current lesson into their experiences with the class so far and engage in a dialogue with the observer to determine the next steps towards their goal. The goal this teacher had set for this academic year was around improving student recall of information between lessons and on assessments. The observer seeking and recording student voice had been a real benefit to the teacher:

> He would go and sit with the pupils: he would ask them for their opinions and it's interesting to hear their perspective on activities and sometimes you'll organize an activity in a certain way because you want to get something out of it and the pupils often recognize that and it was really quite rewarding when they would say how positively they viewed the lesson, what they were doing, what they were learning, and normally you never hear that … you never get that feedback.

It is interesting to note the extent of the teacher's positive response to both using video and to the new approach to using it as part of performance management. Far from exhibiting the reluctance and negativity discussed earlier in this chapter, the teacher's comments are focused on the professional benefits:

> We're going to do it again next year. We've moved towards this cycle of three observations. In the past we would have three observations which didn't really link together, so I found this year working with the same member of staff observing me

with the same class and then being able to watch it back and have those discussions together made a big difference to the quality of the lessons.

This teacher's positive response to 'shaping' his own professionalism (Evans 2011) suggests that growth is possible within the framework of performance management. This has been made possible by a leadership-led commitment to teacher development through performance management processes that include elements of peer observation, coaching and mentoring (Lofthouse et al. 2010) by the line manager. The ability of both parties to view the lesson and engage in dialogic reflection (Mann and Walsh 2016) about the way that the lesson activities showed the teacher actively working towards their goal is key to the process. The teacher could only play as active a role in the process because of the video recording. As the line manager said:

> The technology underpins the process and the process is obviously becoming a more reflective teacher-led process rather than a performance-enhanced top-down judgement process.

Observation that involves video is no longer a one-way process. Performance management carried out in the way this school has re-designed it can be seen as a dialogic process and very different to the one that was presented at the start of this chapter. It is now a process that can be seen through these examples as a process of continuous teacher development.

Conclusions

It is always interesting for educators to learn how other schools interpret and enact policies. As a reflective profession, teachers look to improve their practice and learn from others. In this chapter, we have sought to share the example of a school that has looked at the process of performance management in order to make it more meaningful and productive for its staff. Although the idea of CPD in relation to teacher appraisal is not new, and in fact is presented as an integral part of the legislation, in recent years it is fair to say that schools have been wary of moving away from some of the more restrictive policies that have been seen as necessary. This case study school has re-emphasized the importance of CPD in performance management and taken steps firstly to improve the process of lesson observation as part of performance management, and secondly, to improve the process of lesson observation by embracing video as a means to enhance the quality of lesson observation itself. Looking at the bigger picture of what other schools could take from this practice, there are three key conclusions for schools to consider in terms of using video-enhanced observation to develop their approach to CPD.

1. **Review and update school policies ready for implementation: identify where video-enhanced observation has potential in wider school practices**

A school's performance management or staff appraisal policy is one of several linked policies that needs to be reviewed to make sure that the school is in a position to implement VEO more fully in its work. Policies that relate to any aspect of teacher education and professional development are an obvious starting point: how the school works with beginning teachers on initial teacher education or school-centred training programmes or how they work with early career teachers and middle or senior leadership training, for example. These are areas where video-enhanced lesson observation can be factored into the school's vision for the way they want to work. Allied to that must be policies that relate to responsible technology use, suitable data protection and data storage policies, in keeping with current data protection and GDPR guidelines. Most importantly, school policies around child protection and safeguarding must be reviewed to incorporate the school's considered use of video in their normal ways of working. This will also be important in terms of developing the use of student voice in relation to video. A transparent approach to policy development that has been put before the school community's stakeholders must be the starting point for a school that intends to embrace video-enhanced observation.

2. **Provide training and support so that staff are empowered to use the technology**
   The successful implementation of VEO depends on staff being competent and confident enough to use the technology, which requires some initial time for training and incorporation into regular practice. As intuitive as the technology may be, staff still need time to learn how it works, and a plan to move from novice to expert over time. An initial training programme that can be followed up to ensure progress through the higher levels of practice is important.

3. **Model the practice that you wish to see over time**
   Moving beyond the technical training programme, staff should have access to opportunities to understand the kind of practice that the school wishes to develop in the longer term. If VEO is to be used routinely for lesson observations, then providing CPD on approaches to observation, feedback and dialogue is important. CPD that emphasizes the importance of peer support, coaching and mentoring will help to shape evidence-informed practice that makes the most of the reflective skills of the staff as they begin to see performance management and CPD as collaborative, community-driven opportunities for personal and professional development. Most important is the commitment to CPD as an iterative and supportive process, and the investment of time for the goals to come to fruition.

This chapter has incorporated perspectives from three different levels of school staff in one school involved the VEO Europa project. VEO did not simply substitute one kind of lesson observation for another; it helped to redefine the purpose and the outcome. For a school considering embedding VEO, it is helpful to visualize how the process has worked successfully in this context and to consider how it might be implemented through the classroom teacher, middle and senior leadership roles in their own school. This is especially important because it gives an insight into the importance of developing meaningful policies embedded in practice and from a position of improving the conditions that create good teaching and learning.

11

SETTVEO: Evidence-based Reflective Practice and Professional Development

Steve Walsh
Newcastle University, UK

Introduction

This chapter reports findings from a British Council-funded research project (SETTVEO) which looked at the use of technology-enhanced learning in a CPD (continuing professional development) context (Walsh 2019). The aim of the study was to provide English language teachers with appropriate tools and procedures to enable them to reflect on and improve their practice through the creation and use of the SETT tag set for the VEO app. This extended previous work, using the SETT (Self Evaluation of Teacher Talk) framework (Walsh 2006, 2011, 2013) and VEO (Video Enhanced Observation) app (Miller and Haines 2015). The central argument of the study was that reflective practice (RP) would be enhanced when reflections are evidence-based by giving teachers something to reflect *on* and something to reflect *with*.

In this chapter, the focus of reflection is classroom interaction, which underpins much of what is learnt in any classroom. Understandings of teaching and learning can be greatly enhanced through a detailed understanding of classroom interaction. Specifically, the aim was to help teachers, through reflections on their teaching, to enhance their Classroom Interactional Competence (CIC, Walsh 2013). In the SETTVEO project, and subsequent collective dialogue and reflection, an online international community of practice (CofP) was established, enabling participants to share and comment on examples of English language teaching around the world. The goal was to establish and evaluate a more dialogic, collaborative approach to RP.

The chapter is organized into five sections. In the first two sections, the key constructs underpinning the study are introduced: dialogic reflection and classroom interactional competence. The next two sections detail the methodology used and present some of the main findings. In the final section a brief conclusion is given.

Dialogic Reflection

Although RP has established itself as a 'ubiquitous presence in professional education and practice' (Mann and Walsh 2013: 296), it is probably fair to say that it is not being operationalized in systematic and evidence-based ways, nor do teachers have access to appropriate tools to help them reflect on their practice. Currently, there is a paucity of both data-led research on RP and data-led practice in RP; data is needed from the perspectives of both research and professional development. The argument in this chapter is that teachers' professional development will be greatly enhanced when they have evidence from their own context, when they are able to use that evidence to reflect and develop new practices, and when they have access to appropriate tools for doing reflection.

Much of the work on RP has focused on written forms of reflection. In the study reported here, the focus is on dialogic reflection (Mann and Walsh 2017), whereby professional development is enhanced through collaboration and dialogue with a colleague or critical friend. The claim is not so much that one form of reflection is in any way better than another, rather that there needs to be a rebalancing of written reflection – which tends to be solitary – towards something spoken, dialogic and collaborative.

Dialogic reflection (Walsh and Mann 2015; Mann and Walsh 2017) is a collaborative process of professional learning which entails interaction, discussion and debate with another professional. Dialogic reflection emphasizes learning (and professional development more broadly) as a social process whereby meanings and new understandings of complex phenomena are mediated by language. Dialogue allows meanings to be co-constructed, new understandings to emerge and professional learning to develop. Dialogic processes can either be intrapersonal or interpersonal (private or public, cf. Vygotsky 1978) entailing interactions between individuals or between an individual and an artefact or tool. It is a process which draws heavily on sociocultural theories of learning, which highlight the importance of language as a mediating tool and stress the value of social interaction in professional learning.

Dialogue facilitates understanding by allowing interactants space and support to express their ideas and arrive at new or different takes on a particular practice, issue or concern. Opportunities for reflection and learning are maximized when new concepts, or the meta-language used to realize them, can be both understood and verbalized. However, the centrality of speech to learning has another, more significant dimension in that consciousness, considered by Vygotsky as being central to learning, is developed through social interaction. Learners become more aware, through participation in social activity, of themselves as learners. Dialogic reflection may lead to deeper, longer-lasting professional development and can facilitate the appropriation of good practice.

Central to the notion of dialogic reflection are the various tools and artefacts which can be used as a catalyst (e.g. metaphors, critical incidents, video) and help promote more systematic and focused professional dialogue. Examples include the use of transcripts and recordings of classroom talk, though recent studies have advocated the need to move away from transcription on the basis that it is too time-consuming and not always representative of what 'really happens'. One alternative is the use of 'snapshot' lesson excerpts: short (5–7 minutes) recordings which are then analysed without transcription (see Walsh 2011).

In the next section, a summary is presented of the other central construct in this study: classroom interactional competence.

Classroom Interactional Competence

Classroom Interactional Competence (CIC) is defined as 'Teachers' and learners' ability to use interaction as a tool for mediating and assisting learning' (Walsh 2011: 130). It puts interaction firmly at the centre of teaching and learning and argues that by improving CIC, both teachers and learners will immediately improve learning and opportunities for learning. As discussed previously, the aim of the present study was to give teachers something to reflect *with* – presented in the previous section under dialogic reflection – and something to reflect *on*, discussed in this section under CIC.

The relevance of CIC is clear. If our aim as language educators is to promote dialogic, engaged and 'safe' classroom environments where learners are actively involved and feel free to contribute and take risks, we need to study the interactions which take place and learn from them. The suggestion here is that we need to acquire a fine-grained understanding of what constitutes classroom interactional competence and how it might be achieved. This can only be accomplished by using data from our own context; the starting point has to be evidence from the classroom in the form of a video- or audio-recording, self- or peer-observation. Only by starting to describe interactional processes can we begin to understand in some detail our local context. Not only will such an understanding result in more engaged and dynamic interactions in classrooms, it will also enhance learning.

While it is true to say that CIC is highly context-specific, not just to the particular class, but to a specific moment in the discourse, there are a number of features of CIC which are common to all contexts. First, teachers may demonstrate CIC through their ability to use language which is both convergent to the pedagogic goal of the moment and appropriate to the learners' language use and pedagogic goals must work together. Essentially, this entails an understanding of the interactional strategies which are appropriate to teaching goals and which are adjusted in relation to the co-construction of meaning and the unfolding agenda of a lesson. This position assumes that pedagogic goals and the language used to achieve them are inextricably intertwined and constantly being re-adjusted (see Walsh 2003; Seedhouse 2004).

Secondly, CIC facilitates interactional space: learners need space for learning to participate in the discourse, to contribute to class conversations and to receive feedback on their contributions. In short, CIC creates 'space for learning' (Walsh and Li 2013). There are a number of ways in which space for learning can be maximized. These include increased wait-time, by resisting the temptation to 'fill silence' (by reducing teacher echo), by promoting extended learner turns and by allowing planning time. By affording learners space, they are better able to contribute to the process of co-constructing meanings – something which lies at the very heart of learning through interaction.

170 *Video Enhanced Observation for Language Teaching*

Thirdly, CIC entails teachers *shaping* learner contributions. Shaping involves taking a learner response and doing something with it rather than simply accepting it. For example, a response may be paraphrased, using slightly different vocabulary or grammatical structures; it may be summarized or extended in some way; a response may require scaffolding so that learners are assisted in saying what they really mean; it may be recast: 'handed back' to the learner but with some small changes included. By shaping learner contributions and by helping learners to really articulate what they mean, teachers are performing a more central role in the interaction, while, at the same time, maintaining a student-centred, decentralized approach to teaching.

Having discussed the key theoretical constructs which informed this research project, the methodology used will now be described.

Methodology

In the ELTRA study, teachers were encouraged to collect evidence through the SETTVEO app and then use that evidence to both reflect on current practice and improve their CIC. The VEO app was developed by teacher educators at Newcastle University and allows users to record and tag videos which can be uploaded and saved to a portal. By reviewing short video extracts, teachers are able to categorize a range of interactional features, consider their appropriateness in relation to their pedagogic goals and evaluate each teaching episode. The tags allow the user to jump to the exact instance within the video, presenting a rich view of action, interaction and context that can be shared for further analysis and evaluation.

VEO has been trialled in numerous geographical locations and educational contexts across the globe for various purposes, including improving initial teacher education in the UK and Finland; enabling ongoing teacher CPD in the United States, China and Ghana; researching university-level medical education; and evaluating pupil understanding of taught concepts. The advantages that VEO brings to analysing complex situations make it highly appropriate for studying interaction, where multiple perspectives are possible and where relevant frameworks can clarify and enhance its understanding.

The SETT framework has been used in a range of educational settings since its publication in 2006 and further development in 2011 and 2013. In short, the framework has been used extensively to promote awareness and understanding of the role of interaction in class-based learning and to help teachers improve their practices. SETT comprises four classroom micro-contexts (called *modes*) and fourteen interactional features (called *interactures*). Classroom discourse is portrayed as a series of complex and inter-related micro-contexts or modes, where meanings are co-constructed by teachers and learners and where learning occurs through the ensuing talk of teachers and learners (Walsh 2013).

In the current study, SETT and VEO were combined to help teachers profile their interactions, improve their CIC and enhance learning and learning opportunity. From the original SETT framework, all four modes and eight of the fourteen interactures were included in the SETTVEO tag set (see screenshot below). The modes appear across the bottom of the interface, while the interactures are organized down each

Figure 11.1 Screenshot of the SETTVEO tagset.

side. While watching the playback of a video, participants simply select which mode and which interactures are being observed at any given moment.

By sharing their reflections in an international online community of practice, it was possible to develop a global network of reflections, with teachers identifying and talking about common problems and issues in a range of English language contexts. Online communities were formed between teachers sharing videos of interactions, evaluated according to the SETT framework.

The study was guided by the following research questions:

1. How do VEO and SETT networks promote evidence-based reflection?
2. To what extent are teachers able to improve their Classroom Interactional Competence through the use of SETTVEO?
3. What evidence is there that the process of using SETTVEO, combined with reflection and online discussion, results in more dialogic, engaged learning environments?

Using outcomes and participants from a recent research project, the present study recruited twenty-four English language teachers working in universities in four countries (Spain, Turkey, Chile and Thailand). Over a twelve-month period, data were collected in three phases:

Phase 1. Baseline data were collected to include a short, video-recorded lesson segment of each teacher plus a short reflective commentary on that segment and a follow-up online interview with the research team. In this phase, the aim was to provide an overview of teachers' professional practices in each of the four contexts.

Phase 2. In the second phase of the study, participating teachers each made four 'snapshot' recordings of their teaching (around 10 minutes per recording). Online training in the use of SETTVEO was provided and each recording was then

172   *Video Enhanced Observation for Language Teaching*

reviewed and evaluated using the app. The recordings and reflective commentaries were uploaded to the VEO platform and made available to all participants for further dialogue and discussion.

Phase 3. In the final phase of the study, participating teachers took part in online focus groups and individual interviews to evaluate the extent to which their reflective practices had changed and to consider any changes in CIC.

Data were analysed using multiple methods, comprising:

1. Profiles of each teacher's classroom practices were created using the VEO software and SETT tag set. This provided detailed qualitative and quantitative information about teachers' interactional practices, use of language, levels of learner involvement, use of language in relation to pedagogic goals and so on.
2. Conversation analysis was used to transcribe and analyse a sample of the video-recorded classroom data.
3. Thematic analysis was used to analyse focus group and interview data.
4. Reflective commentaries from teachers' interactions in the online community, together with their posts, were analysed using thematic content analysis.

Findings

Owing to limitations of space, findings will be presented under the main thematic categories emerging from the data.

Theme 1: Developing CIC

One of the key questions posed in this study was the second research question (see above), which asked if and by how much teachers could improve their CIC. A number of teachers made comments on this in their reflections. Teacher A, below, for example, talks about her elicitation strategies and gives reasons for her particular use of display or referential questions, two of the tags used in the SETT tag set.

Extract 1

I asked mostly display questions to help them do brainstorming about the topics and to make most of the students be able to speak about the topics. At the beginning I needed to ask some referential questions (00.20) to refer to the exercises we did in our former lessons. After watching myself in the video I saw that I repeated the same phrases several times, but I think this helped them speak better and self-confidently because they were elementary level students and needed to hear too many repetitions and examples. Firstly, I used content feedback to emphasize how they would find relevant supporting ideas for the topics we discussed, how they would agree/disagree with each other, how they would organize their ideas and list them. Secondly, I mostly preferred form-focused feedback because they were in need of hearing correct forms and learning how to make correct sentences.

(Teacher A)

Of interest in this extract is the extent to which Teacher A uses an appropriate metalanguage to describe her practices – she talks about questions types and (indirectly) teacher echo ('I repeated the same phrases several times'). She goes on to include two additional interactures: content feedback and form-focused feedback. It is also of interest to note that she is able to rationalize her use of particular interactional features which were of help and support to her students.

Indications of CIC include an ability to use an appropriate metalanguage and to be able to justify 'online decision making' (Walsh 2013) – both of which are evidenced by this teacher in her reflective commentary. She refers to five of the eight interactional features included in the app and is able to both justify her interactional decisions and explain how level is an important determiner of these practices.

An important feature of the VEO app is the tagging function, which allows users to 'tag' (i.e. mark) specific features of their interactions and then review these features later. The software then prepares a statistical breakdown showing how features are used, which ones occur most frequently and how this affected the interaction. In extract 2, Teacher C is talking about her teacher echo, a feature which many teachers comment on (in one study (Walsh 2006) it was referred to as a teacher's 'bete noire'!).

Extract 2

Looking at the tagging session report, I observed that the teacher echo was excessive to my standards. It made me realize that I should put an effort to reduce it, because I found it annoying to watch myself saying so many 'oks', 'alrights'. The amount of display questions on the report was high at 40%, compared to the referential questions at 15%. The amount of content feedback and seeking clarification were quite similar at approximately 15%. The lowest rate was form focused feedback with only about 3%. Although I was a bit disappointed at myself for making the tagging session a bit long because of the wait times for the reading and watching the videos, the extended wait time was quite low in the report, with only 5%.

(Teacher C)

Here, Teacher C focuses on her excessive use of discourse markers (sometimes referred to as transition markers). In fact, these tokens perform a very important function in classroom discourse, acting almost like punctuation marks and helping students stay focused and avoid becoming lost in the interaction (see, for example, Breen 1998).

Teacher C then goes on to look at the statistical breakdown of specific features, making a valid comparison between display and referential questions – the former dominate most classroom talk, while teachers often miss opportunities to ask genuine, or referential questions. Again, she demonstrates a high level of CIC through her ability to use an appropriate metalanguage and justify her actions, even being quite critical of her decisions at times.

174   *Video Enhanced Observation for Language Teaching*

Research has shown (see, for example, Carless 2019) that one of the most important ways in which learning in the classroom can be influenced is through the ways in which teachers handle feedback. Feedback, almost without exception, is more likely to affect learning or learning potential than almost any other practice. The ways in which teachers scaffold, shape, clarify, confirm, correct, paraphrase learner responses are vital; it is perhaps one of the hallmarks of effective teaching and a key indicator of CIC.

In extract 3, we witness Teacher G talking about the lack of responses from her students and then commenting on her own feedback.

Extract 3

I felt happy even when I heard a simple one-to-two-word utterances from my students. After watching the video, I saw that I did not provide much feedback; still I could see that some of my reactions could be considered as content feedback.

(Teacher G)

It is not apparent in this comment whether the teacher is attributing the short responses from her students to her absence of detailed feedback; this could certainly be one possible interpretation. The same is true of her comment about content feedback; she demonstrates a high level of awareness (from the video-viewing) of the importance and need for feedback – especially feedback which is focused on the message rather than the language, tagged as 'content feedback' in the app. The value of replaying key features, such as examples of content feedback, through the tagging function is highlighted in this extract: teachers need appropriate tools and the space to reflect and comment on their actions in order to enhance understandings of their practice.

Theme 2: Changes to Practice and Self-awareness

In a project which focuses on RP, there is clearly an interest to note any changes to practice or, rather, if any changes to practice were reported. Here, three extracts have been selected to exemplify some of the changes reported by participating teachers.

The message in extract 4 could not be clearer: the main goal of English Language Education (ELE) is to help students learn to speak the language; again, the emphasis is very much on the students rather than on teacher performance (*the best way of creating self-sufficiency; the better they feel and learn*). One of the main advantages of tagging software like the VEO app is that, while the user may be focusing on their own use of language and interactional features (i.e. the teacher's), they cannot ignore what students are doing. Many of the comments in the data referred to the actions or engagement of learners; a further stage would be to try to explain these in relation to what was said by the teacher since one aspect of CIC is to understand how teacher-learner interaction is inextricably linked.

Extract 4

Speaking and helping them speak is the best way of creating self-sufficiency. The more they speak, the better they feel and learn.

(Teacher M)

The extent to which SETTVEO promoted a focus on learners is illustrated in the next extract. Teacher G in extract 5 focuses on task variety and the need to vary tasks more.

Extract 5

When it comes to the question 'What would I change If I taught the same lesson again?' It would definitely be task variety. I criticize myself about sticking to the same type of task, which can be really boring for unmotivated learners. As far as I observed in my class, due to some personal factors, lack of task variety and restricted time, not all the students talked about the topic which was not my expectation before the class. Had there been small pair or group works, students could have participated and been more productive. I could have distributed worksheets about famous people's life stories; therefore, they could have felt more inspired and orientated to learning more instinctively.

(Teacher G)

Teacher G is able to highlight the main problem or issue in her class (*not all the students talked about the topic*) and suggest a possible way forward: the use of pair/group work and a more interesting worksheet. Of interest, too, is the reference to 'learning more instinctively', which suggests that – for this teacher at least – certain task-types promote more 'instinctive' opportunities for learning. While this idea would need to be explored further with Teacher G, this extract highlights the extent to which a focus on speaking helps students to gain confidence and become more independent as learners.

In the final extract in this section, we learn how one of the teachers has developed through participating in the research project. Teacher A is concerned to highlight the importance of management in teaching, linking the importance of good management to a growth in confidence.

Extract 6

Moreover, my expectation of myself as an educator is that of a good teacher with many management tools. I have grown exponentially in my management skills throughout this experience and have gained a lot of confidence in my ability to improve further with each future classroom. I'm excited to grow and learn as a teacher for many years to come thanks to this experience. Teaching is definitely a 'learning process'.

(Teacher A)

She is very positive about her participation in the study; what is very encouraging is the fact that the SETTVEO project gave her a desire 'to grow and learn as a teacher'. Part of the sub-text of the project is that teachers need to acquire and develop skills which will allow them to make sense of their professional practice, to become researchers of their context and to become autonomous in their ability to change and develop. The comments of Teacher A suggest that this is indeed feasible and even desirable once the right conditions are in place.

In this study, participants were given an opportunity to put their teaching under the microscope and learn from the experience; it would not be inconceivable for such practices to become more widespread, especially with the exponential growth of video in ELTE. The next theme looks at the value of video in RP.

Theme 3: The Advantages of Video

To illustrate and extend the argument which concluded the last section, Theme 3 focuses on the advantages of video in teacher education and professional development, something which several teachers commented on. It is clear when reading the next extract that, for some of the participants at least, the use of video in teacher learning is of great benefit. Previous studies (see, for example, Mann and Walsh 2017; Mann 2018) have highlighted the use of video in ELTE and pointed to this medium as an important and progressive tool in future CPD.

Teacher B, with sixteen years' experience, emphasizes the value of self-observation as a means of understanding classroom dynamics and understanding student feelings and attitudes. Of importance in this observation is the fact that she seems to suggest that her own strengths and weaknesses can be gleaned by focusing on her learners, an acute and mature observation. Rather than 'blaming the learner', this teacher takes responsibility for her professional practice, acknowledging that while her understanding of teaching and learning can be developed through self-observation, a focus on her students will clearly highlight her strengths and weaknesses as a teacher.

Extract 7

I had an opportunity to reflect on my teaching as a teacher having sixteen years' experience considering my classroom video as a part of SETTVEO Project. During this period, I found a chance to make a self-observation which enabled me to be deeply aware of my classroom dynamics, students' attitudes and feelings during the class and as a matter of course, my strengths and weaknesses.

(Teacher G)

Theme 4: Use of Metaphors

Interestingly, some of the teachers in the study made use of metaphors in their evaluations. Metaphors in both English language education (ELE) and English language teacher education (ELTE) have been found to be a very powerful means of enhancing learning and helping learners deal with complex ideas or new knowledge (see, for example, Deignan 2005). Teacher B in extract 5 uses a nautical metaphor, comparing her classroom to a ship, with herself as the captain and her students as her crew. Sensitivity and learner-centredness are shown in her analogy; note, for example, the way in which she describes how she and her students learn from one another and, though one in their common goal, they are unique as individuals. This teacher provides a sense of coherence and cohesion in her account by using vocabulary items which belong to the same word family: *ship, flowing river, captain, journey, squad, route, destination*. While there is no reference to interaction, SETTVEO or the interactures, the extract below confirms that the video-playback has allowed this teacher to think more deeply about her practice and produce this very vivid metaphor.

Extract 8

I aimed to develop students' thinking and speaking skills, get a wide participation and ask them display questions in order to let them talk spontaneously. In this regard, I visualized my classroom as a ship on a flowing river in which we are talking about our ideas, experiences, dreams and learning from each other; me as a captain of the ship having more responsibility in the same journey; and my students as a squad whose members are unique with different backgrounds, but they follow the same route to reach their destination.

(Teacher B)

In the second metaphor example, presented below in extract 9, we witness Teacher D offering a rather negative critique of her lesson.

Extract 9

Basically, two skills, speaking and reading, were fostered during this short session, which started with a whole-class speaking and continued with a pre-reading task (matching interview questions with the responses). The tools and materials that were used in the class were only the textbook and the projector. The main challenge for me, as a teacher, was to activate and inspire my students to speak or at least to provide responses to my questions during the discussion. Therefore, I can use the following metaphors:
- Dead batteries for my students
- A far-fetched marathon for my lesson
- A poor swimmer for myself

Again, no reference is made to the app or its tagging function, but her reflections suggest that she felt somewhat despondent following the video-replay. Her choice of language to capture this episode (*dead batteries, a far-fetched marathon, a poor swimmer*) effectively describes the essential ingredients of any piece of teaching (teacher, students, materials), though her tone is clearly negative.

Perhaps the main rationale for including these metaphorical examples is to highlight the power of video in teacher education and to demonstrate its multifarious

178   *Video Enhanced Observation for Language Teaching*

uses (see above). In the examples presented here, teachers were free to choose their own metaphors to really express their feelings, to give us a genuine and honest sense of their teaching contexts and to help us understand the complexities of teaching and learning. Perhaps by focusing on the detail in their practice, these teachers were able to stand back and see what was really going on – surely something which we all need to do from time to time in our reflections.

Theme 5: Project Evaluation

The final section of analysis offers a brief evaluation of the study. Extracts 10 and 11 are from comments made by two of the four in-country co-ordinators who oversaw teacher recruitment, data collection, training, etc.

Extract 10 exemplifies some of the issues which can arise when conducting this kind of research. Apart from recruiting teachers in the first place, the main issue is retaining them, especially when they are employed on the kind of zero-hour contract described below.

Extract 10

Re SETTVEO, yes, before Xmas I contacted the teachers and asked them if they could work on their reflections. It was difficult to contact them as 1) out of 5 teachers, 4 have left the university and 2) Xmas, summer, other jobs, etc. I believe the main problem we had is that during data collection, they were soooo overwhelmed with teaching that it was impossible for them to do anything else really. That is the problem when teachers work without a contract … they teach in different places to make ends meet. Very common here … I think it's similar to 0 hr contract system in the UK. I was thinking that maybe we should include in the report that this is an issue regarding critical CALL in terms of the challenges we face in contexts where teachers are not given proper time for professional development. I was reading an article about how technology can sometimes complicate things. Perhaps the British Council would find this info useful for their actions regarding teacher education.

(Co-ordinator A (Sara))

As Co-ordinator A, Sara, points out, under such conditions, not only are teachers extremely busy and unable to focus on anything other than their teaching, rapid and high staff turnover is the norm. A project like this one becomes almost unmanageable if there is constant turnover of staff and participants keep changing. And yet, to fully appreciate professional issues and engage in CPD-focused research, we need more longitudinal studies, which, in turn, clearly depend on a constant and unchanging group of participants. Sara quite rightly comments on this in her evaluation. Her second point is perhaps even more telling: the use of technology can actually add to complications and make projects even more difficult to manage. This was certainly the case in the present study – China was forced to withdraw owing to technical issues.

Other studies (see, for example, Li 2008) have identified similar issues with integrating and using technology in educational settings.

To end on an upbeat note, consider extract 11, which comments on some of the issues raised by participants when viewing themselves on video for the first time. Of interest here is the value – once the initial shock of seeing and hearing oneself on camera wears off – of video in affirming and strengthening beliefs about teaching. And this is a valid and important point: through self-observation, we are not always seeking to change or develop; rather, we are looking to be reassured that our practice is appropriate, that we are decent teachers and that our students actually learn something. To that end, the SETTVEO project achieved its goals.

Extract 11

SETTVEO has been an opportunity for participant instructors to raise awareness of what they have employed in their classes. The participants from time to time informed me about the issues which led to raise their awareness of their own experience inside a real classroom context. For example, one of them stated that she had not heard her voice like this in the classroom and it was so strange for her. Also, another participant told me that she had not thought she repeated the same information that much inside the classroom. Besides, it really strengthens the participants' beliefs and ideas about what they are employing inside the classroom as well as their use of the classroom discourse. As a conclusion, SETTVEO is both a challenge and a change for all of us. The project is also a fun and a learning process for us and it contributes into our understanding of teaching–learning process with a genuine classroom-based data.

(Co-ordinator C, Secil)

Conclusions

To conclude this chapter, a brief evaluation is offered of the SETTVEO project as well as consideration of future directions for this kind of research. To recap, the aim of the study was to provide English language teachers with appropriate tools and procedures to enable them to reflect on and improve their practice through the creation and use of the SETT tag set. From the data presented here, there is evidence to suggest that the use of SETTVEO does indeed result in reflections which are evidence-based and informed by interactional data. There is also evidence highlighting the value of the practices and procedures used in the study as a means of developing CIC; by logical extension, it would be fair to claim that the teachers made comments concerning the extent to which their classes had become more engaged and more dialogic.

A clear finding from this small-scale study is that video has an important part to play in ELTE. Recent studies (see, for example, Mann 2018) confirm the value of video in mediating understandings of teaching and in unpacking the complexities of that process. By giving teachers a tool and focus, reflection becomes extremely 'doable' and useful. Note too that relatively short 'snapshot' recordings have value in heightening awareness and deepening understandings; given an appropriate tool and a clear focus, there is no need for wholesale transcription of lessons. Put simply, video creates opportunities for professional development in a relatively short space of time and without an enormous investment of energy.

Future studies would be well-advised to focus on this approach by using short extracts, a clear focus and by employing a mediating tool like the VEO app. There is also much to be learned through research projects which have a longitudinal dimension, something which was not feasible in the present study. One of the most important aspects of the use of video in teacher education is that it quickly, easily and inexpensively provides evidence on which to reflect. Video can be replayed to allow time for greater reflection and it serves as a historical record of a teacher's professional development over time. Few tools offer so many advantages and enable teachers to discuss their teaching so easily. In sum, video is the *sine qua non* of evidence-based reflection.

A second feature of the present study was its focus on CIC, something which has been heralded for some time now as a potential 'third strand' in ELTE programmes. While most teacher education courses around the world highlight the importance of subject knowledge and pedagogical skills as key strands, hardly any emphasize an understanding of interaction. If we accept that interaction is where the action is, the place to look for evidence of learning, then surely it warrants closer scrutiny. Advances in technology and the widespread use of video make this so much easier to achieve. By making CIC a key feature of ELTE programmes, course providers would be taking an important step in highlighting the need for a detailed understanding of interaction.

The final element of the present study was its focus on dialogic reflection. The VEO app with SETT tag set enabled short recordings to be made, shared in a CoP and discussed. The potential from what was essentially a small-scale study is enormous; it would not be difficult, for example, to extend the present project to something much bigger, culminating in an international corpus of professional practice comprising video recordings and reflections from every corner of the globe. The potential to offer such a product is with us now; there are clearly enormous advantages in developing an online resource through which teachers comment on and compare English teaching practices around the world. Not only would such a resource promote greater understandings of teaching and learning, it would result in closer and deeper understandings of context, surely one of the most important elements in English language education.

12

Changing Error Correction Practice over Three Lessons Using an Individualized Video Enhanced Observation Tagset on a Teacher Training Course

Paul Seedhouse and Alison Whelan
Newcastle University, UK

Introduction

In this chapter, we focus on an individual case study of development in which a teacher has an individualized VEO tag set created to help her with her teaching on an in-service teacher training course. AA is an experienced teacher of English to speakers of other languages (TESOL). At the time of this study (2016–17), she had been teaching for thirteen years and held BA and PGCE qualifications. AA was selected for a case study as a good example of the use of VEO for self-directed CPD and of how VEO can be used when writing assignments for professional qualifications. This case study also provides an example of how a tag set was developed in order to help a teacher with a teacher training qualification. At the time of the study, she was taking the Cambridge DELTA course (Diploma in Teaching English to Speakers of Other Languages) – a postgraduate-level qualification http://www.cambridgeenglish.org/teaching-english/teaching-qualifications/delta/, which is open to experienced teachers in the proficient to expert stages on the Cambridge English Teaching Framework. In order to complete the second module of the course, AA needed to compile a portfolio of coursework, including written assignments and assessed teaching practice. AA elected to use VEO for self-recording of lessons in order to develop her practice in line with feedback received on diagnostic observation undertaken by her DELTA tutor. The other reasons for this being an ideal case study are that: the study is longitudinal, looking at three lessons over seven months; for the qualification, AA had to identify an aspect of her practice which needed improving and then produce evidence of improvement, which is clearly shown in the data.

Literature Review

In this chapter, we propose the argument that careful, theory-based tag set design can deliver effective change in an in-service context. To understand this more fully, we must look at previous research on the use of video in teacher training programmes, and how this can support the development of reflective practice and bridge a gap between theory and practice.

It is imperative that trainee teachers in all fields learn to apply knowledge acquired from pedagogical theory and from contexts of practice (Hatton and Smith 1995, in Ajayi 2016: 80). The Cambridge DELTA handbook for tutors and candidates requires that DELTA trainees have 'a sophisticated understanding of language–learning concepts' and demonstrate this consistently when planning and teaching (p5). Smyth's (1989) research found that trainees can struggle to develop a critical perspective on their teaching and 'articulate, critique, and culturally locate principles about their own teaching' (Smyth 1989: 5). This critical engagement with theory and the ability to apply this to practice is a marker of becoming a reflective practitioner, as originally defined by Dewey (1933) and Schön (1983) – in other words, 'learning through and from experience towards gaining new insights of self and practice' (Finlay 2008).

The use of video observation may 'bridge the gap between theory and practice and support pre-service teachers' attempt to apply what they have learned at the university in actual classroom lessons' (Blomberg et al. 2013: 93, in Ajayi 2016: 79). Larrivee (2000) suggests that trainees become reflective practitioners when they are able to modify their practice to the teaching context and develop new strategies (p87). AA's use of VEO for self-observation and reflection is therefore supporting her development as a reflective practitioner. She was able to apply her theoretical knowledge of self-correction when watching her video recording, modifying her subsequent practice and therefore demonstrating her developing reflection and insight.

The DELTA course demands that a pre-service teacher 'consistently reflects critically, observes other colleagues' and 'is highly aware of own strengths and weaknesses' (p5). In his 1989 research, Smyth identified four levels of reflection, defined as firstly describing and explaining concrete teaching events; secondly, informing practice with 'theories-in-use'; thirdly, confronting assumptions and beliefs about teaching by situating theory and practice in a broader context; and fourthly, reconstructing their ideas about teaching (p6).

This echoes Schön's (1987) concept of becoming a reflective practitioner and his identification of reflection-in-action and reflection-on-action, as discussed by Calandra et al. (2006: 137). Reflection-on-action, whereby teachers can 'look beyond the "technical" aspects of teaching to questioning their knowledge and assumptions' (Van Manen 1977; Gay and Kirland 2003) (p137), is enabled by the use of video observation. Teachers have the time and space to 'reflect more deeply, think more widely, and link critical events in the classroom to the broader principles of teaching' (Calandra et al. 2006: 137). Video observation can also provide opportunities to relate theory to classroom practice (Jacobs et al. 2009; Gaudin and Chaliès 2015), as a teacher can observe their practice from a new perspective and identify critical incidents and

Changing Error Correction Practice on a Teacher Training Course 183

details which were unnoticed or which they were unable to reflect on more deeply during the lesson (Marsh and Mitchell 2014, in Gröschner et al. 2018: 225).

Being able to revisit and review their own teaching using the VEO app means that trainee teachers engage in critical reflection and self-assessment, which can improve teacher quality through continual self-improvement and develop skills in self-evaluation and problem solving (Leitch and Day 2000; Cornish and Jenkins 2012). Indeed, Parsons (2005) suggests that trainees who fail in their school practice may be 'unable to identify areas of their practice that require improvement, continually repeating their mistakes' (in Coffey 2014: 87). Engaging in self-observation helps the trainee become 'uniquely capable of accounting for why things went the way they did' (Nunan 1996, in Stillwell 2009: 357). In AA's case, the use of VEO allows her to observe her own practice and identify her own areas for improvement. More specifically, using a bespoke tag set means that she can focus on key areas for development and reflect particularly on critical incidents during the lesson, applying her theoretical knowledge of self-correction in order to modify her practice in subsequent lessons.

Over the past decade, the use of video for self and peer observation has become more prevalent in classrooms. McFadden et al.'s (2014) work into early career science teachers' use of a digital video annotation tool for self-reflection looked at research developments in the field including guidelines in using video annotation software (Rich and Tripp 2011) and the use of video for reflection during teachers' induction period (Martin and Siry 2012). Ajayi (2016) claimed that 'classroom video has become crucially important to changes in teacher education (TE) as governments and the public continue to demand accountability, program accreditation, and effectiveness' (p80). Research has shown the various benefits to using video observation in its guise as both a technical tool and an aid to promote discussion, reflection and analysis of practice (Lofthouse and Birmingham 2010: 5). The latter authors studied trainee teachers using video observation as part of a coaching programme and found that: 89 per cent of them reported a positive impact on the way they reflected on their practice; 80 per cent claimed that video had improved their ability to pick out critical incidents and characteristics in their practice; 78 per cent said that the use of video enabled them to see their own teaching from a different perspective (ibid.: 8).

Whereas an observer can be an invasive presence in the room for the teacher (Master 1983, in Stillwell 2009: 356), video observation helps develop the teacher's ability to 'notice' the teaching and learning taking place in their own classroom, and therefore they are able to make more evidence-based observations and evaluations about it (Sherin and Van Es 2005, in Coffey 2014: 88–9). Video observation is therefore both a technical tool and a psychological tool. Lofthouse and Birmingham (2010) cite Kozulin's (1998) observation of Vygotsky's distinction between these: 'The most essential feature distinguishing the psychological tool from the technical tool, is that it directs the mind and behaviour whereas the technical tool ... is directed towards producing one or other set of changes in the object itself' (p5). A stronger sense of self-efficacy (Bandura 1977, 1997; Pietsch et al. 2003) can develop from this self-evaluation and its subsequent action. This encapsulates the initial premise of VEO: the creators Haines and Miller (2017) wanted to 'encourage and enable teachers to work together to

184   *Video Enhanced Observation for Language Teaching*

identify and gather evidence of their own good and developing practice', to allow them to 'illustrate their progress over time, identify their own professional development needs, undertake action and illustrate impact, leading to greater ownership' (p134). In this chapter, we aim to show that AA's use of VEO and specifically her use of an individualized DELTA tag set allow her to make progress over a series of three lessons by identifying her professional needs (improvement in self-correction) and taking greater ownership of her development through self-reflection and self-evaluation. The study illustrates how teachers apply theory to practice, how reflection can aid development, and how video can support the reflection and evaluation process. The following section explains how an individualized tag set was developed in order to help this teacher deliver effective change and progress in their teacher training qualification lessons.

Research Context

AA was teaching English to classes of adult speakers of other languages at a community-based satellite centre of an urban college of Further Education in the North East of England. The classes were held weekly at 6 pm for two hours. Classes consisted of up to fifteen adult learners in a flexible, modern classroom with an internet-linked computer and interactive whiteboard. Rapid turnover of staff and changing responsibilities meant that VEO was not implemented in a systematic way at the college and was offered as an option for staff to pursue for CPD, which AA decided to take up.

This study uses a mixed methods approach. The approach to analysis of three lessons of L2 classroom interaction is conversation analysis (CA) (Seedhouse 2004). The other sources of data are: an interview with AA; reflections on the project written by AA; written assignments produced by AA as part of the DELTA course; the customized DELTA tag set; the statistics generated by VEO for the three lessons; documentation relating to DELTA. Data has been collected and analysed using a case study approach. Case studies are widely used in educational research, particularly that exploring teacher training and professional development, as the researcher can undertake a more in-depth examination of the chosen teacher's progress, the problems they encounter and the pedagogical strategies they employ. There are several advantages to using a case study approach in this piece of research. Firstly, unpacking a participant's narrative can provide rich data which can help generate new ideas and develop a clearer understanding of a particular phenomenon. In his essay on the misunderstandings associated with case study research, Flyvberg (2006) cites Mattingly (1991: 237), who states that 'narratives not only give meaningful form to experiences we have already lived through. They also provide us a forward glance, helping us to anticipate situations even before we encounter them, allowing us to envision alternative futures' (p25). This means, therefore, that a case study narrative enquiry develops an interpretation of an unfolding phenomenon from the perspective of the participant – in this case, AA – rather than beginning with a theoretical hypothesis. Secondly, the collection and analysis of the data is often conducted within the context of its use (Yin 1984, in Zainal 2007: 4). Thirdly, the depth and detail of the qualitative case study data can help to explain the complexities of real-life situations and environments (Zainal 2007: 4). This makes a case study approach ideal in this context, as the data is collected in the classroom in a real-life situation, allowing AA and the researcher involved to generalize the results and generate modifications to AA's subsequent practice based on her observed experience.

The interactional nature of teaching means that it is impossible to predict exactly how the lesson will unfold. Teachers are 'active, thinking decision-makers who make instructional choices by drawing on complex, practically-oriented, personalized, and context-sensitive networks of knowledge, thoughts, and beliefs' (Borg 2003: 81), while learners are individuals and therefore each interactional discourse between teacher and student is unique. Hamilton and Corbitt-Whittier (2013) refer to Whitehead (1989) who in both his individual work and his work with McNiff (2009) discussed the importance of documenting the unique, personal journey of a teacher in a classroom. These journeys, he maintained, were not solely about the creation of theory and knowledge, but about the experiences, values and reflections being recounted by each individual and the educational theories they embodied. The interactional journey undertaken by a teacher with their student will lead to complex learning opportunities on both sides, and though each case is unique, there are common threads which can be unpacked and linked to educational theory and teacher training criteria. The case of AA is examined through the lens of the DELTA handbook criteria and her progress as a teacher trainee, but the extracted theories of self-directed CPD and the importance of reflection will resonate with both trainee and experienced teachers in all areas of education.

The VEO Story

AA was recruited to the study through initial contact with the college of Further Education. Involvement in the VEO Europa project was optional and she attended two VEO training sessions. She worked with the Newcastle University RA Liz Hidson, who wrote an individualized tag set to match her identified needs based on DELTA feedback from her tutor. This was intended to allow her to focus on these areas, with the video providing both evidence of progress and material for reflection, which could feed into assignments.

Three lessons were video recorded. In her first video session, the lesson was recorded from start to finish by researcher Liz Hidson with no live tagging. Review and reflection took place independently afterwards. In her second video, Liz Hidson used the DELTA tag set to identify key episodes in the lesson. AA reviewed these tags independently afterwards. In the third video Liz Hidson used the same tag set.

In this case it was clear that professional development was supported by VEO in that:

- VEO was used for self-directed CPD
- Usage was mapped to qualification assessment criteria
- AA was able to review her own teaching in light of tutor feedback

186   *Video Enhanced Observation for Language Teaching*

- AA was able to use reflections as part of her portfolio of evidence for the qualification
- Lessons were recorded, then reviewed, feeding into both teaching and assignment

The main points and issues observed in relation to AA were that she showed willingness to be observed and engage in reflection with no obvious signs of discomfort at being observed. She was hindered by lack of institutional access to iPad or other mobile device. She cited lack of time to devote to developing VEO skills and lack of technology as issues. The varied locations for teaching (different campuses) reduced capacity.

The Customized DELTA Tag Set

This case study provides an example of how an individualized tag set was developed in order to help a teacher with a teacher training qualification. The DELTA syllabus states that successful candidates will:

7.1 Review and develop their own practice in the light of data from their own and others' experience and from specific theories of language, language learning and learning theory

7.2 Reflect critically on their own beliefs about learning and teaching and how these influence their approach to teaching

7.3 Reflect on feedback received from learners, colleagues, tutors and managers and how this is used for their own development as a teacher

The tag set was intended to allow the teacher to develop these skills and to focus on specific areas of development. Moreover, the tag set was designed to help AA focus on specific areas for development. As AA put it in her interview: 'I had a diagnostic observation by my DELTA tutor and he pointed out some areas for development and then in response to that Liz created some tags.' The tag set which was developed is shown below.

The tag set features many options for teacher feedback, in line with the identified focus. The tag set enables noting of:

- Explicit explanation of language rules/vocabulary
- Feedback on content
- Feedback on language accuracy
- Dealing with students' language queries in the session
- Opportunities for learners to record new vocabulary
- Contextualized/meaningful language practice

Changing Error Correction Practice on a Teacher Training Course

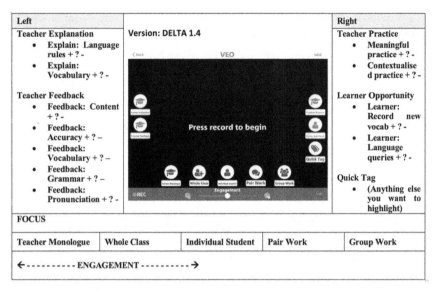

Figure 12.1 The DELTA tagset.

Error Correction: The Specific Area for Development

The teacher had three lessons recorded over a period of about seven months and the tag set customization facility of the VEO app proved useful in enabling the development of the targeted DELTA skills. The following points of development were noted:

AA noted in her action plan that she needed to develop in the areas of correction and creating opportunities for meaningful language practice, providing strategies for achieving this. These two areas might initially be thought to have the potential to work against each other, in that correction typically focuses on errors of linguistic form. By contrast 'meaningful language practice' might imply that meaning and fluency would be prioritized, with linguistic errors being allowed to pass. The customized tag set above incorporates both of the above areas by having tags on 'feedback – content' and 'feedback – accuracy' as well as 'teacher practice – meaningful practice'.

In this chapter, we focus specifically on the development of AA's correction practices in the three lessons. In her DELTA professional development assignment, AA wrote

> I do not correct enough, or make it explicit enough. The belief underlying this is that too much correction will make learners reluctant to speak. This is based on experience of working with a lot of learners who lack confidence ... Not correcting my current elementary learners and not being explicit enough about this is not helping them to form and re-form rules about language ... Summary of key weaknesses ... Lack of explicit correction.

188   *Video Enhanced Observation for Language Teaching*

In her action plan for the DELTA professional development assignment, AA wrote that she would develop in the area of correction in three ways:

- By reading current research on effective correction methods in language learning/ teaching in ELT Journal/English Teaching Professional as well as extracts of these books: Correction (Bartram and Walton 1991); Mistakes and Correction (Edge 1990).
- By identifying and evaluating techniques peers use and trialling at least two new methods in my own lessons and reflecting on this.
- By asking learners how/when they like to be corrected.

Error correction is one of the key practices undertaken by L2 teachers and has a key role in the processes of language learning. As such, error correction is a key component of teaching practices which are assessed on teacher training programmes such as DELTA. Research has explored the different aspects of error correction, often focusing on how the teacher initiates and undertakes the error correction process. Lyster and Ranta (1997) identified the following error correction techniques which are at the disposal of teachers: explicit correction, recasts, clarification requests, metalinguistic feedback, elicitation and repetition. Of these, indirect error correction methods (e.g. clarification request, elicitation or repetition) allow the student to be more proactive in the correction process. Ellis (2010) looked at how students often expect the teacher to correct, and how self-correction is less likely without basic knowledge of the language being used. Teachers may therefore attempt to elicit self-correction, but resort to a more direct teacher correction method if this fails. Li (2014) cites Lantolf (2000), who suggests a 'prompt-then-provide approach', supported by Sociocultural Theory, is the most effective, by which he means that support should be provided only when necessary, and after the student has attempted to self-correct without excessive direct feedback.

Lyster and Ranta (1997) found that following the repair exchange, 'teachers often seize the moment to reinforce the correct form before proceeding to topic continuation by making short statements of approval such as, "Yes!," "That's it!," and "Bravo!" or by repeating the student's corrected utterance' (p51). This reinforcement often also includes metalinguistic information to enable the student to better understand the repair. Teachers therefore undertake a repair sequence and close the sequence with appropriate positive reinforcement before moving on.

However, in the fast-moving dynamic of a lesson, a teacher may struggle to evaluate and reflect on a repair sequence as it occurs, instead reacting to the errors instinctively. Hedge (2000: 289, in Li 2014: 197) suggests that 'teachers should respond to "errors", which are due to a lack of knowledge about a linguistic item, rather than "mistakes", which are non-systematic and occur as a result of factors such as fatigue', but points out that this is easier said than done during spontaneous classroom discourse. Being able to examine a lesson using video after the event (Schön's reflection-on-action 1983) is an invaluable opportunity for a teacher to see the whole repair sequence and begin to understand why they reacted as they did, the interaction which took place between teacher and student, and how this could be modified and improved.

Changing Error Correction Practice on a Teacher Training Course

189

Evidence of Development: Analysis of Interaction in the Three Lessons

We now analyse the interactional evidence of development by using a CA approach with extracts from the three lessons. In this section we use some of the terminology of CA to explain how the error correction is managed in interactional terms. It is important to understand the different trajectories of repair. Initiation and performance of correction can be undertaken by self or others, so a variety of trajectories are possible. We can distinguish self-initiated repair (I prompt repair of the trouble source) from other-initiated repair (somebody else notices the trouble and initiates repair). Self-repair (I carry out repair myself) must also be distinguished from other-repair (somebody else carries out repair on the trouble source). There are therefore normally four repair trajectories, which involve different combinations of the initiation and performance of repair:

- Self-initiated self-repair
- Self-initiated other-repair
- Other-initiated self-repair
- Other-initiated other-repair

In the first video, there is evidence of problematic sequences involving correction for accuracy of language forms:

Lesson 1

Extract 1
```
1    T:    yeah (1.3) °what can you remember about the motorbike°
2          (0.4)
3    L1:   uhh ahh (1.0) drived a motorbike
4    T:    good drive or:?
5    LL:   [(unclear)
6    L1:   [ no
7          (0.7)
8    T:    do you drive a motorbike.
9    L4:   no no
10   T:    wha- what would you say L4 (0.7) [you
11   L4:                                    [i'm not driving a motorbike=
12   T:    =no do we say drive different word (.) not drive a motorbike.
13         (0.7) what do you say for [drive
14   L4:                              [ehh
15         (0.4)
16   T:    a bike
17         (1.2)
18   L4:   not drive
19   T:    ss: (2.3) ruh- (.) ra-
20         (5.0)
21   L1:   this is beginning letter(unclear)
22         (0.7)
23   T:    ri::(0.5) rrr ((T writes R, then I on the board))
24         (2.7)
25   L1:   ride
26   T:    RIDE brilliant L1 well done ride well done
```

Here the error of collocation and tense: 'drive a bicycle' rather than 'rode' in line 3 is not corrected until line 26 and even then the infinitive form is produced rather than the past simple 'rode'. There is no further practice after line 26. Furthermore,

190   *Video Enhanced Observation for Language Teaching*

a long break from meaningful practice has occurred to deal with a problem which did not impede communication. The many pauses and hesitation phenomena suggest difficulty in maintaining the flow of interaction.

The repair technique here in line 4 – teacher initiation of self-repair by the student 'good drive or' – does not make specific what the trouble is to be repaired and the learners are not able to perform the repair. T's subsequent attempt to clarify what is to be repaired in line 8 'do you drive a motorbike' again does not work because as we see in line 10, L takes this to be a genuine question and replies 'I'm not driving the motorbike'.

In retrospect, it seems that a more appropriate correction technique in this context would have been immediate explicit correction, for example, 'he rode a motorbike'. By the end of the above sequence, it is unclear whether the learners are able to produce the correct target form 'he rode a motorbike', since uptake is not displayed by the learners.

Lesson 2

In lessons 2 and 3, by contrast, there are no further examples of such lengthy and problematic repair sequences. In lesson 2, which was delivered four months later, we can see examples of much more economical and successful correction:

```
Extract 2
1       T:      how often do you speak english on the phone
2               L1?
3               (0.3)
4       L1:     yes (0.3) one day for (1.6) one day for (1.1) for
5               for weeks=
6       T:      =yeah: once a week maybe.=
7       L1:     =once a week yeah
8       T:      yeah  do   you   wanna   ask   L2   ask   L2(0.2)   how   often
```

In the above extract, we notice that the error correction sequence is much shorter. It is more successful, in that there is immediate uptake from the student, and very little disruption, as evidenced by the lack of pauses or hesitation phenomena. The correction technique employed in line 6 is a very different one, namely embedded correction (Jefferson 1987: 95), that is, a correction done as a by-the-way occurrence in the context of a social action, which in this case is an action of agreement and confirmation. This form of correction and expansion is highly reminiscent of adult-child conversation, and the technique being used by the teacher here is often termed *scaffolding* (Johnson 1995: 75). The linguistic repair is performed in a mitigated way because it is prefaced by an action of agreement and approval and a tentative 'maybe' is added. Therefore, this type of embedded correction can be treated as a by-the-way matter which does not interrupt the flow of talk. We can see in line 7 that this is how L1 responds to the embedded correction, displaying uptake of the corrected phrase with a 'yeah' of confirmation added. The 'latching' marked by the = symbol shows that the turn-changing is smooth and does not involve pauses.

Changing Error Correction Practice on a Teacher Training Course   191

Extract 3

```
1    T:     (1.8) i'm gonna give you (0.2) some numbers (0.9) okay can you
2           match the number? (1.9) with the information. (0.4) so four
3           billion (.) what's four billion. (0.5)
4    L2:    four billion
5    L1:    four billion is phone number
6    T:     good numbers in the- number of phones in the world:
7    L1:    in the- [in the world
8    L2:            [in the world four billion
9    T:     fantastic yeah good. what's twenty
```

In the above extract, which is also from lesson 2, T has asked a pair of students to match a series of numbers to a series of pieces of information. In line 5, it is evident that L1 has matched the two correctly, but T analyses the statement 'four billion is phone number' as not being sufficiently explicit or well-formed enough. Again the technique employed is embedded correction, with a 'good' providing positive evaluation of the correct matching, followed by a correction of the phrase. Once more we see uptake of the correction by both students in lines 7 and 8 and an absence of pauses or hesitation markers. So the correction has again been achieved economically and without disturbing the flow of activity.

Thus we have seen evidence of a positive change in correction practices between lessons 1 and 2. The successful introduction of embedded correction techniques means that AA is able to both perform correction and promote meaningful interaction, thus achieving both of her targeted objectives.

Lesson 3

Extract 4

```
1    L7:    i can say (0.5) my er (0.2) worst habit (0.4) coming
2           (unclear) too late
3    T:     heheheh
4    L7:    heheheh
5    T:     yes (0.4) L7 perfect (0.3) my worst habit is
6           lateness
7    L7:    yeah lateness (0.3) yeah
```

In the third recorded lesson, three months later, learners are being asked to identify their worst habits. As L7 always arrives late for lessons he or she tries to express that in line 1, but the linguistic formatting is imperfect. After mutual laughter at the aptness of this observation, T provides positive feedback in line 5 aimed at the message and then corrects L7's turn into a well-formed clause. L7 demonstrates uptake of the correction in line 7.

There was a further area of development in relation to error correction practice between lessons 2 and 3. After lesson 2, AA received the feedback from her DELTA tutor that she was not ensuring extended repetition of the corrected item by the

192   *Video Enhanced Observation for Language Teaching*

learners. In an interview, AA reflected that: 'I repeat the word to myself and I think I noticed that in the last one I often say the word to myself but I don't get them to say it' (interview data). So although AA's correction practice had changed in lesson 2, she was still not ensuring sufficiently that the learners were able to produce the target vocabulary correctly, according to the tutor, and AA's reflection shows that she has taken this point on board.

The interactional evidence from lesson 3 was in fact that AA was ensuring more extended repetition by the learners of the target words:

```
Extract 5
1      L4:    irritable
2      T:     irritable
3      L1:    irritable
4      T:     yeah can you say irritable
5      (0.2)
6      LL:    irritable
7      T:     irritable
8      L1:    irritable
9      T:     yeah
(58 lines omitted)
68     T:     good (0.3) which which words are new (0.2) which
69            words are new words
70     L3:    pessimistic
71     L:     pessimistic
72     T:     pessimistic (0.2) yeah
73     L4:    irritable
74     (0.5)
75     T:     irritable
76     (0.3)
77     L4:    irritable
78     (1.7)
79     T:     irritable
80     L:     irritable
81     L4:    irritable
82     T:     good
83     L3:    (unclear)
84     (0.5)
85     L4:    irritable
```

The above extract illustrates the change in AA's correction practice in lesson 3 to explicit, extended pronunciation practice which ensures individual students are able to produce target vocabulary correctly. Lines 1–9 practise correct pronunciation, but the vocabulary revision for the lesson initiated in line 68 requires students to recall and practise the correct pronunciation once again.

Conclusions

In conclusion, we can see that AA and her tutor identified an area of professional practice – correction – which she wished to improve. The interaction and discussion between AA and her tutor were key to AA's professional development, and the use of video observation allowed AA to reflect and evaluate on her own practice in an objective manner. Lofthouse et al. (2010), in their research on coaching, found that teaching could be improved through 'providing feedback to teachers and allowing them to reflect intensively on classroom evidence generated by video' (p4). This discussion between trainee and coach is an excellent example of the development of relational agency (Edwards and D'Arcy 2004; Edwards 2007) which is defined as the 'capacity to offer and give support ... to expand understandings of the work problem as an object of joint activity, and the ability to attune one's responses to the enhanced interpretation to those being made by other professionals' (Edwards 2010: 13, in Kennedy et al. 2015: 199).

AA therefore identified three specific objectives, which were reading key literature on the area of error correction (developing her knowledge of theory); trialling at least two new methods in her lessons, and reflecting on this (developing her practice and reflecting/evaluating); and asking learners how/when they like to be corrected (applying theory to practice). Of these, the second objective, that of implementing new methods in her classroom teaching, was the most difficult for her to evaluate without the opportunity afforded by the use of video observation. As discussed, the dynamic, interactional nature of classroom discourse allows little time for the teacher to reflect-in-action (Schön 1987), so being able to re-examine the lesson using VEO meant that AA could evaluate her correction methods, and begin to reflect on how she could apply her theoretical knowledge and her learners' feedback to her future practice.

The three lessons were recorded over a long time period of seven months, and this gave AA time to reflect on her video observations, discuss them with her tutor and develop a growing awareness of her progress. The customized tag set incorporated the areas of correction and creating opportunities for meaningful language practice, having tags on 'feedback – content' and 'feedback – accuracy' as well as 'teacher practice – meaningful practice', and AA was able therefore to easily identify key moments in the lesson for discussion and reflection.

In lesson 1 we saw an example in which the correction sequence was overlong and not successful in terms of ensuring the learners could produce the target item. By lesson 2, AA had acquired more economical and effective repair techniques and had been able to employ them in class. The tutor had provided feedback after lesson 2 that AA was not checking sufficiently that students were able to produce the target items correctly themselves, and in lesson 3 we see evidence of extended explicit correction sequences requiring the students to produce correct pronunciation.

The improvement appears to be a result of a number of factors: input from the DELTA programme tutor; reflection on her performance and being able to review her lesson on the video. Did the tag set actually help AA focus during the lessons on the areas for development which her tutor had identified? In her interview, AA says: 'knowing what the tags were made me conscious or I tried to consciously focus on those areas so in some sense I suppose it's perhaps a bit more powerful than just having areas to work on that someone writes about.' In her reflection text, AA wrote: 'Planning to teach with the tags in mind made me try and focus on these areas of development. I sort of knew I could be checked up on!' In this case, then, the creation of an individualized tag set specific to the developmental needs of an individual teacher has made a significant contribution to the improvement of her professional practice on a training programme, according to the teacher herself.

Looking at AA's error correction practice from extracts 1 to 5, one could take a contrary view, namely that her practice starts out more 'communicative' in that the learners have lots of interactional space to express themselves. It ends up in extract 5 as more mechanistic, behaviouristic, audio-lingual type drilling. It should of course be pointed out that extract 5 is pronunciation practice of new words and therefore does not imply that AA's error correction practice as a whole has become uniformly mechanistic. AA in her interview reveals that she has reflected on the issues involved in drilling: 'I'm still a bit uncomfortable at making adults repeat single words. I find it is a bit patronising to do that but I don't think it is because if they can't say the word they can't use it.' Oser and Baeriswyl (2001, in Gröschner et al. 2018) point out that classroom discourse is characterized by verbal teacher-student interactions: 'instructional patterns and choreographies of teaching' (p224). The use of VEO in this case allowed AA to 'identify and reframe the pedagogical problem', and to 'think critically about multiple pedagogical options' to address this choreography (Christ et al. 2015: 238). As discussed, this critical engagement with theory and practice demonstrates AA's transition to becoming a reflective practitioner (Schön 1983; Dewey 1933), using her experience to learn and gain new insights of self and practice (Finlay 2008).

Linking AA's case study to the self-directed CPD model below (Figure 12.1), we can see that AA and her tutor first worked together to develop a set of objectives based on agreed areas for improvement. AA then worked with the RA to create an individualized tag set to match those objectives. Over the next seven months, AA recorded three lessons using VEO and viewed them, reflecting on critical incidents and key moments thanks to the use of the tag set. After each recording and reflection, AA's tutor observed the video and gave feedback, and AA was able to modify her practice based on her evaluation, reflection and tutor feedback. As a final step, AA was able to complete

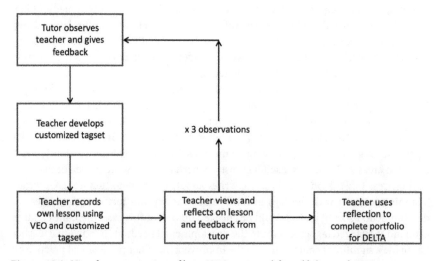

Figure 12.2 Visual representation of how VEO was used for self-directed CPD.

her DELTA portfolio, demonstrating a greater insight into the application of error correction theory to her practice, a heightened awareness of her own progress and further development as a reflective practitioner.

In terms of the DELTA course handbook criteria, a trainee requires (a) evidence that they have been able to use a wide range and variety of error correction techniques in appropriate ways in various contexts, and (b) evidence of some reflection and development in terms of awareness and practice. In this case study, there is clear evidence in both of these areas in relation to AA. The individualized tag set allowed her to examine her progress over the three lessons, identifying her professional needs and areas for improvement, and taking ownership of her development. VEO aims to empower individuals to take control of their own learning, improve specific aspects of what they do and see rapid results over time (VEO website 2020), and the case of AA shows how this empowerment and improvement take place over the series of recorded lessons.

AA also gave feedback in her interviews on aspects of VEO with which she did not feel fully comfortable. She found that it is quite difficult to categorize things you observe and wondered if just bookmarking and making a comment might be more useful for her sometimes. For this purpose, the 'quick tag' marker can be used simply to bookmark and written comments can be added. AA felt that something is lost from the lesson from watching it back and that you don't get the full sense/atmosphere in the room. It is quite true that not all of the five senses are captured in video and that video can never be the same as real life. Finally, AA noted that she was not very good at reflecting on her own in isolation and that she likes dialogue with another professional who could ask why she did things and suggest how she might have done things differently. This point reinforces why it is a good idea to integrate VEO into a programme of reflection in professional development, which is the main thrust of this book. Throughout a teaching training programme, it is imperative that a trainee learns how to critique their own teaching, modifying their practice as a result (Smyth 1989; Larrivee 2000). Video observation does indeed help to bridge the gap between theory and practice, allowing trainees to trial what the theory they have learnt in their classroom practice, as AA did when she trialled her theoretical error correction methods, but this process must be supported by the opportunity for discussion, feedback and coaching from a trusted tutor or mentor.

Implications

We can conclude the following from this study:

1. It is very good practice to produce a customized tag set in relation to the requirements of CPD courses and qualifications, as we have seen in this chapter in relation to DELTA. Such a tag set can then be used by the whole cohort. This then helps to ensure that the focus of the video recording of lessons can be on those specific features which are essential to the course and which are targeted for development.

2. In order to gather clear evidence of development, whether for a portfolio or for research purposes, a problem area for the teacher should be identified, and a series of lessons taught in which the teacher tackles this area. In this chapter the teacher selected correction as an area of weakness for development, but there are many areas of teacher and learner behaviour which could be targeted.
3. Subsequently, data should be gathered to determine the degree and nature of any development in practices. As exemplified in this chapter, a combination of data collection instruments which works well with VEO is (a) statistics which are automatically generated, (b) microanalysis of interaction, (c) self-report data in terms of interview, reflective diary and (d) documents such as lesson plans and tutor feedback. These can all feed into a case study narrative.

Part Three

Making the Most of Video Enhanced Observation

13

A Practical Framework for Integrating Digital Video and Video Enhanced Observation into Continuing Professional Development

Paul Seedhouse
Newcastle University, UK
Paul Miller
VEO Group, UK
Jon Haines
Newcastle University, UK

Introduction

This chapter presents a framework for the use of digital video, and the VEO app in particular, for professional development and reflective practice. The framework is broadly conceived so as to be applicable to any profession in any country which has the required digital infrastructure. The framework is based on the authors' experience of working with a wide range of professional users around the world, as well as on the findings of the empirical studies in Section II of this book. The framework explains the processes which are involved in a CPD programme using digital video for observation and reflection. It demonstrates how processes and procedures can be customized in relation to specific professional settings. The customization process is then exemplified by looking at cases which show how the framework has been adapted to two very different professional settings – teacher training and distance learning. We also show how it is straightforward to adapt schemes for assessing the spoken performance of individuals by developing a VEO tag set and show how these schemes can be used for the professional development of examiners. We further explain how the framework relates to theoretical models of education, CPD and reflective practice, by reference to two existing theoretical models used in two chapters in this volume. Finally, we look at issues of confidentiality and consent, as well as procedures for building up a database of videos of professional practice.

Towards a Practical Framework

In this section we look back at the six models for integrating VEO into CPD which were developed independently during the empirical studies in four different countries and in a variety of educational settings. We then consider what they have in common, prior to merging them into a single framework.

Chapter 5

This model, illustrated in Figure 13.1, is based on the first case study in Germany and illustrates how VEO can be used as an instrument to scaffold processes of reflection among pre-service teachers.

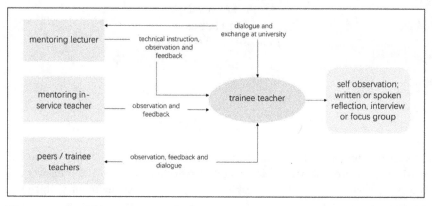

Figure 13.1 Scaffolding processes of reflection among pre-service teachers.

Chapter 6

This linear model represents process of reflective practice for the Primary Teacher Education Programme in Finland. Linking practical episodes to theory is an explicit part of the model.

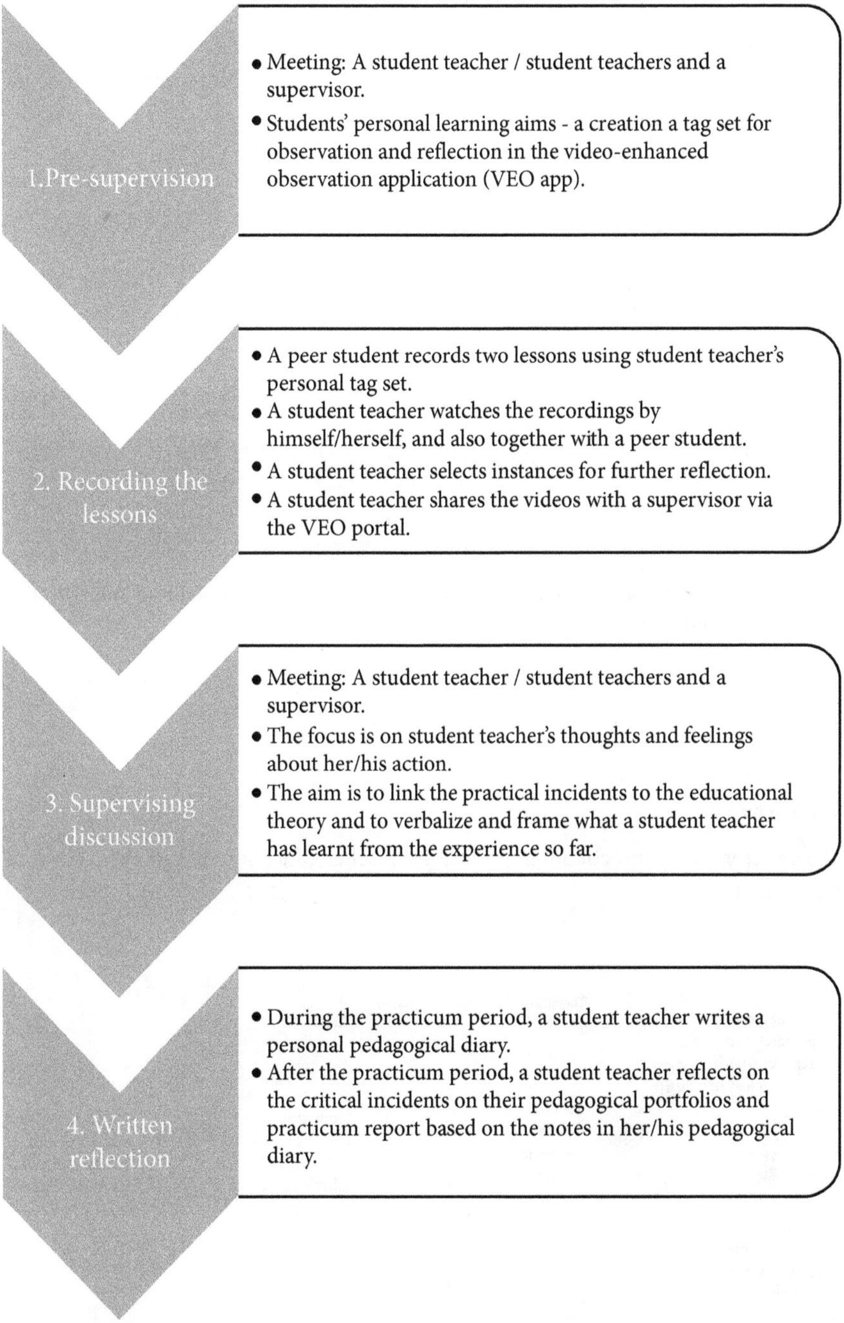

Integrating VEO into CPD 201

1.Pre-supervision
- Meeting: A student teacher / student teachers and a supervisor.
- Students' personal learning aims - a creation a tag set for observation and reflection in the video-enhanced observation application (VEO app).

2. Recording the lessons
- A peer student records two lessons using student teacher's personal tag set.
- A student teacher watches the recordings by himself/herself, and also together with a peer student.
- A student teacher selects instances for further reflection.
- A student teacher shares the videos with a supervisor via the VEO portal.

3. Supervising discussion
- Meeting: A student teacher / student teachers and a supervisor.
- The focus is on student teacher's thoughts and feelings about her/his action.
- The aim is to link the practical incidents to the educational theory and to verbalize and frame what a student teacher has learnt from the experience so far.

4. Written reflection
- During the practicum period, a student teacher writes a personal pedagogical diary.
- After the practicum period, a student teacher reflects on the critical incidents on their pedagogical portfolios and practicum report based on the notes in her/his pedagogical diary.

Figure 13.2 The procedure of guided reflection with VEO.

Chapter 7

As part of the IMDAT teacher education framework in Turkey (Sert 2015), VEO-integrated IMDAT has been put into practice as part of the student teachers' practicum studies (see Figure 13.3).

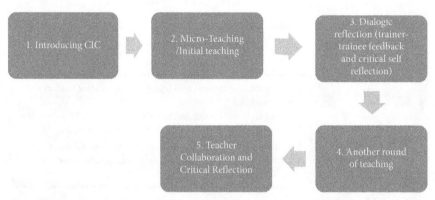

Figure 13.3 IMDAT: a classroom interaction-driven, technology-enhanced and reflective teacher education framework (Sert 2019, p. 223).

Chapter 9

The structure of the practicum in pre-service teacher education in Turkey is shown in Figure 13.4.

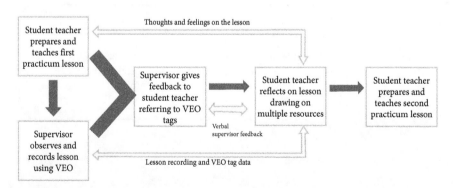

Figure 13.4 Detailed practicum structure using VEO.

Chapter 10

Hidson illustrates in Figure 13.5 the way that VEO was integrated into the performance management cycle in the case study school in the UK.

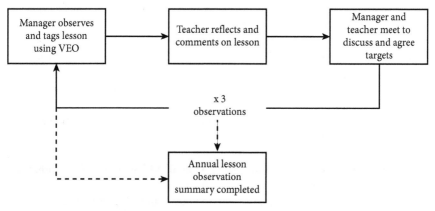

Figure 13.5 Lesson observation using VEO during the performance management cycle in the case study school.

Chapter 12

This figure shows how VEO was integrated into a longitudinal CPD programme as part of an in-service qualification in the UK.

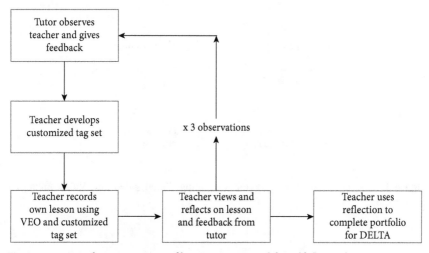

Figure 13.6 Visual representation of how VEO was used for self-directed CPD.

We therefore have six models developed independently during the empirical studies in four different countries and in a variety of educational settings. They have some similar features as follows, which should feed into our overarching practical framework:

- The central feature in each model is a professional event (lesson), which is video-recorded using VEO.
- The individualization of professional development is desirable, where possible.
- Developing an individualized tag set for a specific professional setting is beneficial.
- There is a preparatory meeting before the lesson.
- There is a meeting after the lesson to discuss how it went, to promote reflection and to relate the practice to theory.
- Following discussion and reflection, some development is expected which will be translated into future action.

A Practical Framework for Integrating Digital Video and Video Enhanced Observation into CPD.

The following framework is compatible with the six models presented above and is designed to provide a flexible and overarching framework for the use of digital video, and the VEO app in particular, for professional development and reflective practice. The framework is broadly conceived to be applicable to any profession in any country with the required digital infrastructure.

We now provide more detail of what is involved in all of the stages:

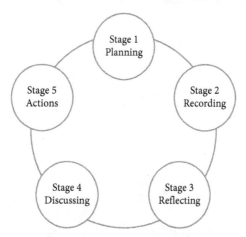

Figure 13.7 A practical framework for integrating digital video and Video Enhanced Observation into CPD.

Stage 1. Planning (Pre-recording) Meeting

Typically this is between a professional/trainee professional and a more experienced supervisor, but peer observation is also possible (see Chapter 8 for an example). There will be discussion and preparation of what will happen in the stage 2 professional event, which will be recorded using VEO. There is consideration of the following: what are the professional's interests and needs? What will the professional/trainee professional's aims will be during the event? How do they visualize the specific characteristics of the event and how will success be evaluated? How will the video recording be conducted in terms of logistics, taking into consideration any specific issues of consent and participation? Ideally, there may be the creation of a tailored VEO tag set to suit the event/programme/qualification (see Chapter 12 for an example), or a discussion of the use of an existing VEO tag set. It is best practice to complete the 'pre-record info' for the VEO recording session at his point.

Stage 2. Recording of a Professional Event(s)

There is a video recording made of the professional event(s). This may be made using any digital video recorder, with the video being uploaded to the VEO portal and tagged retrospectively. Or a supervisor or colleague may record and live-tag the event as it happens. Technical advice on recording is provided in Chapter 4.

Stage 3. Reviewing and Reflection

Following the recording, the professional/trainee professional whose performance was recorded will watch the video, or selected episodes and reflect on it in some way. It is best practice to complete the 'post-record info' for the VEO recording session at his point. A peer or a supervisor may also view the video.

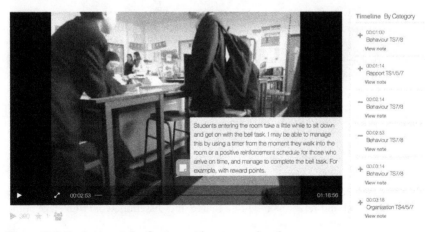

Figure 13.8 Reviewing and reflecting, with notes produced.

Tagging the event may also take place at this stage. By doing so, users are creating key moments on which to focus their reflections. The tags can also be annotated to further capture and scaffold the user's thoughts in written form. Reflections may be linked to existing theoretical models of CPD at this stage.

Stage 4. Meeting for Discussion of the Event

Following review of the video, the professional/trainee professional will discuss the performance and reflect with the peer and/or supervisor on the extent to which his/her aims were fulfilled, discussing thoughts and feelings and identifying issues for future development. This meeting may take place online or face-to-face. This may involve multiple sources and types of data. Qualitative and quantitative data can help inform the discussion and evaluate the impact of the learning event. It is best practice in this meeting to consider how the practice under discussion relates to theoretical issues. VEO also allows the upload of other documents and files which are then associated and linked to this video – providing a useful repository for multiple sources of evidence and triangulation.

Figure 13.9 A meeting with multiple sources and types of data.

Stage 5. Action Following the Event

Following the reflection and discussions, the professional/trainee professional may take actions as a result. This may involve writing or recording a reflective journal or report or producing an action plan for the next professional event, which builds on what has been learnt. There should be consideration of any best practice identified during the event and how this might be shared and disseminated. From stage 5, the procedure may then loop back again to stage 1.

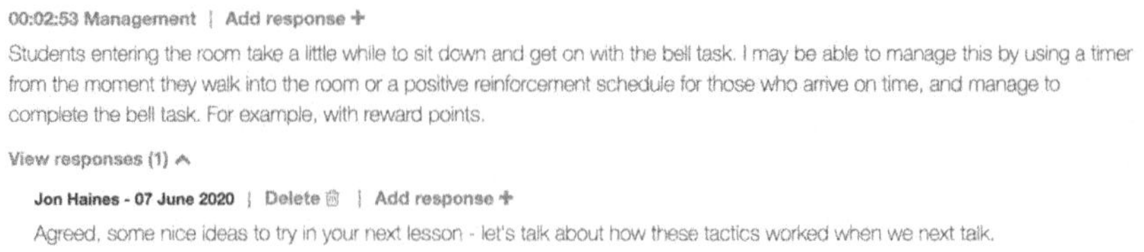

00:02:53 Management | Add response +

Students entering the room take a little while to sit down and get on with the bell task. I may be able to manage this by using a timer from the moment they walk into the room or a positive reinforcement schedule for those who arrive on time, and manage to complete the bell task. For example, with reward points.

View responses (1) ∧

Jon Haines - 07 June 2020 | Delete 🗑 | Add response +

Agreed, some nice ideas to try in your next lesson - let's talk about how these tactics worked when we next talk.

Figure 13.10 Actions agreed for the following lesson.

How the Practical Framework Works

We now provide examples of how the practical framework relates to professional practice in the real world. The first is from teacher training, the second from distance learning and the third from assessment and evaluation.

Example 1: Teacher Training

This example relates to Chapter 12, which shows in effect how the practical framework can be recycled longitudinally over time. The study shows CPD in a teacher training course (DELTA) over the course of three lessons, in which we see the practical framework procedures being repeated and progress being recorded.

Stage 1. Planning (Pre-recording) Meeting

There were three planning meetings which took place before the three lessons. A tailored VEO tag set was produced.

Stage 2. Recording of a Professional Event(s)

Three lessons were recorded using the customized DELTA tag set over a seven-month period, transcribed and analysed in relation to error correction practice.

Stage 3. Reviewing and Reflection

The teacher was able to review the lesson video and reflect on her performance three times, noting development over time.

Stage 4. Meeting for Discussion of the Event

The teacher received feedback from the tutor at three meetings and was able to combine this feedback with insights from stage 3.

Stage 5. Action following the Event

The teacher identified issues in relation to her correction feedback after the first lesson and made plans to change practice in the following lessons. Moreover, she completed a reflective portfolio for her professional qualification which provided evidence of progress.

In this case, then, the practical framework has been utilized in a longitudinal fashion, recycling procedures to provide evidence of a cycle of development.

Example 2: Distance Learning

Firstly, we provide the background to this example of distance learning on a large scale. VEO now works with several training providers across diverse fields within education (and beyond). Once such London-based group partnered with VEO to train several hundred teachers from across Kazakhstan in new pedagogy and approaches to learning. Areas included assessment strategies, utilizing cognition in the classroom and implementing CLIL (content and language-integrated learning). Given that Kazakhstan is larger in area than the whole of Western Europe, the need to train teachers from all corners of the country had provided the training company with huge challenges! They turned to VEO, and by working in partnership we were able to create and apply an effective and engaging remote training programme that was able to evidence considered application of new teaching techniques in classrooms across Kazakhstan. The several hundred teachers were brought together for initial face-to-face training over four days, each day dedicated to four new areas of pedagogy. Initial activities involved being grouped into peer groups of six to eight teachers. Together, using VEO, they tagged the trainers' videos which had been created to demonstrate the new techniques in action and to exemplify differing degrees of successful implementation. Returning to their schools across Kazakhstan, teachers were then tasked with capturing a small number of lessons and tagging just three moments of their choice within each lesson, each of which demonstrated a new technique acquired during their training. They then added a short paragraph of annotation on the moment, describing how and why they had implemented the technique. They tagged using simple tag sets directly related to their training.

Stage 1. Planning (Pre-recording) Meeting

Participants meet to be introduced to new elements of practice. As per the Chapter 3 example, this can be done in person or through VEO, with the trainer uploading and sharing videos for participants to tag, analyse and understand. Tag sets are created that are very specifically targeted to the new areas of practice. Participants are places into small groups, of from three to up to nine.

Stage 2. Recording of a Professional Event(s)

Participants return to their place of work – in this case schools across Kazakhstan. They record a lesson and tag only three specific moments within the lesson, related to the new pedagogy. They write a brief paragraph to reflect on what is happening and how this relates to the new pedagogy.

Stage 3. Reviewing and Reflection

The video is shared through VEO by the participant. They share it directly with their training group, including any coaches, trainers or mentors.

Stage 4. Meeting for Discussion of the Event

On receiving access to the video, the participants' colleagues (and coaches, etc.) respond to their reflections and create an online discussion, at the exact moment of the video in question. Other participants are able to jump straight to the moment in the video and join in with the discussion. A coach or mentor can further prompt discussion. As a result, the participant has feedback from several other colleagues, while these colleagues have had the opportunity to engage with several moments of new practice.

Stage 5. Action following the Event

The participant in the video can enact any advice or changes deriving from the online discussion in new practice. Participants viewing and feeding back on the pedagogy may seek to introduce it into their practice. Further professional learning feedback cycles are then set up to embed the improved and refined pedagogy into their practice.

Example 3: Using VEO for the Assessment and Evaluation of Spoken Performances

The empirical Section II of this collection was concerned with developing the professional competences of teachers in various settings. However, none of the studies were directly concerned with using VEO for the assessment and evaluation of spoken performances. It is of course true that testing, assessment and evaluation are core components of educational systems, sometimes to the extent that teachers may 'teach to the test'. The 'washback effect', referring to the impact of testing on teaching, learning and curriculum practices, has been extensively studied (Cheng et al. 2004). Experience has shown that it is straightforward to adapt schemes for assessing the spoken performance of individuals by developing a VEO tag set. This helps greatly in the one-stop collection, collation, analysis and transmission of data relating to tests of speaking. Once recorded, a test performance can be assessed or second-marked or moderated by an examiner using the same tag set anywhere in the world. This is in line with university assessments in clinical practice, where VEO is used to grade performance at different simulation stations. Technique and communication skills, among other critical human factors, are observed and evaluated through VEO.

In this section we therefore look at one of the world's most widely taken tests of spoken English, namely the IELTS Speaking Test (IST), and see how the VEO app was used to design a possible application for training examiners. The IST is one of the four components of IELTS (International English Language Testing System), the most widely used English proficiency test for overseas applicants to British and Australian universities. In 2017, over 3 million ISTs were administered at more than 1,100 centres, in over 140 countries around the world (http://www.ielts.org). For candidates, this can be a very high-stakes test in that it can determine their access to the degree programme of their choice. IELTS 'measures the language proficiency of people who want to study or work where English is used as a language of communication' (ibid.).

Using VEO for Training Examiners/Assessors/Moderators

It follows, from the number of candidates taking the IST, that there is a very large cohort of certified examiners (estimated at over 7,000 in 2017) conducting the test, who also require professional training, or examiner training. We therefore report on a funded project (Seedhouse and Satar 2021) which shows how an individualized VEO tag set can be adapted for use in grading the IELTS Speaking Test (IST) https://www.ielts.org/ in order to facilitate examiner training. The project created the customized IELTS tag set (Figure 13.11). This has four dropdown menus (see the left-hand side in Figure 13.11) to represent each of the four IST Band Descriptor or columns.[1] Each menu features the numbers 2–9 for scoring options, as can be seen in the centre of Figure 13.11. If, for example, the examiner hears from the start some pronunciation problems, he or she may choose 5 on the pronunciation scale. If the candidate produces some impressive relative clauses, by contrast, the examiner may then choose 8 on the grammar scale. So this creates a recording of **when** exactly in the test the examiners have noticed **which** specific features of candidate talk, and taken **which** specific decisions on scoring as a result. Written notes can also be added at the same time as the rating, or later. These can record **why** the examiners have taken these decisions. The precise format of the tag set was developed by the research team in collaboration with Cambridge Assessment English staff in order to be of maximum value for examiner development. Below we use screenshots to show what a tag set looks like when it is being used. We see how examiners record their grades and notes.

Integrating VEO into CPD 211

Figure 13.11 Making scoring decisions on VEO using the IELTS tagset.

In Figure 13.11 we see how raters record a scoring decision. Having noticed a feature of candidate talk and wanting to grade it, the examiner has pressed the 'grammar' criterion icon on the left. The drop-down score screen has appeared in the centre, covering part of the video screen. We can see the cursor recording a grammar score of 6.

Figure 13.12 Adding notes on VEO using the IELTS tagset.

In Figure 13.12 we see the examiner has added notes in the box to justify the scoring decision. In the right-hand legion we can see that the scoring decision of 6 for grammar has been recorded on the timeline. All notes are added and are then retrievable by clicking on the timeline.

Seedhouse and Satar (2021) conducted individual interviews with four examiners, as well as a subsequent focus group with the same examiners. They asked the question: would using the VEO IELTS tag set with a video be a good way of training IST examiners? In the full report the quotations were provided, interspersed with comments. The answer to this research question was a very clear one. There was complete agreement amongst examiners that the VEO IELTS tag set with a video would be a good way of training IST examiners. Three examiners mentioned that the process could be used during re-certification as well as during initial training. They suggested that the same video could be rated and commented on by all raters separately. The raters could then watch the standardized master video which has been rated and commented on by the lead examiner.

Moreover, the generation of graphs which combine different examiners' ratings of the same candidate using VEO (noticing trajectories) may potentially add further value to examiner development (see Seedhouse and Satar, 2021). This graphical presentation creates a visualization of the decision points examiners made. This in turn enables a comparison of scoring decisions across raters and test criteria that demonstrated relative divergence and convergence. Figure 13.13 shows how VEO enables tracing of convergence and divergence of all decisions about one candidate's performance by four examiners. So it becomes possible to trace when, how and why raters diverge from each other, providing a basis for moderation, harmonization, standardization and examiner development. The graphical presentation also enables research into the **process** of establishing inter-rater reliability, which has traditionally been presented as a statistical outcome. So in this case the VEO customization process was very direct, transferring an existing scoring system onto a tag set. Once this was accomplished, however, it became clear that this could generate an entirely new, graphical means of presentation which would open up entirely new avenues of professional development and research.

Although the above example related to the assessment of spoken performance in relation to language proficiency in a foreign language, it is clear that spoken performances are assessed in many diverse professional settings. In medical settings, the way in which doctors, nurses and other healthcare professionals interact with patients is of great interest. In marketing, there is much emphasis on the charismatic presentation of product information to potential clients using both verbal and non-verbal means. On the VEO app, a number of assessment tagsets are already available for use, including 'Presentation Evaluation', 'Speaking Performance' and 'Coaching Skills', and any assessment scheme can be transferred to a tailored tag set for use in assessment of spoken performance.

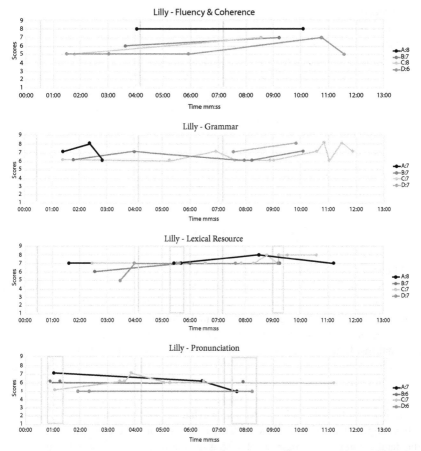

Figure 13.13 Comparison of decisions for four criteria by four examiners for the same candidate.

Integration of VEO with Models and Theories of Professional Development

We saw in Chapters 7 and 11 that it was straightforward to integrate the use of VEO with existing models of reflective professional development: Sert's IMDAT model and Walsh's SETT model. The reason why integration proved straightforward is that VEO tag sets can be produced for any model which specifies behaviours or actions which can be noticed and tagged by observers. So a tag set can transfer not only the professional practice inherent in a model, but also the theoretical assumptions on which it is based. So, for example, Walsh's SETT model is based on the theoretical assumption that L2 classroom interaction can be sub-divided into four different interactional 'modes'. Each of these modes was then transferred to become part of the SETT tag set, so the observer makes a choice as to which of the four modes is currently active in the classroom interaction observed. Theory is therefore inherent in the practice of observation and tagging. The link between theory and practice can be made explicit in academic writing about the model of professional development concerned, but is implicitly included when the VEO tag set is created and employed. This means that VEO can be regarded as an atheoretical tool which is so flexible that it can accommodate any theory-based system for observing spoken behaviour. VEO has now been employed in many professional settings and countries around the world and has been found to be compatible with all theoretical approaches to learning with which it has been used. This is because all theoretical approaches specify certain behaviours and actions by learners and professionals as being particularly advantageous or disadvantageous to learning; these behaviours can then be incorporated into a tag set, which identifies occurences of these behaviours and actions, which in turn provides a focus for reflection, development and/or assessment.

Building Up a Database of Videos

Building up a corpus or database of video-recorded professional interactions for use in professional development and research is an excellent idea. The corpus can then be used as a basis for the planning and delivery of professional development, as well as for research. Building up a corpus is normally fiddly and time-consuming, but one advantage of the VEO system is that your corpus builds up automatically on your personal/institutional login as you make your videos. Furthermore, transmission of the videos to selected people in your organization is very easy to manage securely, using standard social media techniques. It is best practice to write a full set of information on the tabs both prior to and after recording, as well as giving the recording and filename an informative title, for ease of retrieval. In relation to classroom research, Seedhouse (2004) argues that, because of the diversity of classrooms, one should not only specify the database in terms of number of lessons or fragments of lessons, but also in terms of the following background contextual factors, in order that the diversity of the database might be assessed: first language of the learners; multilingual or monolingual classes; culture; country of origin; age of learners; type of institution; level of learners' proficiency in the target language, teaching approach. It is essential in every case to relate the size, nature and diversity of the database to the aims and methodology of the professional development or research. It is also possible to import existing videos from other sources in any format into VEO and subsequently tag them with your own tag set, thus enlarging the corpus. A large number of video-recorded lessons (and other professional events) from around the world are currently freely available online and can be found by searching YouTube and other sites, as well as by doing straightforward internet searches. However, permissions must be obtained for use.

Confidentiality and Consent

Data protection, confidentiality and consent are important factors when using video to record human interaction – the guidance and rules are there to ensure that things are done right, not to prevent things from being done. Each organization will have ethical approval processes and standards, and they will also have policies associated with confidentiality and data protection, all of which may need to be considered in preparation for using video to support professional development and institutional change. These considerations are present, and should be visible at multiple levels, within an organization, as illustrated in Figure 13.14. All stakeholders need to be aware and accepting of the intent and purpose of the use of video. Drawing particular attention to this, the British Educational Research Association highlights that

> the study of facial expressions and gestures and the increasing prevalence of video and multimodal data raise questions about whether concealing identities is always appropriate. Researchers may need to negotiate an ethical course of action here – one that secures very clear agreement about anonymity and about subsequent use of the data. Researchers need to be aware that visual material could be misused by others (for example, as an example of poor practice), and should take steps to prevent this as far as possible.
>
> (BERA 2018)

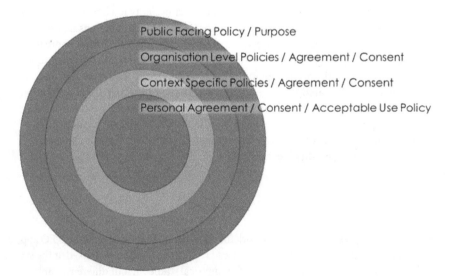

Figure 13.14 Ethical approval processes within an organization.

Video Enhanced Observation as a Pedagogical Method

VEO has the potential to inform a diverse range of pedagogical methods. The basic tools brought together by the app – qualitative video and quantitative tag data – have proven a powerful combination for video based learning. VEO's continuing journey has shown that these can be applied effectively to accelerate diverse learning process.

216   *Video Enhanced Observation for Language Teaching*

Broadly, video is valuable in capturing what has gone before, which supports learning in and for an action, or learning through the experience of doing. Dewey (1997) refers to experience as the 'means and goal of education', and VEO's combination of easily accessible video can be used to align both to achieve this principle. The learning is situated in practice, with the efficiency and clarity brought to reflection and feedback on this experience being used to enhance future practice and experience. This method can be applied to several fields beyond teacher education and is valuable for the wider student population seeking to acquire the skills needed to achieve their own longer-term goals.

Beyond this learning *in* and *for* action, the means to interact at moments within the time span of video, VEO has been proven to make learning *from* video content more immediate and engaging. In practical terms, as more and more video media is used as content, ways to focus attention and to inspire productive communication around the key learning points are increasingly valuable in the 'multi-screen' era. Directing attention onto learning content and away from phones and other distractions can be achieved by inserting questions or discussion points within the video, using VEO's tags. Furthermore, a task requiring users to tag their own actions within video can demonstrate access to concepts or content within, leading to further depth of understanding through enquiry.

VEO's ability to achieve this derives from the system's ability to allow both teachers and learners to create discrete moments in continuous video. This ensures mental focus and creates episodes, building a series of key events out of the longer, more fluid recorded whole. These episodes stimulate future recall and provide a springboard for reflection and comparison. The ability to easily define these moments and interact around them builds a shared language and enhances learning through the collaboration this inspires. As more and more learning takes place online, with people located in more geographically distant and diverse locations, VEO's elegant combination of qualitative and quantitative, focused and continuous, can deliver scalable collaborative pedagogy to meet twenty-first-century needs.

Conclusions

This chapter has presented our framework for the use of digital video, and the VEO app in particular, for professional development and reflective practice. We looked at the six models developed independently during the empirical studies in four different countries and in a variety of educational settings and considered what they have in common. The framework is therefore solidly based on actual practice. The framework graphic (Figure 13.7) is a very simple one, marking out five stages. This means that the framework is easily expandable and adaptable to development in any professional setting round the world. Examples of how the practical framework was related to professional practice in the real world were then provided: from teacher training, distance learning and from assessment and evaluation. Finally, we looked at how to integrate VEO with theory, specifically models of professional development, as well as looking at the practical issues of building up video databases, confidentiality and consent. The framework is therefore up and running, has been tested in the field and has been shown to be highly flexible and adaptable to all kinds of professional practices and approaches.

14

Researching Using the VEO App

Paul Seedhouse
Newcastle University, UK
Paul Miller
VEO Group, UK
Jon Haines
Newcastle University, UK

Introduction

The concluding chapter starts by drawing together all of the points which have emerged from the empirical evidence and discussions in the previous chapters in Section II. The analyses of data and the discussions in this collection have contributed to the development of general principles, procedures and insights in relation to using digital video and specifically the VEO app for professional development and reflective practice. These are summarized in this chapter. Whereas Chapter 13 focused on the use of the VEO app for reflective CPD, this chapter shows how VEO can be used for **research**. One clear finding from this project was that the VEO app is an extremely flexible and useful tool for carrying out research into professional practice, in addition to its core function of promoting professional development. The analyses in Section II of this collection have specialized in researching the areas of educational and applied linguistic research. In the second part of this chapter, however, we present a generic methodological model for researching with the VEO app in relation to professional practices and development in **any** area of research, so these principles may continue to be applied to other contexts in the future.

In the final section of the chapter, we look to the future of the VEO app. We consider the limitations and criticisms of the current version of the app and envisage how it will develop in relation to these. We also consider the areas and ways in which we envisage the app will be used in the future.

Researching Using VEO: Conclusions from the Empirical Chapters

We firstly summarize the lessons learnt about researching using VEO from the empirical research presented in this collection, prior to presenting a generic methodological model for researching professional practices and professional development using the VEO app.

In Chapter 5, Schwab and Oesterle used VEO as a tool to bridge the gap between theory, research and practice in the German secondary teacher training context. They also showed that VEO could be used effectively by a student teacher as a research instrument to collect data for her final thesis. They cautioned that VEO needs to be carefully integrated into the curriculum with clear procedures embedded in order to be effective.

Körkkö, Kyrö-Ämmälä and Turunen show in Chapter 6 how they created a four-stage framework as an intervention in a primary teacher education programme in Finland based on evidence, analysis and theory. This is the kind of useful intervention which can be delivered by integrating VEO into a tailored framework for reflective practice and teacher development. The first trial was not successful. This seemed to be due to the use of a standard tag set and a lack of structure and guidance regarding supervision, discussion and reflection. The second trial showed a considerable improvement due to the creation of an individualized tag set and the development of carefully structured supervision and reflection sessions into which the use of VEO was integrated.

Bozbıyık, Sert and Bacanak show in Chapter 7 how the student teacher changes her questioning practices in the classroom over time as she teaches, gets feedback from an expert and a peer, and reflects on her teaching practices. They also point out that carefully planned integration of the VEO app into the curriculum is vital. The study demonstrates the affordances of the integration of VEO and IMDAT, a technology-enhanced, reflective teacher education framework that puts classroom interaction at the heart of teacher development.

Batlle Rodríguez and Seedhouse show in Chapter 8 how teachers in a Spanish language school develop peer feedback interaction through the use of the VEO app. The striking point is how easily VEO has become integrated into existing peer feedback practice, being used to record and replay the teacher's performance on video and for the observer to record written notes. Although this was the first ever peer feedback session using the new VEO app for this group of eight teachers, they were able to creatively and actively integrate VEO into a central role within their practice. An advantage was that peer feedback interaction becomes more shared and less asymmetrical, since all participants have access to the information (the notes and the video) on the screen.

Tasdemir and Seedhouse show in Chapter 9 that, by reflecting via VEO, a pre-service teacher is able to reflect on her lessons in a level of detail that would not have been possible without the use of tags, and to show improvement in her classroom management skills as a result of the reflective process. The process of reflection generated a very long and self-critical reflective essay by this participant. She would not have been able to produce a reflective document in such detail without having had access to classroom video recordings that are tagged, providing focus points as well as a framework for reflection.

Hidson shows in Chapter 10 how VEO can be integrated into a school's teacher performance management processes by systematizing lesson observation processes within CPD. Use of VEO was found to enhance the dialogic nature of appraisal and also to capture the student voice to feed into the appraisal process.

In Chapter 11, Walsh created the SETT tag set in order to integrate an existing model of reflective teacher development with the VEO app. The study shows that the combined use of the app and tag set results in dialogic reflections which are evidence-based and informed by interactional data.

Seedhouse and Whelan show in Chapter 12 that it is best practice to produce a customized VEO tag set in relation to the requirements of professional development courses and qualifications. This then helps to ensure that the focus of the video recording of lessons can be on those specific features which are essential to the course and which are targeted for development. In order to gather clear evidence of development, a problem area for the teacher should be identified, and a series of lessons taught in which the teacher tackles this area. Longitudinal data should be gathered to determine the degree and nature of any improvement in practices.

We can conclude from the above studies that the best results are obtained for the introduction of VEO when:

- A customized tag set is produced for a specific professional context.
- Time and effort are taken to consider very carefully how exactly VEO can be integrated into reflective professional development in the specific context and the curriculum, rather than 'parachuted in'.
- In order to facilitate such integration, models and procedures are needed – see Chapter 13.
- Training is provided on how to use VEO effectively.
- Consideration is given to how VEO will promote development over time and how this development will be evaluated.
- There is planning to use VEO to promote reflection, which may be written and spoken and can occur before as well as after the observation/recording.

A Methodological Model for Using VEO for Researching Professional Development in Real-world Environments

Having reviewed the research findings, we now present a methodological model for researching and evaluating professional development in real-world professional environments using the VEO app. The fundamental rationale for having a research framework is that professional users inevitably ask what evidence there is that effective professional development and learning take place, as opposed to everyone being excited that this is the latest technology or fashion. Well-designed research can provide convincing evaluator evidence. It is essential that a framework for researching both the process and the product or effectiveness of professional development is put in place from the start, rather than being an afterthought, so here we make explicit how that can be accomplished.

The methodological model for researching professional development using VEO in real-world environments has the following components: (a) a methodology for ensuring the capture of data which are strictly relevant to the research focus; (b) a methodology for the capture of quantitative data relating to professional development; (c) a methodology for recording, describing and analysing the multimodal process of professional development in real-world environments; (d) self-report data and reflections gathered from the users and (e) the full integration of the VEO app into the procedures for professional practice, development, reflection and research. Clearly this is a mixed methods approach and involves a team of researchers gathering different types of data over a period of time. This volume provides a concrete example of how to research professional development in real-world environments by employing this methodological model. Chapters 5, 9, 11 and 12 incorporate quantitative reports of professional development using VEO; Chapters 5, 7, 8 and 12 exemplify CA analyses of the process of professional development; all Chapters 5–12 contain self-report data from participants. Chapters 5, 6, 7, 9, 10 and 12 provide case studies of individual teachers. We justify and elaborate on the five components of this methodological model below.

a) *A methodology for ensuring the capture of data which are strictly relevant to the research focus.* Fortunately, this is in-built in VEO and a major advantage of the app. Users can design their own tag set (see Chapter 4) and this can automatically ensure that what users tag is relevant to the research focus they have chosen. Users decide on their own research focus, develop their own tag set to capture relevant data and then make their own video recordings. Chapters 7, 11 and 12 exemplify the benefits of using a tailored tag set for research.

b) *The next element in the model is to capture quantitative data relating to professional development, in the least obtrusive way possible.* Another major advantage of VEO is that statistics are automatically generated by the system in relation to the chosen tagging set and are immediately available to the researchers in graphical form by pressing the 'statistics report' button. Screenshots can then be inserted in reports, as with Figure 14.1. Professionals invariably ask for hard evidence that an innovative practice does actually produce professional development at a significant level, and quantitative evidence is generally required for this. Moreover, quantification is useful for longitudinal studies of teacher practices, to measure how exactly teachers are able to change their practices over time. If, for example, the teacher and supervisor agree that the teacher talk time percentage was too high in lesson 1, they can then look for a reduction in percentage teacher talk time in lesson 2. If this is tagged by the observer, then the percentage is automatically generated in the statistics report. In addition, it is possible to produce tag sets for assessment. An example is provided later in this chapter in the review of Seedhouse and Satar (2021), in which a tag set for the IELTS Speaking Test was developed and employed to gather assessment data.

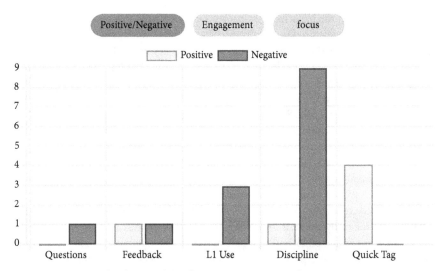

Figure 14.1 Example of screenshot of VEO quantitative tag data.

c) *A methodology for recording, describing and analysing the multimodal process of professional development using VEO in real-world environments.* In the VEO Europa project we used conversation analysis (CA), a multi-disciplinary methodology for the analysis of naturally occurring spoken interaction which is now applied in a very wide range of professional and academic areas. Why is this methodology suitable? According to Seedhouse (2004), one way of presenting the principles of CA is in relation to the questions which it asks. The essential question which we must ask at all stages of CA analysis of data is 'Why that, in that way, right now?' This encapsulates the perspective of interaction as action (why that) which is expressed by means of linguistic forms (in that way) in a developing sequence (right now). In other words, CA is a holistic methodology and is therefore suitable for the analysis of interaction as part of a holistic approach to a complex professional development environment. The aims of analysing the interaction between learners were as follows. Firstly, to uncover the evidence of professional development manifest in the details of the interaction, as illustrated in Chapter 12. Secondly, CA is able to portray the process of professional development in an environment in a holistic and multimodal manner; the analyses in Chapter 8 exemplify multimodal depictions of the professional development feedback process. Thirdly, as Chapters 7 and 12 show, CA is useful for longitudinal studies, to show in micro-detail how exactly teachers are able to change their practices over time; the same point could apply to any professional practices. Examples of CA analysis can be found in Chapters 5, 7, 8 and 12.

d) *Self-report data gathered from the users, in order to collect their reflections on their professional development or professional practices.* There are many ways of gathering self-report data, usually involving variations on questionnaires and interviews. However, the VEO app also offers users the possibility of writing detailed reflective notes, as well as recording reflective video diaries or interviews. Care should be taken to integrate self-report into the overall data-gathering cycle so that the experience does not become

222   *Video Enhanced Observation for Language Teaching*

too burdensome for the participants. Chapter 9 demonstrates that a particularly useful means of data presentation is to place transcripts of classroom interaction side-by-side with teacher reflective diaries, which offers a commentary on the lessons.

e) *The final element in the model is the full integration of the VEO app into the procedures for professional practice, development, reflection and research.* This requires careful planning in advance. As shown in Chapter 6, simply 'parachuting' VEO into a professional setting may not be successful. Serious advance planning is necessary on how VEO will be integrated and how it can make a contribution. Chapters 6, 7, 8, 10 and 12 demonstrate how VEO can achieve a contribution with careful planning and full integration.

We should also conclude that, in view of the complex and multi-dimensional nature of modern learning environments (particularly those integrating technology), it is important to have a complex and multi-dimensional research design in place at the start. This needs to portray both the process and product of professional development, how actions taken by humans and technological systems relate to each other, how physical actions relate to talk and how participants work together to complete relevant tasks. Professional users typically demand concrete evidence of development over time, and this framework is well placed to provide triangulated evidence by using multiple sources of data. For example, both Chapters 7 and 12 provide longitudinal studies which show in interactional micro-detail how exactly teachers are able to change their practices over time. These findings are then corroborated by extracts from the teachers' reflective journals explaining why and how they changed practices.

The VEO App Can Be Used in Combination with a Variety of Methodological and Theoretical Approaches, for Any Language and Culture

As we have seen in Chapter 3, the VEO app was not developed on the basis of any specific theoretical standpoint and appears to be agnostic regarding theories of professional development and teaching. We saw in Chapters 7 and 11 that it was straightforward to integrate the use of VEO with existing models of reflective professional development: Sert's IMDAT model and Walsh's SETT model. The reason why integration proved straightforward is that VEO tag sets can be produced for any model which specifies behaviours or actions which can be noticed and tagged by observers. A tag set can transfer not only the professional practice inherent in a model, but also the theoretical assumptions on which it is based. In this collection, authors have employed a wide range of theoretical and methodological approaches and have found the VEO app to be compatible with all of these, as discussed below.

In Chapter 5, Schwab and Oesterle use CA in combination with quantification (using VEO) of the social actions performed by the teacher. An interesting finding from comparing the pictures presented of the lesson using both means is that: observers tended not to quantify the teacher's praising moves, but did quantify the teacher's correction moves, which gave a distorted picture of the lesson as being about negative feedback. This demonstrates that triangulation by using multiple methods of observation can be useful in providing a balanced portrayal of a lesson.

Körkkö, Kyrö-Ämmälä and Turunen used a case study approach in Chapter 6. As well as recording video, they gathered data using focus groups and recording discussions between supervisor and supervisee, which were analysed using thematic analysis. Supervisors played the key role in getting trainees to reflect on their teaching in a theorized way, specifically by asking them to relate specific practical episodes to the theory they had learnt.

Bozbıyık, Sert and Bacanak report in Chapter 7 on a case study of the development of a pre-service teacher in Turkey. They integrate CA analyses of classroom interaction with analyses of spoken feedback and written reflections. The detailed interactional analyses show a clear change in teacher practices from yes/no to more open questions, which is triangulated by the teacher's written reflections.

Batlle Rodríguez and Seedhouse use a multimodal CA approach in Chapter 8 to demonstrate that the teachers have developed multimodal speech exchange systems appropriate to the peer feedback task using VEO, in which verbal, non-verbal elements, artefacts and task-relevant actions are inextricably intertwined. Moreover, VEO is able to become the central organizing focus for their peer feedback CPD practice.

Tasdemir and Seedhouse show in Chapter 9 that a particularly effective data presentation technique is to combine side-by-side transcripts of classroom interaction with excerpts of reflective essays, which enables the reader to compare the teacher's comments on their own performance with evidence of the performance.

Hidson's case study approach in Chapter 10 includes interviews from three different perspectives on the introduction of VEO into a school: a senior leader, a line manager and one experienced teacher who was observed.

In Walsh's Chapter 11, data were analysed using multiple methods, comprising CA, thematic analysis of interviews and teacher reflections. Of particular interest were the profiles of each teacher's classroom practices, created using the VEO software and SETT tag set. These provided detailed qualitative and quantitative information about teachers' interactional practices, use of language, levels of learner involvement and use of language in relation to pedagogic goals.

As Seedhouse and Whelan exemplified in Chapter 12, a combination of data collection instruments which works well with VEO is (a) statistics which are automatically generated; (b) microanalysis of interaction; (c) self-report data in terms of interview, reflective diary; and (d) documents such as lesson plans and tutor feedback. These can all feed into a case study narrative, which in this case is of the improvement of error correction practices.

The VEO app can be used in conjunction with any language or culture. As part of the VEO Europa Project, we developed the interface for German, Finnish, Bulgarian and Turkish, and this can be done with other languages. As can be seen in Section II, the VEO app has been used successfully in a variety of countries and cultures.

The Future of VEO

In this section we look to the future of the VEO app. We discuss the current limitations of the VEO app and how it is likely to develop in the future in relation to these. We

224 *Video Enhanced Observation for Language Teaching*

also consider which other professional settings might be suitable for a VEO-based professional development programme.

Limitations and Criticisms of VEO

In general terms, the preceding chapters have painted a positive picture of what can be achieved through the application of the VEO app to professional development in education. However, there are limitations and drawbacks to any innovation, so in this section we discuss some limitations and criticisms.

First of all, there are general disadvantages which apply to all technological innovations with digital video, rather than specifically to VEO. The first of these is the amount of time and energy required for busy professionals (a) to learn how to use digital video recording hardware and the VEO software (b) to find the time to set up recording equipment for a lesson, review the videos and engage in reflection and discussions (c) to deal with technical problems involving hardware, software, Wi-Fi, internet, etc. This requirement should not be underestimated, and for this reason we have stressed throughout the book that it is most suitable for the VEO app to be embedded at the centre of a properly resourced ongoing programme of professional development. Proper financing and support for such a programme are essential because of the time, energy and skills development involved. The empirical studies in Section II demonstrate that it is indeed possible to develop such programmes, and that the results amply reward the investment. Another problem is that it can be difficult to capture all of the relevant interaction which takes place in a classroom, unless large numbers of video cameras and audio recorders are involved. The teacher in Seedhouse and Whelan's Chapter 12 reports that something is lost from the lesson from watching it back and you don't get the full sense/atmosphere in the room. As Körkkö, Kyrö-Ämmälä and Turunen report in Chapter 6, 'student teachers sometimes resist sharing videos with others ... They may struggle with watching the videos of their own teaching and fear that others will judge their teaching if they see the video.' 'Student teachers are not automatically able to notice integral aspects of teaching and learning in videos; instead, they might concentrate on superficial issues, such as their appearance and their behaviour .... Student teachers can find it difficult to criticise their own or their peers' teaching, which may hinder a deeper discussion of their developmental needs.' Extra work must therefore sometimes be done on building a supportive community which is able to engage in reflection and constructive criticism of professional practices.

The second general problem relates to data permissions, protection and storage and depends to some extent on the country and type of organization collecting the data; in the EU, the GDPR directive regulates all issues. Schwab and Oesterle in Chapter 5 report some reluctance from some parents and teachers at lessons being filmed. Furthermore, they had to follow certain local government procedures before even being allowed to contact schools about the possibility of filming: 'use of video at university and in schools has become a rather complicated and sometimes frustrating endeavour in Germany'. It is therefore important to embed use of VEO in a system for dealing with the ethics and proper management of digital video as part of the overall programme of professional development. Timescales and information on procedures need to be a central part of any project planning. Walsh in Chapter 11 reports on the problems of reflective CPD in schools where there is a high turnover of staff without proper contracts or time allocation for CPD, which emphasizes the point that the successful introduction of VEO may involve a stable professional environment with secure long-term funding for reflective CPD.

Next, we move on to limitations and criticisms of the VEO app in particular. Some of the projects reported in the empirical chapters noted specific technical problems with VEO, but some of these related to specific equipment (video and audio quality of iPad mini). Others related to lack of zooming or selective blurring for faces. These technical problems may be dealt with in future versions and updates of the app.

In theory, the strength of VEO is the ability to tag using pre-defined categories. However, according to Schwab and Oesterle in Chapter 5 'some students reported that using VEO can be rather challenging. Students from both case studies seemed to have problems with exact tagging due to some vagueness in the chosen categories. … all students commented on the importance of clearly defining and discussing the categories and "what actually is meant by it' …. That said, defining the categories can also be seen as a chance for professional development.' The teacher in Seedhouse and Whelan's Chapter 12 also found it quite difficult to categorize the things she observed using tags. However, her solution was to use the 'quick tag' marker to bookmark and then write comments.

A number of the empirical studies concluded that the VEO app cannot simply be 'parachuted' into a school and make a significant difference. The findings of Schwab and Oesterle in Chapter 5 'suggest making processes of reflection more transparent and integrating them systematically into our programme. Simply having the students use the VEO app does not seem to be enough; they need to be guided and given time and incentives by the lecturer to engage in reflective practices.' A very similar conclusion was reached by Körkkö, Kyrö-Ämmälä and Turunen in Chapter 6: 'The results showed that it was necessary to provide student teachers with a strong external reflection guide to support their video analysis and to connect individual video-based reflection to collaborative video-based reflection with their peers and supervisors in supervisory processes.' This was delivered successfully in their second trial. The studies suggest great benefits for CPD programmes in which VEO is centrally integrated, but some of the studies suggest that additional time commitment for training will be necessary to achieve this, in terms of learning to use the software and how to integrate it into reflective CPD procedures and communities.

The Future for VEO-based Professional Development Programmes

As a SaaS system, with licences available to purchase, VEO is being continually developed to increase and extend fit for the diverse use cases that have been identified and touched upon in this book. While some of these are at the more cutting-edge end of the spectrum of development, many others are simpler tweaks and redesigns intended

226   *Video Enhanced Observation for Language Teaching*

to improve user experience. These changes derive, not only from user feedback, but are also based on the best research evidence available for what works in professional development.

Many of these upcoming developments speak to the issues uncovered by researchers in this book and aim to improve accessibility via improved process within the technology, as well as the technology itself. VEO currently provides a very flexible video tagging tool that can be used for a range of professional development, quality assurance and research purposes. However, upcoming developments will bundle process into the product to direct initial use and to reduce the training and onboarding needed to get started and to generate value from the system. These user journeys and pathways will follow a logical order for and be tailored to the purposes behind using VEO, as pioneered by early users and researchers of the system and demanded by identified large-scale opportunities to create impact. These will be complemented by tool-tips and some (optional) AI and auto-suggestion of pathways. As a result, effective deployments of VEO can be quickly and easily replicated by others.

While VEO is currently fully compliant with GDPR (see https://veo.co.uk/data-security-and-safeguarding/), the above journeys will make this explicit in VEO's use.

Regularly requested features such as face blurring and enhanced reporting will be designed and implemented in close consultation with users.

Where VEO will push its own boundaries with more innovative product developments, direct research evidence will necessarily be limited. However, VEO has identified useful means to deploy artificial intelligence and machine learning to make suggestions as to patterns in data that might direct users' reflections, pathways and connections. At the time of writing, these are in development.

Finally, VEO is busy working on integrations with other learning platforms. The VEO API is fully documented so that it is a relatively simple job for developers to pull through the required data, displays and functionality into other software systems. By embedding VEO in organizations' own systems, easier adoption will be facilitated through familiarity with legacy products.

All of the above will reduce the time and effort needed by the user to create value from VEO. At the same time, care will be taken to ensure that user autonomy is not diluted and the simplicity heart of VEO will be maintained. This will allow VEO to work with trainers, publishers and examination bodies, as well as individual trainers and learners to accelerate learning at scale.

The Legacy of the VEO App and VEO-based Programmes

It is hoped that the results of the work to date with VEO and the upcoming system enhancements will lead to a greater ease of collaboration in learning, through the seamless provision of tools on which to base this communication. VEO's aim has been to centre learning on people, their interaction and performance. By giving a simple but focussed means to reflect and feedback on this activity, greater depth of understanding and evaluation can be engendered, while providing transparency of video evidence. The ability to accurately review action can not only give greater access to its improvement, but also deepen understanding and consensus of the meaning and value of such action. VEO's initial work across various fields from teacher training to pupil learning, medical training to academic research, can provide a catalyst to enhanced focus in action learning and research, as well as heighten the learning and collaboration potential of video as a resource. By accessing and sharing the key moments that really matter, learners, teachers and researchers can gain transformational insight to build accelerated and lasting improvement in thought and action.

Notes

Chapter 5

1   This is basically the same in all six Universities of Education in the Federal State of Baden-Wuerttemberg but can differ in other parts of Germany, especially in programmes for grammar schoolteachers.

2   In Germany, students in teaching programmes usually read two majors (here: English and German), some even an additional minor – e.g. arts, music or PE – and also take a major in pedagogy along with a couple of classes in sociology and psychology.

3   Selting, M. et al. (2011). A system for transcribing talk-in-interaction: GAT 2 translated and adapted for English by Elizabeth Couper-Kuhlen and Dagmar Barth-Weingarten. Gesprächsforschung. 12. 1–51 (online version).

Chapter 6

1   The practicum included practice teaching of the mainstream compulsory subjects stated in the national core curriculum for basic education (Finnish National Board of Education 2014).

2   The Finnish school system follows an inclusive approach, and therefore children are taught together in the same classroom whenever possible. Some pupils study part-time in separate special education groups, which consist of pupils from different grades.

Chapter 7

1   The tag set is based on the authors' review of years of classroom interaction research, including the frameworks by Seedhouse (2004) and Walsh (2011). It should also be noted that some aspects of VEO-tags were also discussed during the first project meeting in 2015 in Newcastle; therefore, the second author is grateful for the inspiration by Paul Seedhouse and Götz Schwab.

2   TEOG is a national student placement exam in Turkey.

Chapter 13

1   The IELTS band descriptors can be found on https://www.ielts.org/-/media/pdfs/speaking-band-descriptors.ashx?la=en

References

Chapter 1

Körkkö, M. (2020), 'Beneath the surface: Developing video-based reflective practice in the primary school teacher education programme', Doctoral diss., Faculty of Education, University of Lapland, Finland.

Chapter 2

Aydin, Z. and Yildiz, S. (2014), 'Use of wikis to promote collaborative EFL writing', *Language Learning & Technology*, 18 (1): 160–80.

Balzaretti, N., Ciani, A., Cutting, C., O'Keeffe, L. and White, B. (2019), 'Unpacking the potential of 360 degree video to support pre-service teacher development', *Research on Education and Media*, 11 (1): 63–9.

Baecher, L., Kung, S. C., Jewkes, A. M. and Rosalia, C. (2013), 'The role of video for self-evaluation in early field experiences', *Teaching and Teacher Education*, 36: 189–97.

Bao, W. (2020). 'COVID-19 and online teaching in higher education: A case study of Peking University', *Human Behavior and Emerging Technologies*, 2: 113–15.

Blake, R. (2016), 'Technology and the four skills', *Language Learning & Technology*, 20 (2): 129–42.

Botero, G. G. and Questier, F. (2016), 'What students think and what they actually do in a mobile assisted language learning context: New insights for self-directed language learning in higher education', *CALL Communities and Culture–Short Papers from EUROCALL*, 150–4.

Breen, M. P., Hird, B., Milton, M., Oliver, R. and Thwaite, A. (2001), 'Making sense of language teaching: Teachers' principles and classroom practices', *Applied Linguistics*, 22 (4): 470–501.

Burston, J. (2013), 'Language learning technology MALL: Future directions for BYOD applications', *The IALLT Journal for Language Learning Technologies*, 43 (2): 89–96.

Cobb, T. (2007), 'Computing the vocabulary demands of L2 reading', *Language Learning & Technology*, 11 (3): 38–63.

Compton, L. K. (2009), 'Preparing language teachers to teach language online: A look at skills, roles, and responsibilities', *Computer Assisted Language Learning*, 22(1): 73–99.

Dewey, J. (1933). *How We Think: A Restatement of the Relation of Reflective Thinking to the Educative Process*. Boston, MA: D.C. Heath & Co Publishers.

Diez-Gutierrez, E. and Gajardo-Espinoza, K. (2020), 'Educar y Evaluar en Tiempos de Coronavirus: la Situación en España', *Multidisciplinary Journal of Educational Research*, 10 (2): 102–34. doi: 10.4471/remie.2020.5604.

Farrell, T. S. C. (2018). 'Reflective practice for language teachers', in Liontas, J. I. (ed.), *The TESOL Encyclopedia of English Language Teaching*, 1st edn., vol. 7, 1–6, Oxford: Wiley-Blackwell. doi:10.1002/9781118784235.eelt0873.

Finlay, L. (2008), 'Reflecting on "Reflective practice"', *Practice-based Professional Learning Paper 52*. The Open University.

Fouz-González, J. (2017), 'Pronunciation instruction through Twitter: The case of commonly mispronounced words', *Computer Assisted Language Learning*, 30 (7): 631–63.

Freeman, D., Webre, A. C. and Epperson, M. (2019), 'What counts as knowledge in English language teaching', in Walsh, S. and Mann, S. (eds), *The Routledge Handbook on English Language Teacher Education*, 13–24. London: Routledge.

Gaudin, C. and Chaliès, S. (2015), 'Video viewing in teacher education and professional development: A literature review', *Educational Research Review*, 16: 41–67.

Hampel, R. and Stickler, U. (2005), 'New skills for new classrooms: Training tutors to teach languages online', *Computer Assisted Language Learning*, 18 (4): 311–26.

Hampel, R. and Stickler, U. (eds) (2015), *Developing Online Language Teaching: Research-Based Pedagogies and Reflective Practices*. Houndmills: Palgrave Macmillan.

Healey, D., Hanson-Smith, E., Hubbard, P., Ioannou-Georgiou, S., Kessler, G. and Ware, P. (2011), *TESOL Technology Standards: Description, Implementation, Integration*. Alexandria, VA: TESOL.

Helm, F. (2015), 'The practices and challenges of telecollaboration in higher education in Europe', *Language Learning & Technology*, 19 (2): 197–217.

Hinkelman, D. and Gruba, P. (2012), 'Power within blended language learning programs in Japan', *Language Learning & Technology*, 16 (2): 46–64.

Hockly, N. (2015), 'Developments in online language learning', *ELT Journal*, 69 (3): 308–13.

Hockly, N. (2018), 'Video-based observation in language teacher education', *ELT Journal*, 72 (3): 329–35.

Hubbard, P. (2006), 'Teacher education in CALL: The seven central questions', *Keynote speech at the International Conference on Computer Assisted Language Learning*. Beijing, China. June 2006.

Jackson, D. O. and Cho, M. (2018), 'Language teacher noticing: A socio-cognitive window on classroom realities', *Language Teaching Research*, 22 (1): 29–46.

Jarvis, H. and Krashen, S. (2014), 'Is CALL obsolete? Language acquisition and language learning revisited in a digital age', *Tesl-Ej*, 17(4): 1–6.

Kessler, G. and Hubbard, P. (2017), 'Language teacher education and technology', in Chapelle, C. and Sauro, S. (eds), *The Handbook of Technology and Second Language Teaching and Learning*, 278–92, Oxford: Wiley-Blackwell.

Kessler, G. (2018), 'Technology and the future of language teaching', *Foreign Language Annals*, 51: 205–18. doi: 10.1111/flan.12318

Kukulska-Hulme, A. and Shield, L. (2008), 'An overview of mobile assisted language learning: From content delivery to supported collaboration and interaction', *ReCALL*, 20 (3): 271–89. doi:10.1017/S0958344008000335.

Levy, M. (1997), *Computer-assisted Language Learning: Context and Conceptualization*. Oxford: Oxford University Press.

Levy, M. and Hubbard, P. (2005), 'Why call CALL "CALL"?' *Computer Assisted Language Learning*, 18 (3): 143–9.

Mann, S. and Walsh, S. (2017), *Reflective Practice in English Language Teaching: Research-based Principles and Practices*. New York: Taylor & Francis.

References

Marsh, B. and Mitchell, N. (2014), 'The role of video in teacher professional development', *Teacher Development*, 18 (3): 403–17.

Mezirow, J. (2000), *Learning as Transformation: Critical Perspectives on a Theory in Progress. The Jossey-Bass Higher and Adult Education Series*. San Francisco, CA: Jossey-Bass Publishers.

Mosley Wetzel, M., Maloch, B. and Hoffman, J. V. (2017), 'Retrospective video analysis: A reflective tool for teachers and teacher educators', *The Reading Teacher*, 70 (5): 533–42.

Mumford, S. and Dikilitaş, K. (2020), 'Pre-service language teachers reflection development through online interaction in a hybrid learning course', *Computers & Education*, 144: 103706.

Park, J., Yang, J. and Hsieh, Y. C. (2014), 'University level second language readers' online reading and comprehension strategies', *Language Learning & Technology*, 18 (3): 148–72.

Rosell-Aguilar, F. (2018), 'Twitter: A Professional Development and Community of Practice Tool for Teachers', *Journal of Interactive Media in Education*,1: 6, DOI: http://doi.org/10.5334/jime.452

Salmon, G. (2012), *E-moderating: The Key to Online Teaching and Learning*. London: Routledge.

Schön, D. A. (1984), *The Reflective Practitioner: How Professionals Think in Action*, Vol. 5126. New York: Basic books.

Seedhouse, P. (ed.) (2017), *Task-based Language Learning in a Real-World Digital Environment: The European Digital Kitchen*. London: Bloomsbury.

Seidel, T., Stürmer, K., Blomberg, G., Kobarg, M. and Schwindt, K. (2011), 'Teacher learning from analysis of videotaped classroom situations: Does it make a difference whether teachers observe their own teaching or that of others?' *Teaching and Teacher Education*, 27 (2): 259–67.

Smith, S. and Wang, S. (2013), 'Reading and grammar learning through mobile phones', *Language Learning & Technology*, 17 (3): 117–34.

Steeg, S. M. (2016), 'A case study of teacher reflection: Examining teacher participation in a video-based professional learning community', *Journal of Language and Literacy Education*, 12 (1): 122–41.

Stockwell, G. and Hubbard, P. (2013), 'Some emerging principles for mobile-assisted language learning', *The International Research Foundation for English Language Education*, 1–15.

Sun, Y. C. and Chang, Y. J. (2012), 'Blogging to learn: Becoming EFL academic writers through collaborative dialogues', *Language Learning & Technology*, 16 (1): 43–61.

Ur, P. (2019), 'Theory and practice in language teacher education', *Language Teaching*, 52 (4): 450–9.

Van Es, E. A. and Sherin, M. G. (2002), 'Learning to notice: Scaffolding new teachers' interpretations of classroom interactions', *Journal of Technology and Teacher Education*, 10 (4): 571–96.

Van Es, E. A. (2012), 'Examining the development of a teacher learning community: The case of a video club', *Teaching and Teacher Education*, 28 (2): 182–92.

Vygotsky, L. S. (1978), *Mind and Society: The Development of Higher Psychological Processes*. Cambridge, MA: Harvard University Press.

232 References

Chapter 3

Christensen, C. M., Horn, M. B. and Johnson, C. W. (2008), *Disrupting Class: How Disruptive Innovation Will Change the Way the World Learns*. New York: McGraw-Hill.

Clegg, D., Du Rose, A. and Byfield, D. (2018), 'The effect of psychomotor skills training feedback using video enhanced observations (VEO) on VIVA outcomes: platform presentation', WFC/ACC 10th Chiropractic Education Conference, London, United Kingdom, 24 October 2018–27 October 2018.

Kirkpatrick, D. (1996), 'Revisiting Kirkpatrick's four-level-model', *Training & Development*, 50 (1): 54–7.

Lofthouse, R. and Birmingham, P. (2010), 'The camera in the classroom: Video-recording as a tool for professional development of student teachers', *Tean Journal*, 1 (2) December [Online]. Available online: http://ojs.cumbria.ac.uk/index.php/TEAN/article/view/59 (Accessed on 29 February 2020).

Lofthouse, R., Leat, D. and Towler, C. (2010), *Coaching for Teaching and Learning: A Practical Guide for Schools*. Reading: CfBT Education Trust.

Chapter 5

Abendroth-Timmer, D. (2011), 'Reflexive Lehrerbildung: Konzepte und Perspektiven für den Einsatz von Unterrichtssimulation und Videographie in der fremdsprachendidaktischen Ausbildung', *Zeitschrift für Fremdsprachenforschung*, 22 (1): 3–41.

Allen, J. M. and Wright, S. E. (2014), 'Integrating theory and practice in the pre-service education practicum', *Teachers and Teaching: Theory and Practice*, 20 (2): 136–51.

Batlle, J. and Miller, P. (2017), 'Video enhanced observation and teacher development: Teachers' beliefs as technology users', *EDULEARN17 Proceedings*, 2017: 2352–61.

Baecher, L., Schieblie, M., Rosalia, C. and Rorimer, S. (2013), 'Blogging for academic purposes with English language learners: An online fieldwork initiative'. *Contemporary Issues in Technology and Teacher Education*, 13 (1): 1–21.

Baumert, J. and Kunter, M. (2006), 'Stichwort: Professionelle Kompetenz von Lehrkräften', *Zeitschrift für Erziehungswissenschaft*, 9 (4): 469–520.

Blomberg, G., Renkl, A., Sherin, M. G., Borko, H. and Seidel, T. (2013), 'Five research-based heuristics for using video in pre-service teacher education', *Journal for Educational Research Online*, 5 (1): 90–114.

Breidbach, S. (2007), *Bildung, Kultur, Wissenschaft. Reflexive Didaktik für den bilingualen Sachfachunterricht*. Münster: Waxmann.

Bresges, A., Harring, M., Kauertz, A., Nordmeier, V. and Parchmann, I. (2019), 'Die Theorie-Praxis-Verzahnung in der Lehrerbildung – eine Einführung in die Thematik', in Bundesministerium für Bildung und Forschung [BMBF] (ed.), *Verzahnung von Theorie und Praxis im Lehramtsstudium. Erkenntnisse aus Projekten der "Qualitätsoffensive Lehrerbildung"*, 4–7. Frankfurt a. M.: Druck- und Verlagshaus Zarbock. Available online: https://www.bmbf.de/upload_filestore/pub/Verzahnung_Theorie_Praxis_Lehramtsstudium_Erkenntnisse_QLB.pdf (Accessed 3 June 2020).

References

233

Burnett, P. C. and Mendel, V. (2010), 'Praise and feedback in the primary classroom: Teachers' and students' perspectives', *Australian Journal of Educational & Developmental Psychology*, (10): 145–54.

Caspari, D. (2016), 'Wechselspiele zwischen Theorie und Forschung', in Caspari, D., Klippel, F., Legutke, M. K. and Schramm, K. (eds), *Forschungsmethoden in der Fremdsprachendidaktik. Ein Handbuch*, 364–69. Tübingen: Narr.

Cavar, D. (2020), 'Mobile Technologien zur Videografie im Englischunterricht', unpublished final thesis, University of Education, Karlsruhe.

Dörnyei, Z. (2007), *Research Methods in Applied Linguistics: Quantitative, Qualitative, and Mixed Methodologies*. Oxford [u.a.]: Oxford University Press.

Elsner, D. and Keßler, J.-U. (2013), *Bilingual Education in Primary School*. Tübingen: Narr.

Fantilli, R. D. and McDougall, D. E. (2009), 'A study of novice teachers: Challenges and supports in the first years', *Teaching and Teacher Education*, 25 (6): 814–25.

Gröschner, A., Müller, K., Bauer, J., Seidel, T., Prenzel, M., Kauper, T. and Möller, J. (2015), 'Praxisphasen in der Lehrerausbildung – Eine Strukturanalyse am Beispiel des gymnasialen Lehramtsstudiums in Deutschland', *Zeitschrift für Erziehungswissenschaft*, 18 (4): 639–65.

Häusler, J., Jurik, V., Schindler, A.-K., Gröschner, A. and Seidel, T. (2018), 'Videografie im Unterricht', in Harring, M., Rohls, C. and Gläser-Zikuda, M. (eds), *Handbuch Schulpädagogik*, 831–40. Münster: Waxmann/utb.

Hattie, J. (2012), *Visible Learning for Teachers*. London: Routledge.

Haudeck, H. and Schwab, G. (2011), 'Merkmale bedeutungsvoller Interaktion im frühen Fremdsprachenunterricht der Grundschule', in Kötter, M. and Rymarczyk, J. (eds), *Fremdsprachenunterricht in der Grundschule: Forschungsergebnisse und Vorschläge zu seiner weiteren Entwicklung*, 135–52. Frankfurt et al.: Peter Lang.

Hilzensauer, W. (2017), *Wie kommt die Reflexion in den Lehrberuf? Ein Lernangebot zur Förderung der Reflexionskompetenz bei Lehramtsstudierenden*. Münster: Waxmann.

Hockly, N. (2018), 'Video-based observation in language teacher education', *ELT Journal*, 72 (3): 32–35.

Hosenfeld, A. and Helmke, A. (2008), 'Welche Rolle spielen Lehrpersonenmerkmale für eine erfolgreiche Nutzung von Feedback in Form von Unterrichtsvideos?' in Lankes, E.-M. (ed.), *Pädagogische Professionalität als Gegenstand empirischer Forschung*, 47–60. Münster: Waxmann.

Jäkel, O. (2010), *The Flensburg English Classroom Corpus (FLECC)*. Flensburg: Flensburger University Press.

Lyster, R. (2007), *Learning and Teaching Languages through Content: A Counterbalanced Approach*. Amsterdam: John Benjamins Publishing.

Mann, S. and Walsh, S. (2017), *Reflective Practices in English Language Teaching. Research-Based Principles and Practices*. London: Routledge.

Mattson, M., Eilertsen, T. V. and Rorrison, D. (2011), *A Practicum Turn in Teacher Education*. Rotterdam: Sense Publishers.

McDonagh, C., Roche, M., Sullivan, B. and Glenn, M. (eds) (2019), *Enhancing Practice through Classroom Research: A Teacher's Guide to Professional Development*, 2nd edn. London: Routledge.

Mehisto, P., Marsh, D. and Frigols, M. J. (2008), *Uncovering CLIL*. Oxford: Macmillan.

Mühlhausen, U. (2012), 'Mit multimedialen Unterrichtsdokumenten und Eigenvideos dem Theorie-Praxis-Dilemma der Lehrerbildung entgegenwirken', in Blell, G. and Lütge, C. (eds), *Fremdsprachendidaktik und Lehrerbildung. Konzepte, Impulse und Perspektiven*, 156–70. Münster: LIT Verlag.

Nickerson, R. S. (1998), 'Confirmation bias: A ubiquitous phenomenon in many guises', *Review of General Psychology*, 2 (2): 175–220.

Oliver, R. (2000), 'Age differences in negotiation and feedback in classroom and pairwork', *Language Learning*, 50: 119–51.

Schramm, K. and Aguado, K. (2010), 'Videographie in den Fremdsprachendidaktiken', in Aguado, K., Schramm, K. and Vollmer, H. J. (eds), *Fremdsprachliches Handeln beobachten, messen, evaluieren. Neue methodische Ansätze der Kompetenzforschung und der Videographie*, 185–214. Frankfurt a. M.: Peter Lang.

Schwab, G. (2014), 'LID - Lehrerprofessionalisierung im Diskurs. Eine Pilotstudie zur gesprächsanalytischen Beratung von Englischlehrkräften in der Realschule', in Pieper, I., Frei, P., Hauenschild, K. and Schmidt-Thieme, B. (eds), *Was ist der Fall. Fallarbeit in Lehrerbildung und Bildungsforschung*, 89–105, Wiesbaden: VS Verlag.

Schwab, G. (2020a), 'Observation in the language classroom', in Lenz, F., Frobenius, M. and Klattenberg, R. (eds), *Classroom Observation: Researching Interaction in English Language Teaching*, 9–29. Frankfurt a.M.: Peter Lang.

Schwab, G. (2020b), 'Conversation analysis gets mobile. Student participation in a bilingual primary classroom in Germany', in Lenz, F., Frobenius, M. and Klattenberg, R. (eds), *Classroom Observation: Researching Interaction in English Language Teaching*, 85–115. Frankfurt a.M.: Peter Lang.

Seedhouse, P. (2007), 'Interaction and constructs', in Hua, Z., Seedhouse, P. and Cook, V. (eds), *Language Learning and Teaching as Social Interaction*, 9–21. Basingstoke: Palgrave Macmillan.

Seidel, T., Blomberg, G. and Stürmer, K. (2010), 'Observer – Validierung eines videobasierten Instruments zur Erfassung der professionellen Wahrnehmung von Unterricht. Projekt OBSERVE', in Klieme, E., Leutner, D. and Kenk, M. (eds), *Kompetenzmodellierung. Zwischenbilanz des DFG-Schwerpunktprogramms und Perspektiven des Forschungsansatzes* (56th supplement to Zeitschrift für Pädagogik), 296–306. Weinheim: Beltz.

Seidel, T., Stürmer., K., Blomberg, G., Kobarg, M. and Schwindt, K. (2011), 'Teacher learning from analysis of videotaped classroom situations: Does it make a difference whether teachers observe their own teaching or that of others?' *Teaching and Teacher Education*, 27 (2): 259–67.

Selting, M. et al. (2011), 'A system for transcribing talk-in-interaction: GAT 2' translated and adapted for English by Elizabeth Couper-Kuhlen and Dagmar Barth- Weingarten, *Gesprächsforschung*, 12: 1–51. (online version) Available online: (Access on 30 March 2020).

Sert, O. (2015), *Social Interaction and L2 Classroom Discourse*. Edinburgh: Edinburgh University Press.

Sherin, M. G. and Van Es, E.-A. (2009), 'Effects of video club participation on teachers' professional vision', *Journal of Teacher Education*, 60 (1): 20–37.

Terhart, E. (2006), 'Standards und Kompetenzen in der Lehrerbildung', in Hilligus, A. H. (ed.), *Paderborner Beiträge zur Unterrichtsforschung und Lehrerbildung. Bd. 11: Standards und Kompetenzen - neue Qualität in der Lehrerausbildung? Neue Ansätze und Erfahrungen in nationaler und internationaler Perspektive*, 29–41. Berlin: LIT Verlag.

Treetzen, I. (2016), 'Teaching in the early English classroom. Using the VEO app to observe teacher feedback', unpublished final thesis, University of Education, Karlsruhe.

Tripp, T. R. and Rich, P. J. (2012), 'The influence of video analysis on the process of teacher change', *Teaching and Teacher Education*, 28 (5): 728–39.

Van Lier, L. (1996), *Interaction in the Language Curriculum: Awareness, Autonomy and Authenticity*. London: Longman.

Chapter 6

Blomberg, G., Stürmer, K. and Seidel, T. (2011), 'How pre-service teachers observe teaching on video: Effects of viewers' teaching subjects and the subject of the video', *Teaching & Teacher Education*, 27 (7): 1131–40. doi:10.1016/j.tate.2011.04.008

Blömeke, S., Gustafsson, J.-E. and Shavelson, R. (2015), 'Beyond dichotomies: Competence viewed as a continuum', *Zeitschrift Für Psychologie*, 223 (1): 3–13. doi:10.1027/2151-2604/a000194

Borko, H., Jacobs, J., Eiteljorg, E. and Pittman, M. (2008), 'Video as a tool for fostering productive discussions in mathematics professional development', *Teaching and Teacher Education*, 24 (2): 417–36. doi:10.1016/j.tate.2006.11.012

Bryan, L. and Recesso, A. (2006), 'Promoting reflection among science student teachers using a web-based video analysis tool', *Journal of Computing in Teacher Education*, 23 (1): 31–9. Available online: https://www.learntechlib.org/p/55277/

Christ, T., Arya, P. and Chiu, M. (2014), 'Teachers' reports of learning and application to pedagogy based on engagement in collaborative peer video analysis', *Teaching Education*, 25 (4): 349–74. doi:10.1080/10476210.2014.920001

Ellis, J., McFadden, J., Anwar, T. and Roehrig, G. (2015), 'Investigating the social interactions of beginning teachers using a video annotation tool', *Contemporary Issues in Technology and Teacher Education*, 15 (3): 404–21.

Fadde, P. and Sullivan, P. (2013), 'Using interactive video to develop preservice teachers' classroom awareness', *Contemporary Issues in Technology and Teacher Education*, 13 (2): 156–74.

Finnish National Board of Education (2014), *Perusopetuksen Opetussuunnitelman Perusteet [The National Core Curriculum for Basic Education]*. Helsinki: Finnish National Board of Education.

Goldman, R., Pea, R., Barron, B. and Derry, S. (2007), *Video Research in the Learning Sciences*. Mahwah, NJ: Lawrence Erlbaum Associates.

Gröschner, A., Seidel, T., Kiemer, K. and Pehmer, A.-K. (2014), 'Through the lens of teacher professional development components: The "dialogic video cycle" as an innovative program to foster classroom dialogue', *Professional Development in Education*, 41 (4): 729–56. doi:10.1080/19415257.2014.939692

Gröschner, A., Schindler, A.-K., Holzberger, D., Alles, M. and Seidel, T. (2018), 'How systematic video reflection in teacher professional development regarding classroom discourse contributes to teacher and student self-efficacy', *International Journal of Educational Research*, 90: 223–33. doi:10.1016/j.ijer.2018.02.003

Harford, J. and MacRuairc, G. (2008), 'Engaging student teachers in meaningful reflective practice', *Teaching and Teacher Education*, 24 (7): 1884–92. doi:10.1016/j.tate.2008.02.010

Husu, J., Toom, A. and Patrikainen, S. (2008), 'Guided reflection as a means to demonstrate and develop student teachers' reflective competencies', *Reflective Practice*, 9 (1): 37–51. doi:10.1080/14623940701816642

References

Jay, J. and Johnson, K. (2002), 'Capturing complexity: A typology of reflective practice for teacher education', *Teaching and Teacher Education*, 18 (1): 73–85. Available online: https://eric.ed.gov/?id=EJ640181

Kansanen, P. (1993), 'An outline for a model of teachers' pedagogical thinking', in Kansanen, P. (ed.), *Discussions on Some Educational Issues IV*, 51–65. Research Report 121. Helsinki: University of Helsinki.

Körkkö, M. (2019). 'Towards meaningful reflection and a holistic approach: Creating a reflection framework in teacher education', *Scandinavian Journal of Educational Research*, 65 (2): 258–75. doi: 10.1080/00313831.2019.1676306.

Körkkö, M. (2020). 'Beneath the surface: Developing video-based reflective practice in the primary school teacher education programme', Doctoral diss., Faculty of Education, University of Lapland, Finland.

Körkkö, M., Kyrö-Ämmälä, O. and Turunen, T. (2016), 'Professional development through reflection in teacher education', *Teaching and Teacher Education*, 55 (2): 198–206. doi:10.1016/j.tate.2016.01.014

Körkkö, M., Morales-Rios, S. and Kyrö-Ämmälä, O. (2019), 'Using a video App as a tool for reflective practice', *Educational Research*, 61 (1): 22–37. doi:10.1080/00131881.2018.1562954

Korthagen, F. (2004), 'In search of the essence of a good teacher: Towards a more holistic approach in teacher education', *Teaching & Teacher Education*, 20 (1): 77–97.

Korthagen, F. (2017), 'Inconvenient truths about teacher learning: Towards professional development 3.0', *Teachers & Teaching*, 23 (4): 387–405. doi:10.1080/13540602.2016.1211523

Korthagen, F., Kessels, J., Koster, B., Lagerwerf, B. and Wubbels, T. (eds) (2001), *Linking Practice and Theory: The Pedagogy of Realistic Teacher Education*. Mahwah, NJ: Lawrence Erlbaum Associates.

Kyrö-Ämmälä, O. (2019), 'Initial teacher education at the University of Lapland', in Paksuniemi, M. and Keskitalo, P. (eds), *Introduction to the Finnish Educational System*, 51–66. Leiden: Brill/Sense.

Mayring, P. (2014), *Qualitative Content Analysis: Theoretical Foundation, Basic Procedures and Software Solution*. Klagenfurt: GESIS Leibniz Institute for the Social Sciences. Available online: http://nbn-resolving.de/urn:nbn:de:0168-ssoar-395173

Santagata, R. and Angelici, G. (2010), 'Studying the impact of the lesson analysis framework on preservice teachers' abilities to reflect on videos of classroom teaching', *Journal of Teacher Education*, 61 (4): 339–49. doi:10.1177/0022487110369555

Santagata, R. and Guarino, J. (2011), 'Using video to teach future teachers to learn from teaching', *ZDM Mathematics Education*, 43 (1): 133–45. doi:10.1007/s11858-010-0292-3

Schön, D. (1987), *Educating the Reflective Practitioner: Toward a New Design for Teaching and Learning in the Professions*. San Francisco: Jossey-Bass.

Sherin, M. (2004), 'New perspectives on the role of video in teacher education', in Brophy, J. (ed.), *Using Video in Teacher Education*, 1–28. Amsterdam: Elsevier.

Snoeyink, R. (2010), 'Using video self-analysis to improve the "withitness" of student teachers', *Journal of Digital Learning in Teacher Education*, 26 (3): 101–10.

Vaugh, S., Schumm, J. and Sinagub, J. (1996), *Focus Group Interviews in Education and Psychology*. Thousand Oaks, CA: Sage.

Zanting, A., Verloop, N. and Vermunt, J. (2003), 'How do student teachers elicit their mentor teachers' practical knowledge?' *Teachers & Teaching*, 9 (3): 197–211. doi:10.1080/1354060032000116602

Chapter 7

Appleton, K. and Kindt, I. (2002), 'Beginning elementary teachers' development as teachers of science', *Journal of Science Teacher Education*, 13 (1): 43–61.

Aşık, A. and Kuru Gönen, I. S. (2016), 'Pre-service EFL teachers' reported perceptions of their development through SETT experience', *Classroom Discourse*, 7 (2): 164–83.

Aus der Wieschen, M. V. and Sert, O. (2021). 'Divergent language choices and maintenance of intersubjectivity: The case of Danish EFL young learners. *International Journal of Bilingual Education and Bilingualism*, 24 (1): 107–23.

Balaman, U. (2018), 'Embodied resources in a repetition activity in a preschool L2 classroom', *Novitas-ROYAL (Research on Youth and Language)*, 12 (1): 27–51.

Baumgart, J. (2019), 'The quality of teacher talk in TESOL Classroom: A critical-reflective analysis of discourse', in De Dios Martinez Agudo, J. (eds), *Quality in TESOL and Teacher Education. From Results Culture towards Quality Culture*, 84–93. New York: Routledge.

Bozbıyık, M. (2017), 'The implementation of VEO in an English language education context: A focus on teacher questioning practices', Unpublished MA diss., Gazi University, Turkey.

Çelik, S., Baran, E. and Sert, O. (2018), 'The affordances of mobile-app supported teacher observations for peer feedback', *International Journal of Mobile and Blended Learning*, 10 (2): 36–49.

Dalton-Puffer, C. (2006), 'Questions as strategies to encourage speaking in content-and-language-integrated classrooms', in Uso-Juan, E. and Martirez-Flor, A. (eds), *Current Trends in the Development and Teaching of the Four Language Skills*, 187–214. New York: M. deGruyter.

Heritage, J. (2012), 'The epistemic engine: Sequence organization and territories of knowledge', *Research on Language and Social Interaction*, 45 (1): 30–52.

Jacknick, C. M. (2011), '"But this is writing": Post-expansion in student-initiated sequences', *Novitas-ROYAL (Research on Youth and Language)*, 5 (1): 39–54.

Jakonen, T. (2018), 'Retrospective orientation to learning activities and achievements as a resource in classroom interaction', *The Modern Language Journal*, 102 (4): 758–74.

Jefferson, G. (2004), 'Glossary of transcript symbols with an introduction', *Pragmatics and Beyond New Series*, 125: 13–34.

Kärkkäinen, E. and Thompson, S. A. (2018), 'Language and bodily resources: "Response packages" in response to polar questions in English', *Journal of Pragmatics*, 123: 220–38.

Kim, Y. and Silver, R. E. (2016), 'Provoking reflective thinking in post observation conversations', *Journal of Teacher Education*, 67 (3): 203–19.

Koshik, I. (2002a), 'Designedly incomplete utterances: A pedagogical practice for eliciting knowledge displays in error correction sequences', *Research on Language and Social Interaction*, 35: 277–309.

Koshik, I. (2002b), 'A conversation analytic study of yes/no questions which convey reversed polarity assertions', *Journal of Pragmatics*, 34: 1851–77.

Koshik, I. (2003), 'Wh-questions used as challenges', *Discourse Studies*, 5: 51–77.

Koshik, I. (2005), 'Alternative questions used in conversational repair', *Discourse Studies*, 7: 193–211.

Koshik, I. (2010), 'Questions that convey information in teacher-student conferences', in Freed, A. and Ehrlich, S. (eds), *"Why Do You Ask?" The Function of Questions in Institutional Discourse*, 159–86. New York: Oxford University.

Körkkö, M., Morales Rios, S. and Kyrö-Ämmälä, O. (2019), 'Using a video app as a tool for reflective practice', *Educational Research*, 61 (1): 22–37.

Li, L. (2017), *Social Interaction and Teacher Cognition*. Edinburgh: Edinburgh University Press.

Li, L. (2020). *Language Teacher Cognition*. Basingstoke, UK: Palgrave Macmillan.

Long, M. H. and Sato, C. J. (1983), 'Classroom foreigner talk discourse: Forms and functions of teachers' questions', in Seliger, H. W. and Long, M. H. (eds), *Classroom Oriented Research in Second Language Acquisition*, 268–85. Rowley, MA: Newbury House.

Lyster, R. and Ranta, L. (1997), 'Corrective feedback and learner uptake', *Studies in Second Language Acquisition*, 19 (1): 37–66.

Mann, S. and Walsh, S. (2015), 'Reflective dimension of CPD: Supporting self-evaluation and peer evaluation', in Howard, A. and Donaghue, H. (eds), *Teacher Evaluation in Second Language Education*, 17–33. New York: Bloomsbury.

Mann, S. and Walsh, S. (2017), *Reflective Practice in English Language Teaching: Research-based Principles and Practices*. London: Routledge.

Markee, N. (2008), 'Toward a learning behavior tracking methodology for CA-for-SLA', *Applied Linguistics*, 29: 404–27.

Markee, N. (2013), 'Emic and etic in qualitative research', in C. Chapelle, (eds), *Encyclopedia of Applied Linguistics*, 404–27. Oxford: Wiley-Blackwell.

Mehan, H. (1979), "What time is it Denise?' Asking known information questions in classroom discourse', *Theory into Practice*, 28 (4): 285–94.

Mondada, L. (2018), 'Multiple temporalities of language and body in interaction: Challenges for transcribing multimodality', *Research on Language and Social Interaction*, 51 (1): 85–106.

Pekarek Doehler, S. (2018), 'Elaborations on L2 interactional competence: The development of L2 grammar-for-interaction', *Classroom Discourse*, 9 (1): 3–24.

Pomerantz, A. (2005), 'Using participants' video stimulated comments to complement analyses of interactional practices', in Te Molder, H. and Potter, J. (eds), *Conversation and Cognition*, 93–113. Cambridge: Cambridge University.

Raymond, G. (2003), 'Grammar and social organization: Yes/no interrogatives and the structure of responding', *American Sociological Review*, 68 (6): 939–67.

Raymond, G. (2013), 'At the intersection of turn and sequence organization: On the relevance of "slots" in type-conforming responses to polar interrogatives', in Szczepek Reed, B. and Raymond, G. (eds), *Units of Talk – Units of Action*, 169–206. John Benjamins, Amsterdam.

Sacks, H., Schegloff, E. A. and Jefferson, G., (1974), 'A simplest systematics for the organization of turn-taking for conversation', *Language*, 50 (4): 696–735.

Searle, J. R. (1969), *Speech Acts: An Essay in the Philosophy of Language*. Cambridge: Cambridge University.

Seedhouse, P. (2004), *The Interactional Architecture of the Language Classroom: A Conversation Analysis Perspective*. Malden, MA: Blackwell.

Seedhouse, P. (2008), 'Learning to talk the talk: Conversation analysis as a tool for induction of trainee teachers', in Garton, S. and Richards, K. (eds), *Professional Encounters in TESOL*, 42–57. New York: Palgrave Macmillan.

Sert, O. (2010), 'A proposal for a CA-integrated English language teacher education program in Turkey', *Asian EFL Journal*, 12 (3), 62–97.

Sert, O. (2013), "Epistemic status check' as an interactional phenomenon in instructed learning settings', *Journal of Pragmatics*, 45 (1), 13–28.

Sert, O. and Walsh, S. (2013), 'The interactional management of claims of insufficient knowledge in English language classrooms', *Language and Education*, 27 (6): 542–65.

Sert, O. (2015), *Social Interaction and L2 Classroom Discourse*. Edinburgh: Edinburgh University Press.

Sert, O. (2017), 'Creating opportunities for L2 learning in a prediction activity', *System*, 70: 14–25.

Sert, O. (2019), 'Classroom interaction and language teacher education', in Walsh, S. and Mann, S. (eds), *The Routledge Handbook of English Language Teacher Education*, 216–38. London: Routledge.

Sert, O. (2021). 'Transforming CA findings into future L2 teaching practices: Challenges and prospects for teacher education', in Kunitz, S., Sert, O. and Markee, N. (eds), *Classroom-based Conversation Analytic Research: Theoretical and Applied Perspectives on Pedagogy*, 259–79. New York: Springer.

Sert, O. and Aşık, A. (2020), 'A corpus linguistic investigation into online peer feedback practices in CALL teacher education', *Applied Linguistics Review*, 11 (1): 55–78.

Sert, O., Gynne, A. and Larsson, M. (2020), 'Digi-REFLECT/Towards digitalization in teaching and teacher education: Enhancing the roles and leadership of teachers in classrooms through digitally-enhanced reflection', *A Research and Development Project supported by MKL*. https://mindresearchgroup.org/digi-reflect/

Sinclair, J. and Coulthard, M. (1975), *Towards an Analysis of Discourse*. Oxford: OxfordUniversity.

Svennevig, J. (2013), 'Reformulation of questions with candidate answers', *International Journal of Bilingualism*, 17 (2): 189–204.

Ten Have, P. (2007), *Doing Conversation Analysis*. London: Sage.

Tharp, G. and Gallimore, G. R. (1988), *Rousing Minds to Life: Teaching, Learning, and Schooling in Social Context*. Cambridge: Cambridge University.

Walsh, S. (2006), *Investigating Classroom Discourse*. New York: Routledge.

Walsh, S. (2011), *Exploring Classroom Discourse: Language in Action*. London: Routledge.

Walsh, S. (2013), *Classroom Discourse and Teacher Development*. Edinburgh: Edinburgh University Press.

Walsh, S. and Sert, O. (2019), 'Mediating L2 learning through classroom interaction', in Gao, X. (ed.), *Second Handbook of English Language Teaching*, 737–55, Switzerland: Springer.

Waring, H. Z. (2008), 'Using explicit positive assessment in the language classroom: IRF, feedback, and learning opportunities', *The Modern Language Journal*, 92 (4): 577–94.

Waring, H. Z. (2011), 'Learner initiatives and learning opportunities in the language classroom', *Classroom Discourse*, 2 (2): 201–18.

Waring, H. Z. (2012), 'Yes-no questions that convey a critical stance in the language classroom', *Language and Education*, 26 (5): 451–69.

Waring, H. Z. (2013), "How was your weekend?': Developing the interactional competence in managing routine inquiries', *Language Awareness*, 22 (1): 1–16.

Waring, H. Z. (2021), 'Harnessing the power of heteroglossia: How to multi-task with teacher talk', in Kunitz, S., Sert, O. and Markee, N. (eds), *Classroom-Based Conversation Analytic Research: Theoretical and Applied Perspectives on Pedagogy*. 281–301. New York: Springer.

Weatherall, A. (2011), 'I don't know as a prepositioned epistemic hedge', *Research on Language & Social Interaction*, 44 (1): 317–37.

Willemsen, A., Gosen, M. N., Van Braak, M., Koole, T. and De Glopper, K. (2018), 'Teachers' open invitations in whole-class discussions', *Linguistics and Education*, 45: 40–9.

Wyatt, M. (2010), 'One teacher's development as a reflective practitioner', *Asian EFL Journal*, 12 (2): 235–61.

Wyatt, M. and Borg, S. (2011), 'Development in the practical knowledge of language teachers: A comparative study of three teachers designing and using communicative tasks on an in-service BA TESOL programme in the Middle East', *Innovation in Language Learning and Teaching*, 5 (3): 233–52.

Chapter 8

Bell, M. (2001), 'Supported reflective practice: A programme of peer observation and feedback for academic teacher development', *International Journal for Academic Development*, 6 (1): 29–39.

Cockburn, J. (2005), 'Perspectives and politics of classroom observation', *Research in Post-Compulsory Education*, 10 (3): 373–88.

Copland, F. (2010), 'Causes of tension in post-observation feedback in pre-service teacher training: An alternative view', *Teaching and Teacher Education*, 26 (3): 466–72.

De Lange, T. and Wittek, L. (2018), 'Creating shared spaces: Developing teaching through peer supervision groups', *Mind, Culture, and Activity*, 25 (4): 324–39.

Dobrowolska, D. and Balslev, K. (2017), 'Discursive mentoring strategies and interactional dynamics in teacher education', *Linguistics and Education*, 42: 10–20.

Engin, M. (2015), 'Trainer talk in post-observation feedback sessions: An exploration of scaffolding', *Classroom Discourse*, 6 (1): 57–72

Farr, F. (2003), 'Engaged listenership in spoken academic discourse: The case of student-tutor meetings', *Journal of English for Academic Purposes*, 2: 67–85.

Farr, F. (2011), *The Discourse of Teaching Practice Feedback*. London, England: Routledge.

García García, M. (2016), 'La alternancia de turnos y la organización temática en la conversación entre alemanes aprendientes de ELE', *Linred*, 14: 1–34.

Goodwin, C. and Goodwin, M. H. (1987), 'Concurrent operations on talk: Notes on the interactive organization of assessments', *IPrA Papers in Pragmatics*, 1 (1): 1–52.

Gosling, D. (2002), *Models of Peer Observation of Teaching*. London: LTSN Generic Centre.

Hammersley-Fletcher, L. and Orsmond, P. (2005), 'Reflecting on reflective practices within peer observation', *Studies in Higher Education*, 30 (2): 213–24.

Hazel, S. (2014), 'Visual motifs as meaning making practices', in Nevile, M., Haddington, P., Heinemann, T. and Rauniomaa, M. (eds), *Interacting with Objects: Language, Materiality, and Social Activity*, 169–94. 1st edn. Amsterdam: John Benjamins.

Jakonen, T. (2015), 'Handling knowledge: Using classroom materials to construct and interpret information requests', *Journal of Pragmatics*, 89: 100–112.

Kolb, D. A. (1984), *Experiential Learning Experience as a Source of Learning and Development*. New Jersey: Prentice Hall.

Kohut, G., Burnap, C. and Yon, M. (2007), 'Peer observation of teaching: Perceptions of the observer and the observed', *College Teaching*, 55 (1): 19–25.

Körkkö, M., Morales, S. and Kyrö-Ämmälä, O. (2019), 'Using a video app as a tool for reflective practice', *Educational Research*, 61 (1): 22–37.

Mann, S. and Walsh, S. (2013), 'RP or "RIP": A critical perspective on reflective practice', *Applied Linguistics Review*, 4 (2): 291–315.

Mann, S. and Walsh, S. (2017), *Reflective Practice in English Language Teaching: Research-Based Principles and Practices*, 1st edn. London: Routledge.

Martin, G. A. and Double, J. M. (1998), 'Developing higher education teaching skills through peer observation and collaborative reflection', *Innovations in Education & Training International*, 35 (2): 161–70.

McMahon, T., Barrett, T. and O'Neill, G. (2007), 'Using observation of teaching to improve quality: Finding your way through the muddle of competing conceptions, confusion of practice and mutually exclusive intentions', *Teaching in Higher Education*, 12 (4): 499–511.

Mikkola, P. and Lehtinen, E. (2014), 'Initiating activity shifts through use of appraisal forms as material objects during performance appraisal interviews', in Nevile, M., Haddington, P., Heinemann, T. and Rauniomaa, M. (eds), *Interacting with Objects: Language, Materiality, and Social Activity*, 57–78. 1st edn. Amsterdam: John Benjamins.

Mondada, L. (2007), 'Multimodal resources for turn-taking: Pointing and the emergence of possible speakers', *Discourse Studies*, 9 (2): 194–225.

Mondada, L. (2012), 'Video analysis and the temporality of inscriptions within social interaction: The case of architects at work', *Qualitative Research*, 12 (3): 304–33.

Mondada, L. (2018), 'Multiple Temporalities of language and body in interaction: Challenges for transcribing multimodality', *Research on Language and Social Interaction*, 51 (1): 85–106.

Mondada, L. (2019), 'Contemporary issues in conversation analysis: Embodiment and materiality, multimodality and multisensoriality in social interaction', *Journal of Pragmatics*, 145: 47–62.

Mortensen, K. (2012), 'Conversation analysis and multimodality', in Wagner, J., Mortensen, K. and Chapelle, C. A.(eds), *Conversation Analysis and Applied Linguistics: The Encyclopedia of Applied Linguistics*, 1061–8. Oxford: Oxford University Press.

Nevile, M., Haddington, P., Heinemann, T. and Rauniomaa, M. (eds) (2014a), *Interacting with Objects: Language, Materiality, and Social Activity*, 1st edn. Amsterdam: John Benjamins.

Nevile, M., Haddington, P., Heinemann, T. and Rauniomaa, M. (2014b), 'On the interactional ecology of objects', in Nevile, M., Haddington, P., Heinemann, T. and Rauniomaa, M. (eds), *Interacting with Objects: Language, Materiality, and Social Activity*, 3–26, 1st edn. Amsterdam: John Benjamins.

Nielsen, M. F. (2012), 'Using artifacts in brainstorming sessions to secure participation and decouple sequentiality', *Discourse Studies*, 14 (1): 87–109.

O'Leary, M. (2014), *Classroom Observation. A Guide to the Effective Observation of Teaching and Learning*, 1st edn. New York: Routledge.

O'Leary, M. (ed.) (2017), *Reclaiming Lesson Observation. Supporting Excellence in Teacher Learning*, 1st edn. New York: Routledge.

O'Leary, M. and Price, D. (2017), 'Peer observation as a springboard for teacher learning', in O'Leary, M. (ed.), *Reclaiming Lesson Observation. Supporting Excellence in Teacher Learning*, 114–23. New York: Routledge.

References

Phillips, D. (1999), *The Feedback Session within the Context of Teacher Training and Development: An Analysis of Discourse, Role and Function*, PhD diss., University of London.

Richards, J. C. (2005), *Professional Development for Language Teachers: Strategies for Teacher Learning*. Cambridge: Cambridge University Press.

Rossano, F. (2010), *Gaze Behaviour in Face-to-Face Interaction*, PhD Thesis, Radboud University Nijmegen, Nijmegen.

Sachs, J. and Parsell, M. (eds) (2014), *Peer Review of Learning and Teaching in Higher Education*, 1st edn. Dordrecht: Springer.

Schön, D. (1983), *The Reflective Practitioner: How Professionals Think in Action*, 1st edn. New York: Basic books.

Schön, D. (1987), *Educating the Reflective Practitioner*, 1st edn. San Francisco: Jossey-Bass.

Shortland, S. (2004), 'Peer observation: A tool for staff development or compliance?' *Journal of Further and Higher Education*, 28 (2): 219–28.

Shortland, S. (2010), 'Feedback within peer observation: Continuing professional development and unexpected consequences', *Innovations in Education and Teaching International*, 47 (3): 295–304.

Streeck, J. (1996), 'How to do things with things: Objets trouvés and symbolization', *Human Studies*, 19: 365–84.

Strong, M. and Baron, W. (2004). 'An analysis of mentoring conversations with beginning teachers: Suggestions and responses', *Teaching and Teacher Education*, 20: 47–57.

Thorne, S., Hellermann, J., Jones, A. and Lester, D. (2015), 'Interactional practices and artefact orientation in mobile augmented reality game play', *PsychNology Journal*, 13 (2–3): 259–86.

Walsh, S. and Mann, S. (2015), 'Doing reflective practice: A data-led way forward', *ELT Journal*, 69 (4): 1–12.

Chapter 9

Akcan, S. (2010), 'Watching teacher candidates watch themselves: Reflections on a practicum program in Turkey', *Profile Issues in Teachers' Professional Development*, 12 (1): 33–45.

Alpan, G. B. *et al.* (2014), 'The development of a student teacher concerns scale', *Eurasian Journal of Educational Research*, 14 (54): 151–70.

Batlle, J. and Miller, P. (2017), 'Video enhanced observation and teacher development: Teachers' beliefs as technology users', *EDULEARN17 Proceedings*, 1: 2352–61.

Braun, V. and Clarke, V. (2006), 'Using thematic analysis in psychology', *Qualitative Research in Psychology*, 3 (2): 77–101.

Celen, K. M. and Akcan, S. (2017), 'Evaluation of an ELT practicum programme from the perspectives of supervisors, Student Teachers and Graduates', *Journal of Teacher Education and Educators*, 6 (3): 251–74.

Çelik, S., Baran, E. and Sert, O. (2018), 'The affordances of mobile-App supported teacher observations for peer feedback', *International Journal of Mobile and Blended Learning*, 10(2): 36–49.

Coskun, A. and Daloglu, A. (2010), 'Evaluating an English language teacher education program through peacock's model', *Australian Journal of Teacher Education*, 35 (6): 24–42.

Dewey, J. (1933), *How We Think. A Gateway*. New York: Henry Regnery Company.

First, E. (2019), *Education First: English Proficiency Index 2019*. Miami Beach: EF.

Evertson, C. M. and Weinstein, C. S. (2011), 'Classroom management as a field of inquiry', in Evertson, C. M. and Weinstein, C. S. (eds), *Handbook of Classroom Management: Research, Practice and Contemporary Issues*, 3–15. New York: Routledge.

Farrell, T. S. C. (2018), *Research on Reflective Practice in TESOL*. New York: Routledge.

Gaudin, C. and Chaliès, S. (2015), 'Video viewing in teacher education and professional development: A literature review', *Educational Research Review* (16): 41–67.

Gebhard, J. G. (2009), 'The practicum', in Burns, A. and Richards, J. C. (eds), *The Cambridge Guide to Second Language Teacher Education*, 250–8. New York: Cambridge University Press.

Haines, J. and Miller, P. (2017), 'Video enhanced observation: Developing a flexible and effective tool', in O'Leary, M. (ed.), *Reclaiming Lesson Observation: Supporting Excellence in Teacher Learning*, 127–40. Oxon: Routledge.

Hidson, E. (2018), 'Video-enhanced lesson observation as a source of multiple modes of data for school leadership: A videographic approach', *Management in Education*, 32 (1): 26–31.

Jones, V. (2011), 'How do teachers learn to be effective classroom managers?' in Evertson, C. M. and Weinstein, C. S. (eds), *Handbook of Classroom Management: Research, Practice, and Contemporary Issues*, 887–907. New York: Routledge.

Kong, S. C. (2010), 'Using a web-enabled video system to support student-teachers' self-reflection in teaching practice', *Computers and Education*, 55 (4): 1772–82.

Körkkö, M., Morales Rios, S. and Kyrö-Ämmälä, O. (2019), 'Using a video app as a tool for reflective practice', *Educational Research*. Routledge, 61 (1): 22–37.

Kyriacou, C. (2018), *Essential Teaching Skills*, 5th edn. Oxford, UK: Oxford University Press.

Larrivee, B. (2011), 'The convergence of reflective practice and effective classroom management', in Evertson, C. M. and Weinstein, C. S. (eds), *Handbook of Classroom Management: Research, Practice and Contemporary Issues*, 983–1001. New York: Routledge.

Levin, J. and Nolan, J. F. (2014), *Principles of Classroom Management: A Professional Decision-Making Model*, 7th edn. New Jersey: Pearson.

Lewis, M. (2002), 'Classroom management', in Richards, J. C. and Renandya, W. A. (eds), *Methodology in Language Teaching: An Anthology of Current Practice*, 40–8. Cambridge, UK: Cambridge University Press.

Lofthouse, R. and Birmingham, P. (2010), 'The camera in the classroom: Video-recording as a tool for professional development of student teachers', *TEAN Journal*, 1 (2011): 1–18.

Loughran, J. J. (2002), 'Effective reflective practice in search of meaning in learning about teaching', *Journal of Teacher Education*, 53 (1): 33–43.

Mann, S. and Walsh, S. (2017), *Reflective Practice in English Language Teaching: Research-Based Principles and Practices, ESL & Applied Linguistics Professional Series*. New York: Routledge.

MEB (1998), Öğretmen Adaylarının Milli Eğitim Bakalığına Bağlı Eğitim Öğretim Kurumlarında Yapacakları Öğretmenlik Uygulamasına İlişkin Yönerge, Tebliğler Dergisi.

MEB (2018), Öğretmenlik Uygulaması Yönergesi, Tebliğler Dergisi: Haziran-Ek 2018.

Özen, E. N. et al. (2013), *Turkey National Need Assessment of State School English Language Teaching*. Ankara: British Council.

244 *References*

Rich, P. J. and Hannafin, M. (2009), 'Video annotation tools: Technologies to scaffold, structure, and transform teacher reflection', *Journal of Teacher Education*, 60 (1): 52–67.

Richards, J. C. and Lockhart, C. (1996), *Reflective Teaching in Second Language Classrooms, Cambridge Language Education*. New York, UK: Cambridge University Press.

Richards, J. C. and Nunan, D. (1990), *Second Language Teacher Education*. Cambridge, UK: Cambridge University Press.

Saraç, H. S., Zorba, M. G. and Arikan, A. (2015), 'What happens when pre-service English language teachers are in action and researchers are recording?' in Dikilitaş, K., Smith, R. and Trotman, W. (eds), *Teacher-Researchers in Action*, 399–417. Kent, UK: IATEFL.

Schön, D. A. (1983), *The Reflective Practitioner*. United States of America: Basıc Books.

Scrivener, J. (2005), *Learning Teaching: A Guidebook for English Language Teachers*, 2nd edn. Oxford, UK: Macmillan Books for Teachers.

Scrivener, J. (2012), *Classroom Management Techniques*. Cambridge, UK: Cambridge University Press.

Sert, O. (2010), 'A proposal for a CA-integrated English language teacher education program in Turkey', *The Asian EFL Journal Quarterly*, 12 (3): 62–97.

Sherin, M. G. and Van Es, E. A. (2005), 'Using video to support teachers' ability to notice classroom interactions', *Journal of Technology and Teacher Education*, 13 (3): 475–91.

Stake, R. E. (1995), *The Art of Case Study Research*. Thousand Oaks, California: SAGE Publications.

Todorova, R. and Ivanova, I. (2020), 'Classroom management and good language teachers', in Griffiths, C. and Tajeddin, Z. (eds), *Lessons from Good Language Teachers*, 133–50. United Kingdom: Cambridge University Press.

Tripp, T. and Rich, P. (2012), 'Using video to analyze one's own teaching', *British Journal of Educational Technology*, 43 (4): 678–704.

Tülüce, H. S. and Çeçen, S. (2016), 'Scrutinizing practicum for a more powerful teacher education: A longitudinal study with pre-service teachers', *Educational Sciences: Theory and Practice*, 16(1): 127–51.

Welsch, R. G. and Devlin, P. A. (2007), 'Developing preservice teachers' reflection: Examining the use of video', *Action in Teacher Education*, 28 (4): 53–61.

Wright, T. (2005), *Classroom Management in Language Education, Research and Practice in Applied Linguistics*. Hampshire, UK: Palgrave Macmillan.

Wright, T. (2006), 'Managing classroom life', in Gieve, S. and Miller, I. K. (eds), *Understanding the Language Classroom*, 64–87. Hampshire, UK: Palgrave Macmillan.

Yin, R. K. (2018), *Case Study Research and Applications: Design and Methods*, 6th edn. Los Angeles: SAGE.

Yüksek Öğretim Program Atlası (2020), İngilizce Öğretmenliği (DİL) | TYT-AYT Net Sihirbazı. Available at: https://yokatlas.yok.gov.tr/netler-tablo.php?b=10108 (Accessed 7 May 2020).

Chapter 10

aus der Wieschen, M. V. and Sert, O. (2021), 'Divergent language choices and maintenance of intersubjectivity: The case of Danish EFL young learners'. *International Journal of Bilingual Education and Bilingualism*, 24 (1): 107–23.

Cladingbowl, M. (2014), 'Why I want to try inspecting without grading teaching in each individual lesson', June 2014, No. 140101. Available at https://webarchive.

nationalarchives.gov.uk/20141107094517/http://www.ofsted.gov.uk/resources/why-i-want-try-inspecting-without-grading-teaching-each-individual-lesson.

Coe, R. (2014), 'Classroom observation: It's harder than you think', *CEMblog*, 9 January 2014. Available online: https://www.cem.org/blog/414/.

Coe, R., Aloisi, C., Higgins, S. and Major, L. E. (2014), 'What makes great teaching? Review of the underpinning research', London: Sutton Trust. Available online: http://dro.dur.ac.uk/13747/.

Cremin, H., Mason, C. and Busher, H. (2011), 'Problematising pupil voice using visual methods: Findings from a study of engaged and disaffected pupils in an urban secondary school', *British Educational Research Journal*, 37 (4): 585–603

Czerniawski, G. (2012), 'Repositioning trust: A challenge to inauthentic neoliberal uses of pupil voice', *Management in Education*, 26 (3): 130–9. doi:10.1177/0892020612445685

Department for Education (2011), 'Teachers' standards', Available online: https://www.gov.uk/government/publications/teachers-standards.

Department for Education (2012a), 'The Education (School Teachers' Appraisal) (England) Regulations 2012', Available online: http://www.legislation.gov.uk/uksi/2012/115/contents/made.

Department for Education (2012b), 'Teacher appraisal and capability: Model policy', Available online: https://www.gov.uk/government/publications/teacher-appraisal-and-capability-model-policy

Dixie, G., (2011), *The Ultimate Teaching Manual: A Route to Success*. London: Bloomsbury.

Edgington, U. (2016), 'Performativity and the power of shame: Lesson observations, emotional labour and professional habitus', *Sociological Research Online*, 21 (1): 1–15. doi:10.5153/sro.3802

Evans, L. (2011), 'The "shape" of teacher professionalism in England: Professional standards, performance management, professional development and the changes proposed in the 2010 white paper', *British Educational Research Journal*, 37 (5): 851–70. doi:10.1080/01411926.2011.607231

Hidson, E. (2019), *Video-Enhanced Observation: A Case Study of Lesson Feedback in a PGCE School Placement*. Impact: Journal of the Chartered College of Teaching.

Kilburn, D., (2014), *Methods for Recording Video in the Classroom: Producing Single and Multi-camera Videos for Research into Teaching and Learning*. NCRM Working Paper. NCRM. Available online: http://eprints.ncrm.ac.uk/3599/

Lofthouse, R., Leat, D. and Towler, C. (2010), 'Coaching for teaching and learning: A practical guide for schools' (Guidance report). NCSL. Available online: https://eprints.ncl.ac.uk/file_store/production/157251/413164CA-AE18-47D7-AB09-9BA2DF13C1E8.pdf.

Mann, S. and Walsh, S. (2016), *Reflective Practice in English Language Teaching: Research-based Principles and Practices*. London: Routledge.

Ofsted (2019), 'Ofsted inspections: Myths'. Available online: https://www.gov.uk/government/publications/further-education-and-skills-inspection-handbook/ofsted-inspections-myths

O'Leary, M. (Ed.). (2016), *Reclaiming Lesson Observation: Supporting Excellence in Teacher Learning*. Abingdon: Routledge.

Pine, G. (2009), *Teacher Action Research: Building Knowledge Democracies*. London: Sage.

Rosaen, C. L., Lundeberg, M., Cooper, M., Fritzen, A. and Terpstra, M. (2008), 'Noticing noticing: How does investigation of video records change how teachers reflect on their experiences?' *Journal of Teacher Education*, 59 (4): 347–60. doi:10.1177/0022487108322128

246 *References*

Shulman, L. S. (2005), 'Signature pedagogies in the professions', *Daedalus*, 134 (3): 52–9.
Teacher Development Trust (2020), 'Guidance on teacher goal-setting: Balancing autonomy and coherence', Available at http://tdtrust.org/wp-content/uploads/2020/01/Guidance-on-Teacher-Goal-Setting.pdf
Van Es, E. A. and Sherin, M. G. (2002), 'Learning to notice: Scaffolding new teachers' interpretations of classroom interactions', *Journal of Technology and Teacher Education*, 10 (4): 571–96.
Van Es, E. A. (2012), 'Examining the development of a teacher learning community: The case of a video club', *Teaching and Teacher Education*, 28(2): 182–92.
Webb, R. (2006), *Changing Teaching and Learning in the Primary School*. Maidenhead: OUP.

Chapter 11

Alexander, R. J. (2008), *Towards Dialogic Teaching: Rethinking Classroom Talk*, 4th edn. York: Dialogos.
Breen, M.P. (1998), 'Navigating the discourse: On what is learned in the language classroom', in Renandya, W.A. and G.M. Jacobs (eds), *Learners and Language Learning, Anthology Series 39* (Singapore: SEAMO Regional Language Centre).
Deignan, A. H. (2005), *Metaphor and Corpus Linguistics*. Amsterdam: John Benjamins.
Dewey, J. (1933), *How We Think. A Restatement of the Relation of Reflective Thinking to the Educative Process*, rev. edn. Boston: D. C. Heath.
Farrell, T. S. C. (ed.) (2006), *Language Teacher Research in Asia*. Alexandria, VA: TESOL.
Grayling, A. (2003), *Meditations for the Humanist: Ethics for a Secular Age*. Oxford: Oxford University Press.
Johnson, K. E. (2009), *Second Language Teacher Education: A Sociocultural Perspective*. London and New York: Routledge.
Larrivee, B. (2004), 'Assessing teachers' level of reflective practice as a tool for change', Paper presented at the Third International Conference on Reflective Practice, Gloucester, UK.
Lyster, R. (1998), 'Recasts, repetitions and ambiguity in L2 classroom discourse', *Studies in Second Language Acquisition*, 20: 51–81.
Mann, S. and Walsh, S. (2013), 'RP or "RIP": A critical perspective on reflective practice', *Applied Linguistics Review*, 4 (2): 291–315.
Mann, S. and Walsh, S. (2017), *Reflective Practice in English Language Teaching: Research-Based Principles and Practices*. London and New York: Routledge.
Mercer, N. (2009), *Words and Minds: How We Use Language to Think Together*. London: Routledge.
Miller, P. (2015), 'Video-enhanced observation: A new way to develop teacher practice', *Optimus Education*. Available online at: http://my.optimus-education.com/video-enhanced-observation-new-way-developteacher-practice (Accessed 20 April 2016).
Schön, D. A. (1983), *The Reflective Practitioner*. London: Temple Smith.
Seedhouse, P. (2004), *The Interactional Architecture of the Second Language Classroom: A Conversational Analysis Perspective*. Oxford: Blackwell.
Van Lier, L. (1996), *Interaction in the Language Curriculum: Awareness, Autonomy and Authenticity*. New York: Longman.

Van Lier, L. (2000), 'From input to affordance: Social interactive learning from an ecological perspective', in Lantolf, J. P. (ed.), *Sociocultural Theory and Second Language Learning*, 116–23, Oxford: Oxford University Press.

Vygotsky, L. S. (1978), *Mind in Society: The Development of Higher Psychological Processes*. Cambridge, MA: Harvard University Press.

Walsh, S. (2006), *Investigating Classroom Discourse*. London: Routledge.

Walsh, S. (2011), *Exploring Classroom Discourse: Languagein Action*. London and New York: Routledge.

Walsh, S. (2013), *Classroom Discourse and Teacher Development*. Edinburgh, UK: Edinburgh University Press.

Walsh, S. (2019), 'SETTVEO: Evidence-based reflection and teacher development', *ELT Research Papers*, British Council.

Walsh, S. and Li, L. (2013), 'Conversations as space for learning', *International Journal of Applied Linguistics*, 23/2: 247–66.

Walsh, S. and Mann, S. (2015), 'Doing reflective practice: A data-led way forward', *ELT Journal*, 69 (4): 351–62.

Chapter 12

Ajayi, L. (2016), 'How intern teachers use classroom video for self-reflection on teaching', *Educational Forum*, 80 (1): 79–4.

Bandura, A. (1977), 'Self-efficacy: Toward a unifying theory of behavioral change', *Psychological Review*, 84, (2): 191–15.

Bandura, A. (1997), *Self-efficacy: The Exercise of Control*. New York: W.H. Freeman.

Bartram, M. and Walton, R. (1991), *Correction – Mistake Management: A Positive Approach to Language Mistakes*. Boston, MA: Heinle/Thomson.

Blomberg, G., Sherin, M., Renkl, A., Glogger, I. and Seidel, T. (2013), 'Understanding video as a tool for teacher education: Investigating instructional strategies to promote reflection', *Instructional Science*, 42 (3): 443–63.

Borg, S. (2003), 'Teacher cognition in language teaching: A review of research on what language teachers think, know, believe, and do', *Language Teaching*, 36: 81–109.

Calandra, B., Brantley-Dias, L. and Dias, M. (2006), 'Using digital video for professional development in urban schools: A preservice teacher's experience with reflection', *Journal of Computing in Teacher Education*, 22 (4): 137–45.

Christ, T., Arya, P. and Chiu, M.M. (2015), 'A three-pronged approach to video reflection: Preparing literacy teachers of the future', in Ortlieb, E., Mcvee, M.B. and Shanahan, L.E. (eds), *Video Reflection in Literacy Teacher Education and Development: Lessons from Research and Practice* (Literacy Research, Practice and Evaluation, Vol. 5), 235–56. Bingley: Emerald Group Publishing Limited.

Coffey, A. M. (2014), 'Using video to develop skills in reflection in teacher education students', *Australian Journal of Teacher Education*, 39 (9): 1–13. Edith Cowan Univ., Perth: Research Online.

Cornish, L. and Jenkins, K. (2012), 'Encouraging teacher development through embedding reflective practice in assessment', *Asia-Pacific Journal of Teacher Education*, 40 (2): 159–70.

Dewey, J. (1933 orig. 1910), *How We Think*, rev. edn. Boston: Heath.

Edge, J. (1989), *Mistakes and Correction*. London: Longman.

Edwards, A. (2007), 'Relational agency in professional practice: A CHAT analysis', *An International Journal of Human Activity Theory*, 1: 1–17.

Edwards, A. (2010), 'Relational agency: Working with other practitioners', in Edwards, A. (ed.), *Being an Expert Professional Practitioner*, 61–79. Dordrecht: Springer.

Edwards, A. and D'Arcy, C. (2004), 'Relational agency and disposition in sociocultural accounts of learning to teach', *Educational Review*, 56(2): 147–55.

Ellis, R. (2010) 'Cognitive, social, and psychological dimensions of corrective feedback', in Batstone, R. (ed.), *Sociocognitive Perspectives on Language Use and Language Learning*, 151–65. Oxford: Oxford University Press

Finlay, L. (2008), 'Reflecting on "reflective practice"', *Practice-based Professional Learning* Paper 52, The Open University.

Flyvbjerg, B. (2006), 'Five misunderstandings about case-study research', *Qualitative Inquiry*, 12 (2): 219–45.

Gaudin, C. and Chaliès, S. (2015), 'Video viewing in teacher education and professional development: A literature review', *Educational Research Review*, 16: 41–67.

Gay, G. and Kirland, K. (2003), 'Developing cultural critical consciousness and self-reflection in preservice teacher education', *Theory into Practice*, 42 (3): 181–7.

Gröschner, A., Schindler, A. K., Holzberger, D., Alles, M. and Seidel, T., (2018), 'How systematic video reflection in teacher professional development regarding classroom discourse contributes to teacher and student self-efficacy', *International Journal of Educational Research*, 90: 223–33.

Haines, J., and Miller, P. (2016), 'Video-enhanced observation: Developing a flexible and effective tool', in O'Leary, M. (ed.), *Reclaiming Lesson Observation: Supporting Excellence in Teacher Learning*, 127–40. London: Routledge.

Hatton, N. and Smith, D. (1995), 'Reflection in teacher education: Towards definition and implementation', *Teaching & Teacher Education*, 11 (1): 33–49.

Hedge, T. (2000), *Teaching and Learning in the Language Classroom*. Oxford: Oxford University Press.

Jacobs, J., Borko, H. and Koellner, K. (2009), 'The power of video as a tool for professional development and research: Examples from the Problem-Solving Cycle', in Janik, T. and Seidel, T. (eds), *The Power of Video Studies in Investigating Teaching and Learning in the Classroom*, 259–73. Munster, Germany: Waxmann.

Jefferson, G. (1987). 'On exposed and embedded correction in conversation', in G. Button and Lee, J. (eds), *Talk and Social Organisation*, 86–100. Clevedon: Multilingual Matters.

Johnson, K. (1995). *Understanding Communication in Second Language Classrooms*. Cambridge: Cambridge University Press.

Kennedy, H., Landor, M. and Todd, L. (eds) (2015), *Video Enhanced Reflective Practice: Professional Development through Attuned Interactions*. London: Jessica Kingsley Publishers.

Lantolf, J. (2000), *Sociocultural Theory and Second Language Learning*. Oxford: Oxford University Press.

Larrivee, B. (2000), 'Transforming teaching practice: Becoming the critically reflective teacher', *Reflective Practice*, 1 (3): 293–307.

Leitch, R. and Day, C. (2000), 'Action research and reflective practice: Towards a holistic view', *Educational Action Research*, 8 (1): 179–93.

Li, S. (2014), 'Oral corrective feedback', *ELT Journal*, 68 (2): 196–8.

Lofthouse, R., Leat, D., Towler, C., Hall, E. and Cummings, C. (2010), *Improving Coaching: Evolution Not Revolution*. Reading: CfBT Education Trust.

References

Lofthouse, R. and Birmingham, P. (2010), 'The camera in the classroom: Video-recording as a tool for professional development of student teachers', *Tean Journal*, 1 (2): 1–18.

Lyster, R. and Ranta, L. (1997), 'Corrective feedback and learner uptake: Negotiation of form in communicative classrooms', *Studies in Second Language Acquisition*, 20: 37–66.

Marsh, B. and Mitchell, N. (2014), 'The role of video in teacher professional development', *Teacher Development*, 10: 403–17.

Martin, S. N. and Siry, C. (2012), 'Using video in science teacher education: An analysis of the utilization of video-based media by teacher educators and researchers', in Fraser, B., Tobin, K. and McRobbie, C. J. (eds), *Second International Handbook of Science Education*, 417–34. Dordrecht, Heidelberg, London and New York: Springer.

McFadden, J., Ellis, J., Anwar, T. and Roehrig, G. (2014), 'Beginning science teachers' use of a digital video annotation tool to promote reflective practices', *Journal of Science Education and Technology* 23: 458–70.

Nunan, D. (1996), 'Hidden voices: Insiders' perspectives on classroom interaction', in Bailey, K. and Nunan, D. (eds), *Voices from the Language Classroom: Qualitative Research in Second Language Education*, 41–56. New York: Cambridge University Press.

Parsons, M. and Stephenson, M. (2005), 'Developing reflective practice in student teachers: Collaboration and critical partnerships', *Teachers and Teaching Theory and Practice*, 11(1): 95–116.

Pietsch, J., Walker, R. and Chapman, E. (2003), 'The relationship among self-concept, self-efficacy, and performance in mathematics during secondary school', *Journal of Educational Psychology*, 95(3): 589–603.

Schön, D. (1983), *The Reflective Practitioner*. New York: Basic Books.

Schön, D. (1987), *Educating the Reflective Practitioner*. San Francisco, CA: Jossey-Bass.

Seedhouse, P. (2004), *The Interactional Architecture of the Language Classroom: A Conversation Analysis Perspective*. Malden, MA: Blackwell.

Sheen, Y. (2004), 'Corrective feedback and learner uptake in communicative classrooms across instructional settings', *Language Teaching Research*, 8 (3): 263–300.

Smyth, J. (1989), 'Developing and sustaining critical reflection in teacher education', *Journal of Teacher Education*, 40 (2): 2–9.

Stillwell, C. (2009), 'The collaborative development of teacher training skills', *ELT Journal*, 63 (4): 353–62.

Tripp, T. and Rich, P. (2011), 'Using video to analyze one's own teaching', *British Journal of Educational Technology*, 43 (4): 678–704.

Van Manen, M. (1977), 'Linking ways of knowing with ways of being practical', *Curriculum Inquiry*, 6: 205–28.

Yin, R. K. (1984), *Case Study Research Design and Methods*. Newbury Park, CA: Sage.

Zainal, Z. (2007), 'Case study as a research method', *Jurnal Kemanusiaan* bil.9: 1–6.

Chapter 13

British Educational Research Association (BERA), (2018), *Ethical Guidelines for Educational Research*, 4th edn. London: BERA. Available at: https://www.bera.ac.uk/researchers-resources/publications/ethical-guidelines-for-educational-research-2018 (Accessed 15 June 2020).

Cheng, L., Watanabe, Y. and Curtis, A. (eds) (2004), *Washback in Language Testing: Research Contexts and Method*. Mahwah: Lawrence Erlbaum and Associates.

250 *References*

Dewey, J. (1997), *Experience and Education*. New York: Touchstone.
Seedhouse, P. (2004), *The Interactional Architecture of the Language Classroom: A Conversation Analysis Perspective*. Malden, MA: Blackwell.
Seedhouse, P. and Satar, M. (2021). 'Which specific features of candidate talk do examiners orient to when taking scoring decisions?', *IELTS Research Reports Online Series*, 5. British Council, Cambridge Assessment English and IDP: IELTS Australia. Available at https://www.ielts.org/teaching-and-research/research-reports
Sert, O. (2015), *Social Interaction and L2 Classroom Discourse*. Edinburgh: Edinburgh University Press.
Sert, O. (2019), 'Classroom interaction and language teacher education', in Walsh, S. and Mann, S. (eds), *The Routledge Handbook of English Language Teacher Education*, 216–38. London: Routledge.

Chapter 14

Seedhouse, P. (2004), *The Interactional Architecture of the Language Classroom: A Conversation Analysis Perspective*. Malden, MA: Blackwell.
Seedhouse, P. and Satar, M. (2021). 'Which specific features of candidate talk do examiners orient to when taking scoring decisions?', *IELTS Research Reports Online Series*, 5. British Council, Cambridge Assessment English and IDP: IELTS Australia. Available at https://www.ielts.org/teaching-and-research/research-reports

Index

annotating 36, 39, 44, 49

appraisal 76, 132, 153–4, 156, 161, 164–5, 219

CALL 10–14, 20, 178, 220, 223, 224

classroom interaction 66, 77, 97–9, 101–2, 105–6, 110–11, 114–15, 167, 169, 171, 184, 202, 213, 218, 222–3

classroom management 16, 101, 122, 135–6, 140, 143–6, 148–52, 154, 218

classroom observation 11, 16–17, 120

coaching 21, 28, 30, 78, 153, 164–5, 183, 193, 195, 212

Community of Practice 167, 171

Confidentiality 199, 214–16

consent 28, 103, 199, 205, 214, 216

Continuing Professional Development (CPD) *see also Professional Development* 65, 117–19, 121, 132, 153–7, 164–5, 167, 170, 176, 178, 181, 184–5, 194, 195, 199–201, 203–7, 217, 219, 223, 225

Conversation Analysis (CA) 97–8, 100, 104, 115, 118, 172, 184, 221

Covid-19 9, 35

curriculum 80, 115, 135, 209, 218–19

DELTA 181–2, 184–8, 191, 193, 195, 203, 207, 219

digital video 3–5, 9, 11–12, 17, 18, 20, 65, 67, 156, 183, 197, 201–2, 213, 215, 222

discipline 135, 136, 140, 143–4, 145, 151, 219

distance learning 199, 207–8, 216

engagement 6, 22, 26, 43, 48, 50–1, 69, 71, 79, 98, 109, 145, 148, 150, 155, 174, 182, 194, 221

English language teaching 135, 137–8, 167

error correction 181, 187–91, 193–95, 207, 223

evaluation 9, 18, 29, 30, 36, 69, 87, 90, 98, 100, 117, 120, 133, 167, 170, 176, 178–9, 183, 184, 191, 194, 204, 207, 209, 212, 216

feedback 9, 13, 23–4, 26, 32–4, 36–7, 46–8, 50–2, 55, 58, 60, 66–8, 70, 74–7, 79, 87–8, 91, 94–5, 97–9, 100–1, 103–6, 108, 110, 112–15, 117–25, 127–8, 131–3, 138, 139–45, 148–9, 151, 154, 157–61, 163, 165, 169, 172–4, 181, 185–8, 191, 193–6, 202–3, 207–9, 216, 218, 221–3

foreign language teacher education 65, 67

Finland 83, 156, 170, 200, 218

Germany 65–8, 80, 156, 200, 224

holistic approach 84, 221

IELTS 53, 210–12, 220

IMDAT 97–9, 101–5, 109, 114–15, 202, 218, 222

interaction 9, 10, 13–14, 16–18, 22, 27–8, 33–5, 42–3, 58, 66, 70, 73, 75, 77, 89, 92–4, 97–102, 105–7, 110–11, 114–16, 118–22, 124, 127–33, 160, 167–74, 177, 179–80, 184–5, 188–94, 196, 202, 213–14, 218–19, 221–4

interactional competence 99, 101, 105, 110, 114–15, 167, 169, 171

language teacher education 15, 65, 67, 97, 135–6, 176, 218

limitations 22–3, 35, 87, 172, 217, 224–5

methodological model 217, 219–20

motivation 14, 16, 67, 69, 71, 84–5, 87, 91, 95

multimodal 12, 13, 16, 18–19, 68, 99, 101, 118, 121–2, 132, 215, 220–21, 223

252   *Index*

online community 171–2

pedagogy 15, 31–2, 106, 137, 154–5, 208–9, 216
peer observation 16, 36, 115, 117–23, 125, 127–9, 133, 137–8, 158, 164, 169, 183, 205
performance management 153–9, 161–5, 203, 219
post-observation 98, 101, 103–7, 110–14, 118–19, 121
practicum 18, 29, 67–70, 83, 86–9, 91, 95, 101, 136–40, 151–2, 201–202
pre-service 11, 16–19, 21, 66, 78, 80–1, 97–9, 101, 105, 120, 135–8, 141, 152, 182, 200, 202, 223
primary 66, 68, 74, 77, 79, 83, 86, 115, 135, 137, 142, 149, 162, 200, 218
primary school teacher education 83, 86
Professional Development *see also Continuing Professional Development (CPD)* 10–12, 14, 16–17, 19–24, 28, 36, 65–7, 79, 81, 83, 85–7, 92, 117–19, 136–8, 141, 151–6, 161, 165, 167–8, 176, 178, 180, 184–5, 187–8, 192, 195, 199, 204, 212–222, 224–26
professional practice 15, 27, 79, 86, 91, 93, 133, 156, 171, 176, 180, 192–3, 199, 207, 210, 213–18, 220–2, 224

qualification 53, 90, 181, 184–6, 195, 203, 205, 208, 219
quantitative 35, 46, 79, 115, 172, 206, 215–16, 220–1, 223
questioning 23, 30–2, 40–1, 53, 84, 97–101, 104–5, 109–10, 114–15, 148, 158, 182, 218

reflection 14–21, 23, 29–30, 34, 36, 46, 48, 51, 65–7, 69, 73, 77–80, 83–5, 87, 88–99, 101, 103, 106, 108, 109–11, 113–15, 118, 120, 136–8, 141–3, 146, 148, 150–2, 156, 158–61, 164, 167–9, 171–2, 177–80, 182–6, 188, 192–5, 199–207, 209, 214, 216, 218–221, 223–6

reflective practice 15–17, 27, 83–4, 86–87, 89–91, 93, 95, 97, 117–20, 133, 136, 167, 182, 199–200, 204, 216–18
research 12–15, 18, 26, 65–9, 73–5, 77–81, 83, 85–6, 89–90, 92, 95–100, 114–15, 118, 137, 140–2, 151, 153, 155–62, 167–8, 170–2, 174–6, 178–80, 182–5, 188, 193, 196, 210, 212, 214–215, 217–23, 225–6
review 30, 39, 41, 43–4, 46, 48, 55, 66, 78, 92, 98, 101, 103, 104, 115, 120, 136, 141, 156, 160, 163, 164, 170, 172, 173, 182–3, 185, 186, 193, 205–7, 209, 219–20, 224, 226

secondary 83, 99, 101, 153, 157, 162, 218
SETTVEO 167, 169–71, 173, 175–9
Spain 9, 117, 121, 171
student voice 153, 160–1, 163, 165, 219
supervisor 18, 67, 83–4, 87–96, 101, 105, 115, 138–44, 151–2, 201–2, 205–6, 220, 223

tagging 30–2, 35–6, 39–41, 43–4, 46, 49–51, 53, 55–6, 58–9, 69–72, 76–7, 79, 93, 97, 99, 101, 106, 142–3, 151, 156, 160, 173–4, 177, 185, 206, 208, 214, 220, 223–6
tagset 54, 102, 181, 212
teacher training 18, 25, 29, 58, 65–8, 73, 78, 80, 120, 136, 181–9, 191, 199, 207, 216, 218, 227
teaching practice 11, 14–15, 18–20, 68, 79, 83, 85, 97–8, 109, 118, 120, 135–8, 156, 180–1, 188, 218
TESOL 18, 136–7, 181
Turkey 16, 97, 101, 115, 135–7, 139, 156, 171, 202, 223, 227

UK 21, 24, 27, 29, 39, 49–50, 53–4, 57–8, 61, 117, 135, 153, 167, 170, 178, 181, 199, 203, 217, 226

video-based reflection 78, 83–5, 87–8, 137, 225
video observation 17–19, 67, 78, 137, 140, 151, 182–3, 192–3, 195